Pictures for Organizations

How and why they work as communication
by Philip N. Douglis

Lawrence Ragan Communications, Inc.
Chicago

Cover photograph:
Laughter in the afternoon
by Ed Eckstein. See page 32.

Copyright 1982
by Lawrence Ragan Communications, Inc.

Library of Congress Catalog Card No.: 82-060042
ISBN 0-931368-10-3

Lawrence Ragan Communications, Inc.
407 South Dearborn Street
Chicago, IL 60605

Contents

Introduction iv

1/Symbols in juxtaposition:
the incongruous image 1

2/Spontaneous responses:
the moment picture 19

3/Machines and equipment:
beyond the thing itself 35

4/Pictures of buildings:
What makes them special? 53

5/At work in the office:
more than papers and desks 69

6/Hospital scenes, symbols:
human beings in crisis 85

7/Camera in the classroom:
capturing the essence
of education 101

8/Meetings, speeches:
beyond the talking head 115

9/The sporting life:
people in action 129

10/Ceremonies and rituals:
turning lemons into lemonade .. 145

11/Photographing hobbies
and arts: using one art
to define another 159

12/Photojournalism and
religion: interpreting
issues of our times 173

13/Portraits: revealing
the person inside 187

14/The group portrait:
the bonds we share 203

15/The sequence: when the sum
means more than any part 221

The photographers 228

The organizations 230

Technical notes 231

Selected resources 232

About the author 233

Introduction

Pictures for Organizations is, to my knowledge, the first book ever to explore the reasons how—and why—specific photographs work as communication in the editorial media of organizations.

It is intended to help editors and photographers who work for company, hospital, association, governmental, educational, and religious publications to recognize the concepts, techniques, and stylistic approaches that make the difference between an effective photograph and an ineffective one.

To do this, I have invited a cross section of editor/photographers, in-house photographers, and freelancers to send me examples of what they feel is their most successful work. From this resource, I have selected 100 examples for analysis. Some of these photographers are veteran professionals. Others have only been on the job for a year or two. But all of them have made images that have something to offer the readers of their publications.

The 100 examples discussed in this book should not be considered as the "best" photos of their kind. I do not intend this book as a "gallery of classics." But each image does represent a valuable approach, which any of us can draw upon in conceiving, executing, and using photographs for organizational publications.

I have grouped the photographs into chapters by the nature of their subject matter. These subjects are common organizational content: portraits, people at work and at play, ceremonies and rituals, buildings and machines. In addition, specialized areas—such as hospital, educational, and religious scenes—are included.

Some images could lend themselves to a number of different categories. A picture made in a hospital, for example, might also be an outstanding example of employee portraiture and may well appear in the portraiture chapter instead of with other hospital scenes.

I consider most of these photographs to be unusually strong examples of organizational photography. Others are competent examples of approaches we see quite frequently. But all of them, I feel, can help us to understand the hows and whys of editorial photography on behalf of organizations.

It is my hope that this book will act as a useful supplement to my previous book, *Communicating with Pictures*, published by Ragan Communications in 1976 and now out of print. In that book, I tried to provide editor/photographers, particularly beginners, with very basic how-to guidelines for editorial photography. This book, on the other hand, is intended to offer *examples* of those concepts and techniques, from which the reader can draw inspiration and, with the support of the accompanying text, obtain practical insights into making pictures for organizations.

I want to acknowledge the help of the 26 photographers, representing 35 organizations, who have graciously contributed examples of what they considered their finest work. Without their help, a book of this scope would not be possible. Never before, in my view, have so many good examples of organizational photographs been presented in one place at one time. I dedicate this book to these photographers, and to their collective vision.

I am also grateful to John Szarkowski, the director of the department of photography at the Museum of Modern Art in New York, who first conceived the idea of a book of this type. His *Looking at Photographs,* which analyzes 100 photographs from the museum's collection in terms of why they work as photographic art, provided me a model upon which to base this book.

Finally, a few words of caution. It is easy to look at a picture and see only its subject matter and, if that subject matter is not *our* particular kind of subject matter, to dismiss it as "irrelevant." That would be a mistake. The concepts and techniques *behind* the picture—no matter what the subject might be—could be equally valid for our use as well. Likewise, it is easy to let ourselves become intimidated by the excellence of a particular photograph, prompting us to find excuses why we can't do likewise.

Instead of finding reasons why we *can't* take a particular approach to a given subject, I'd suggest we find ways in which we *can.* I believe that every one of these photographs can help us see the *possibilities* inherent in our own jobs as visual communicators. I hope you will take it from there.

Philip N. Douglis
Swarthmore, Pennsylvania
1982

Chapter 1

Symbols in juxtaposition: the incongruous image

The camera, by its very nature, sees out of context. It can arrest a moment in time, taking it out of its flow. It can change relationships in space. It can refine and reproduce the contrasts between light and dark far more dramatically than the eye can.

Because of this, it is not difficult to isolate and contrast opposing elements to achieve the incongruous. It is incongruity, more than any other principle, that brings forth symbolic values within the photographic image. Yet, for some inexplicable reason, most photographs made by organizations for their employees, shareholders, and external audiences are anything but incongruous.

They are literal. They record only what can be "shown" in a picture, instead of placing symbols in juxtaposition to create contrasts which activate the imagination and the emotions of the viewer.

Simple description becomes boring when used in editorial photography. Incongruous images, on the other hand, are highly interpretive. They reflect the wit, wisdom, and vision of the photographers who make them.

It is the ability to see and capture the incongruous that marks the level of a photographer's performance as a communicator.

A great city, a great loneliness

**John Gerstner, editor, *JD Journal*
Deere & Company
Moline, Illinois**

Few editor/photographers working for organizational publications use incongruity as expertly, and as consistently, as does John Gerstner, who works largely in color and seeks, through his images, to raise as many questions as answers.

The back cover of his award-winning magazine, *JD Journal*, invariably features an image that stands by itself, one designed solely to make his readers *think*, an objective quite rare in the field of organizational publications.

This picture, taken along Lake Michigan, looking toward downtown Chicago, juxtaposes skyline, a human figure, and a pile of garbage. The Latin proverb "A great city, a great loneliness" is the only context the reader is offered.

A number of years ago, the late Minor White, a great photographer, teacher, and editor in his own right, said "a photograph is a function, not a thing. It acts as a catalyst, is a step in a process, not an end product. The image in a viewer's mind is more important than the photograph itself." And so Gerstner sees the role of this image. The incongruities allow the reader to ponder the nature of the individual, the society, the monuments we build to our civilization, and the droppings we leave behind. The answers, if any, will be supplied not by the sender of this message, but by the receiver.

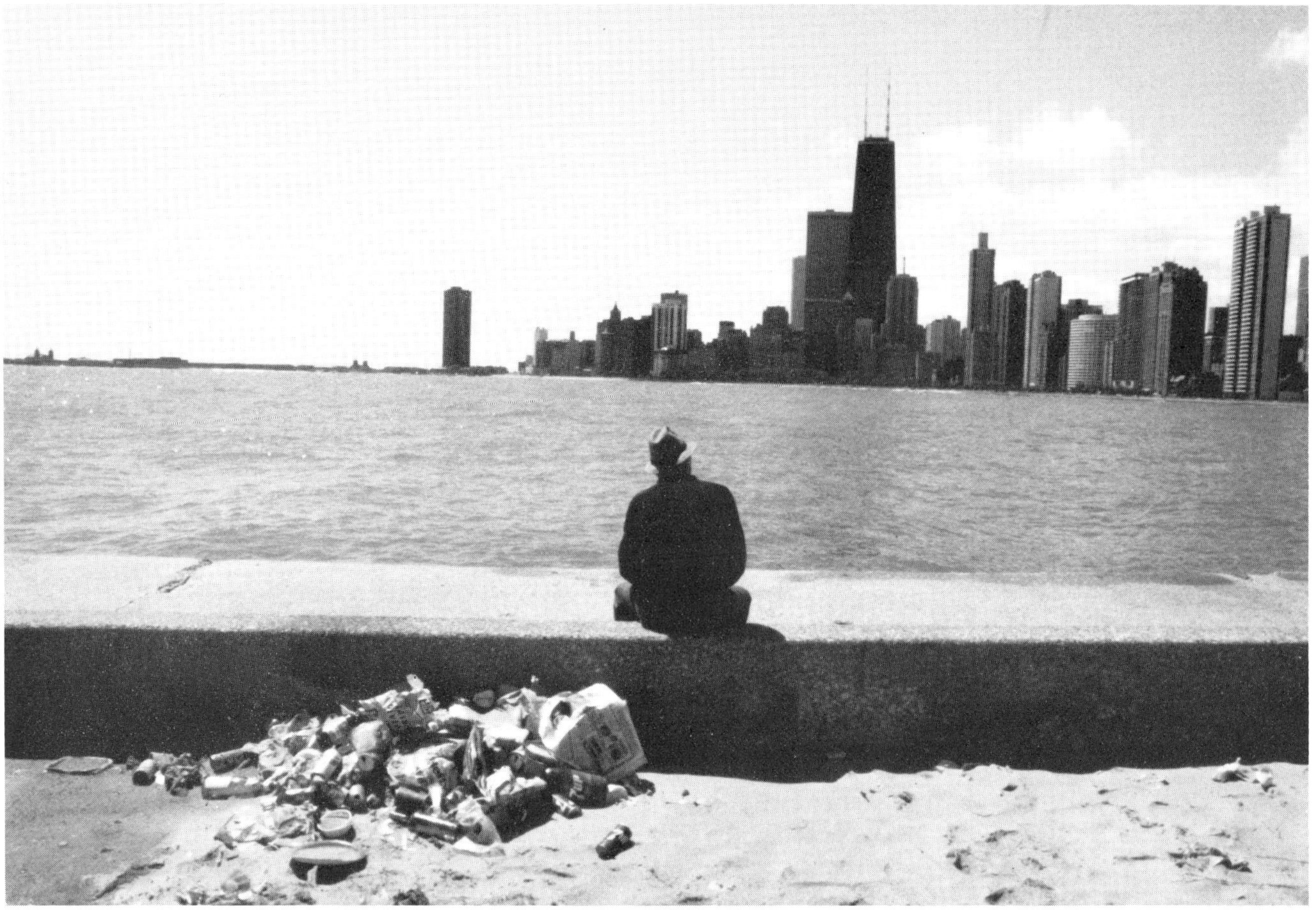

Lassoed

Baron Wolman, freelance photographer
Client: Levi Strauss & Co.
San Francisco, California

Incongruity is at the very basis of humor. And Baron Wolman uses it here to place art and life into bizarre juxtaposition.

Levi's decided to decorate 40-foot trailer trucks with super graphics for advertising and asked Wolman to shoot a story on it for the company's magazine. The final stage was the application of the design, accomplished by placing huge decals on the sides of the trucks.

Recognizing an incongruous idea when he sees one, Wolman waits until half the design is already in place and watches while the worker aligns the other half. At precisely the moment when the worker is affixing the extension of the lasso, Wolman shoots. The body language of both man and decoration contrast humorously, particularly the placement of legs and arms. The picture not only shows the reader how the job was done, but it does so with a touch of wit and whimsy. The picture—and the story—become unforgettable.

Humor is all too rare in organizational publications, probably because it is not easy to capture such incongruous moments. Such events are usually spontaneous. The photographer must be in the right place at the right time, have the eye to recognize a good thing when it happens, and be able to skillfully get it on film.

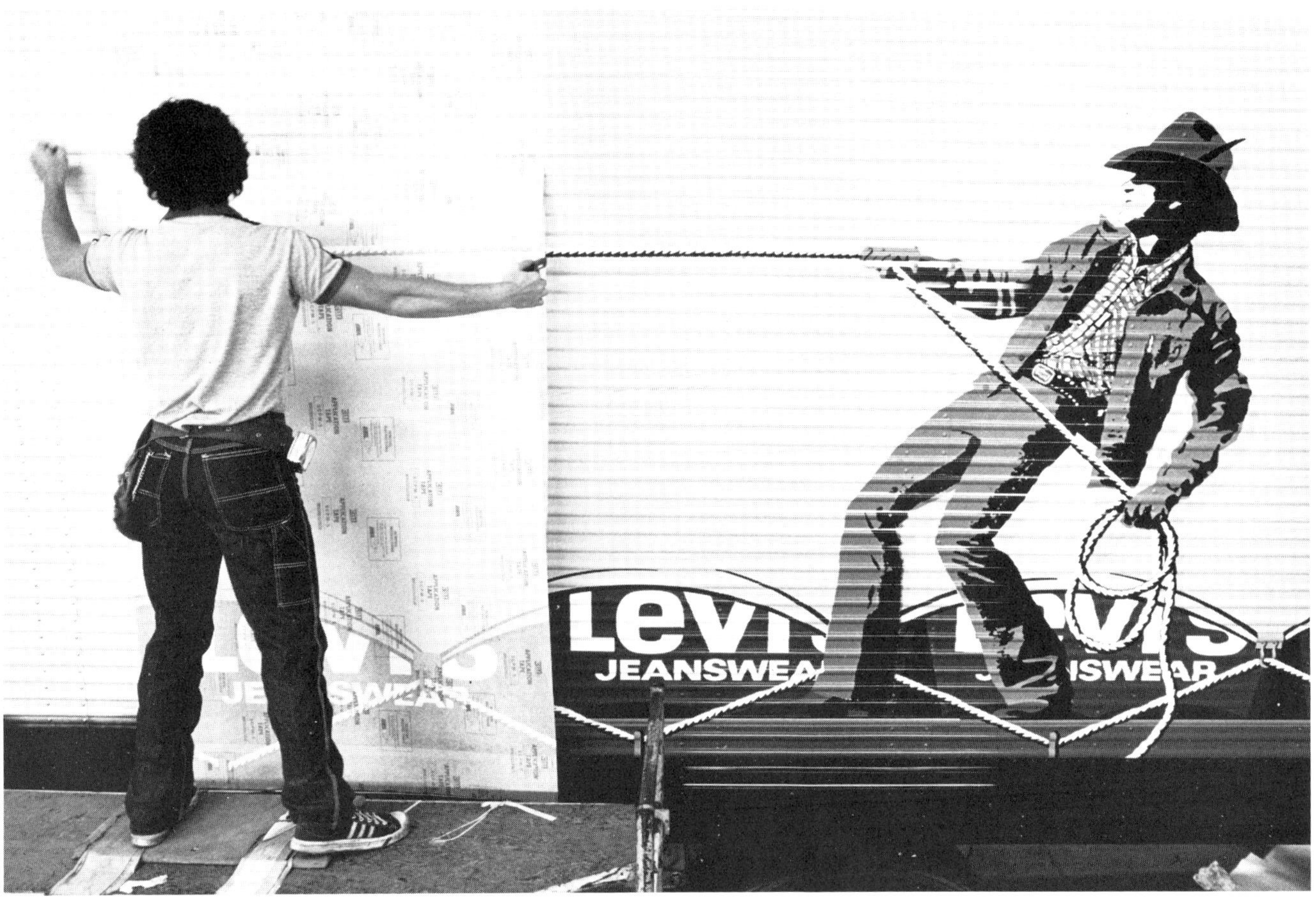
JEANSWEAR

Landfill

Kurt Foss, photojournalist
Hennepin County Public Affairs
Minneapolis, Minnesota

In the early 80s, Hennepin County faced a problem: Its landfills were filling up. By mid-decade, the county would need another means of waste disposal. Plans called for a plant that could convert solid waste into energy, and that plant would be built at taxpayer expense.

It was important that the taxpayer be made aware of the problem, in order to pave the way for public acceptance of the new plant. The county's annual report would be the vehicle for this communication attempt.

Photojournalist Foss, among the finest photographers at work in the field of government public relations, and his editorial colleagues decided to stress the *problem* in visual terms and rely on the text to discuss the solutions.

Foss uses the principle of incongruous contrast to the utmost. He chooses a 24mm wide-angle lens, exaggerating subject matter close to the camera and reducing the distant bulldozer in scale.

His low vantage point places the bulldozer high in the frame. He selects a small lens opening, to make both garbage and machine sharp. The problem is defined through a contrast in scale relationships. Given the context of the accompanying text, the reader has to get the point.

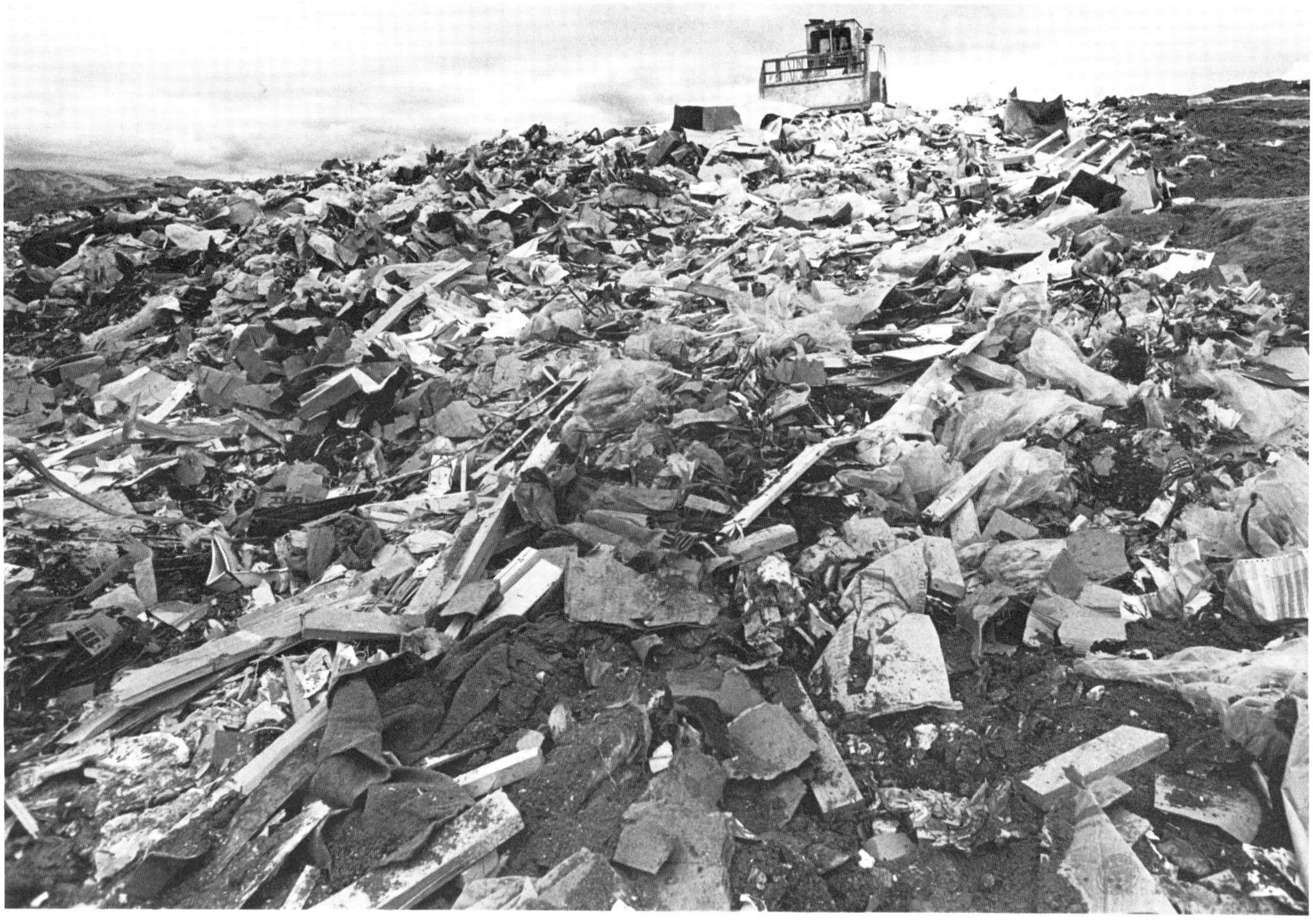

Door prize

Mark Sandlin, manager,
  photographic services
Home Mission Board, Southern
  Baptist Convention
Atlanta, Georgia

It was incongruous, to say the least, to find an image like this one in a religious publication. But *Missions USA*, the magazine of the SBC's Home Mission Board, draws repeatedly on incongruity to communicate the issues faced by its missionaries.

In September 1980, the magazine ran a story on the resurgence of the Klan. Along with the familiar shots of flaming crosses in the night, SBC photographer Mark Sandlin captured the moment when a Thompson submachine gun was raffled off as a door prize by the secretary of the Antioch, Tennessee, chapter.

The incongruities within this image make it work as a symbol for what the SBC Home Mission Board sees as the point of its story. The sight of a woman holding a lethal weapon is incongruous. The costume itself is incongruous. So are sunglasses —at a night rally. The placement of the subject between the flags of the Klan and the nation adds still another discordant note. And to underscore the point, the woman's response is joyful.

The viewers are left to read into the scene what they will. Given the nature of the task before a missionary, the desired message will, no doubt, come home loud and clear.

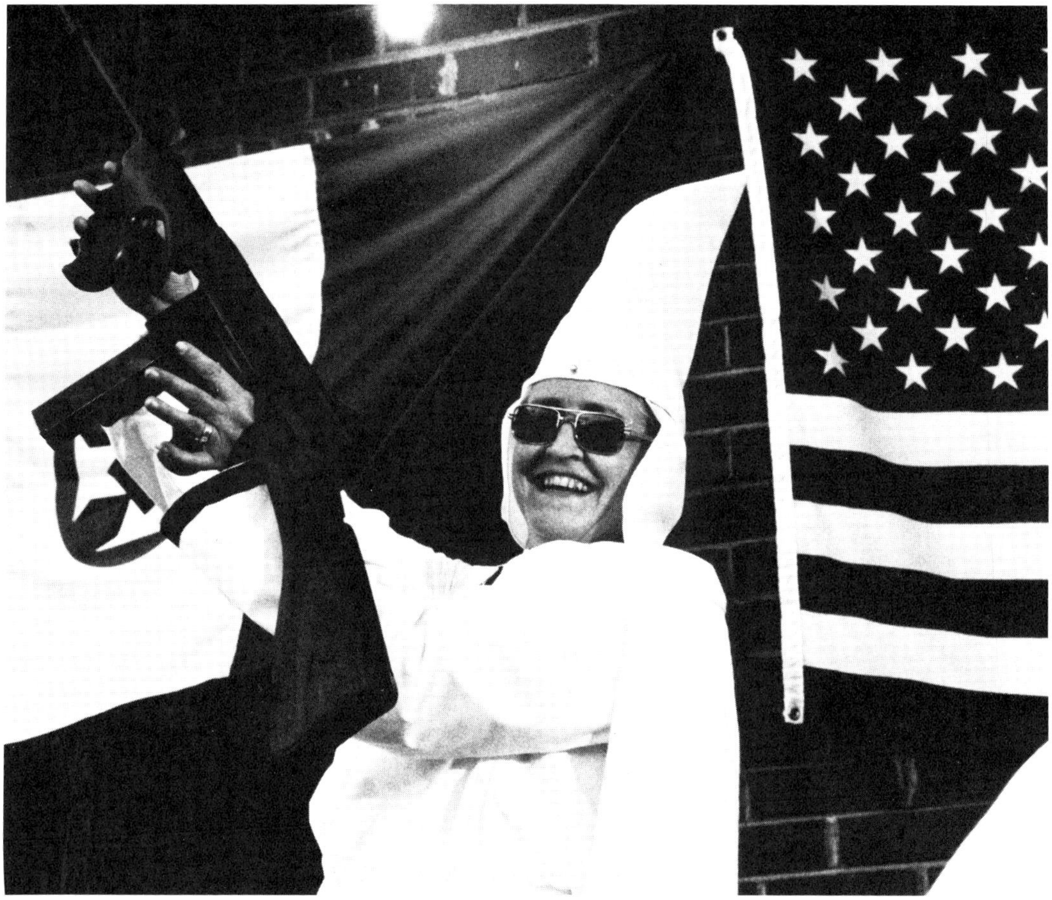

Bailey King on his farm, Quentin, Mississippi, 1979

**Don Rutledge, photojournalist
Home Mission Board, Southern
  Baptist Convention
Atlanta, Georgia**

One of the most profound photo-essays yet produced for an organizational publication was created by Don Rutledge for *Missions USA* in late 1979. It dealt with the issue of poverty and attempted to give SBC missionaries an understanding of the problem by focusing on one man, his family, his life, deep in rural Mississippi.

Bailey King, disabled farmer, father of ten, deeply impoverished, allowed Rutledge to live with his family over a period of many weeks. Rutledge acquired a deep respect for his subject, and in this portrait of King, one of several in the essay, he expresses that respect eloquently.

It is obvious that King has long become accustomed to the presence of Rutledge's Nikons, which consumed more than 4,000 frames of film. He broods amidst his animals, one of which, incongruously, is curled up in his lap.

He is oblivious to the animals. His mind is obviously elsewhere. Yet they seem dependent on him, and he in a sense is dependent on them. The tiny white dog, in particular, turns an ordinary backyard scene into an extraordinary moment. For this small animal becomes virtually a physical part of his master, who provides a makeshift resting place. As for King, his battle against poverty also involves making-do.

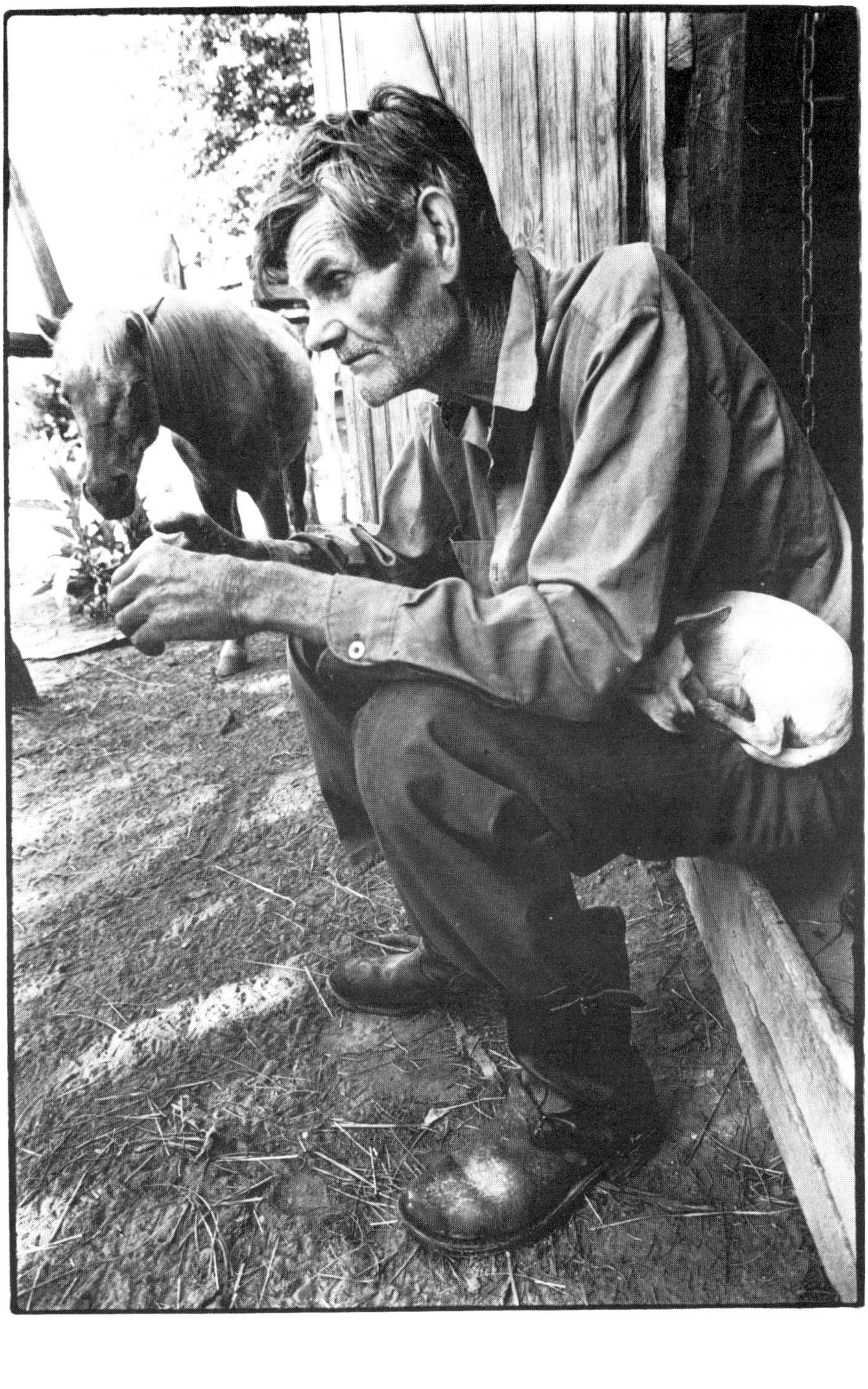

Christmas party

Tom Treuter, supervisor,
 publication photography and
 design
William Beaumont Hospital
Royal Oak, Michigan

Pictures of young patients having fun at Christmas parties are often printed in hospital publications. No matter how crude the photographic technique, such pictures are almost always appealing because of the nature of the subject itself. But every so often, photographic form and content mesh to make such an image transcend the event, projecting the simple joy of childhood in a universal way.

Such a picture was made by Tom Treuter in 1980, as a fitting finale for a story on how a local Lions Club grant was helping the hospital teach sick children to speak again. Some members of the Detroit Tigers baseball team were present at the party. We don't see them, we don't need to. What we do see is the incongruous result of their kindness to this young patient.

A Tiger baseball cap, many sizes too large, spins on the head of the youngster, obviously captivated by the moment. Treuter uses a long telephoto lens to reach across distance and simplify the image, throwing the busy background out of focus. The double incongruity of a big hat on a small child, a gift from a professional athlete to a frail little girl, fuses with the child's uninhibited response. She expresses that most fragile of emotions—absolute ecstasy.

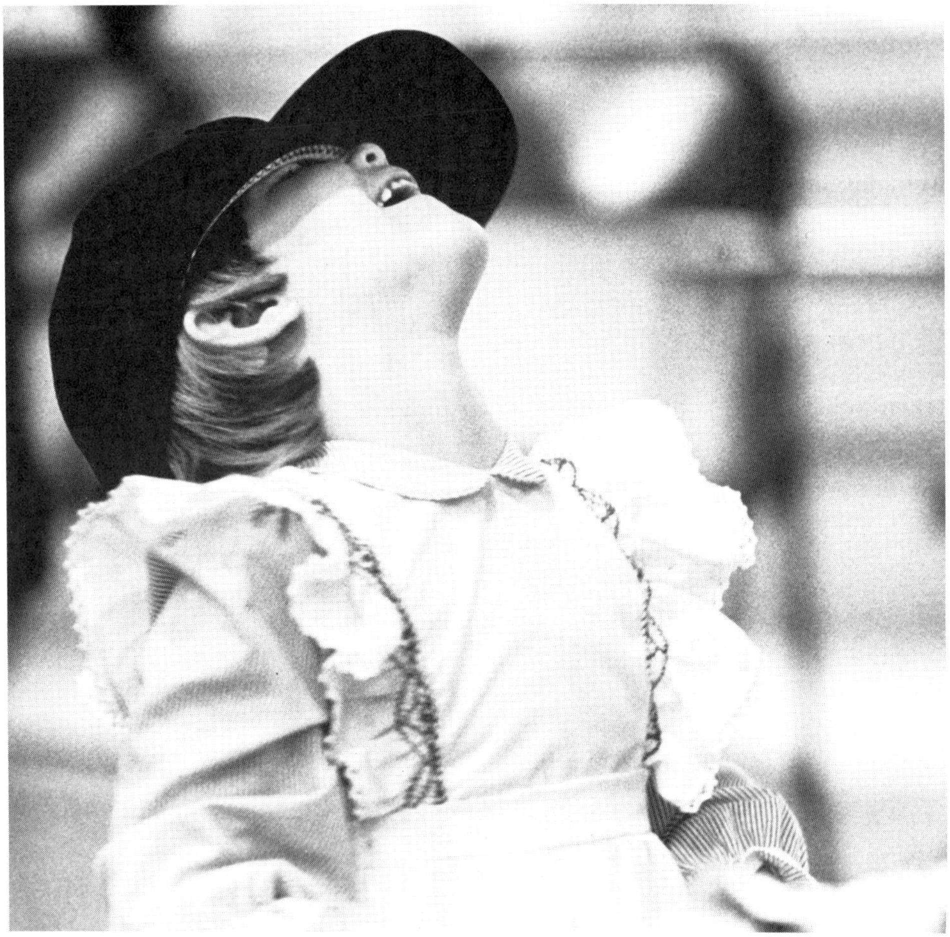

Counselor

Bruce Stromberg, freelance photographer
Client: Episcopal Community Services
Philadelphia, Pennsylvania

One of the many services the Episcopal Church provides to the community is prison counseling. For its 1979 annual report, Episcopal Community Services of Philadelphia asked freelancer Bruce Stromberg to capture the essence of that service in a picture.

Stromberg is able to simplify the image, preserve the anonymity of the prisoner, and draw on incongruous juxtaposition of elements in this striking fulfillment of his assignment.

He contrasts light against dark, juxtaposing incarceration against freedom, carefully dividing the image right down the center. In the profile of the counselor, we sense compassion. His rounded beard rhythmically echoes his tousled forelock.

The rhythms of the bars are broken only by the grasping fingers of the prisoner. A sense of tension is created, and it is the resolution of that tension that is at the core of the counselor's assignment.

Drawing on light, rhythm, response, selective focus, and a close vantage point, Stromberg allows the incongruities of the scene to speak for themselves.

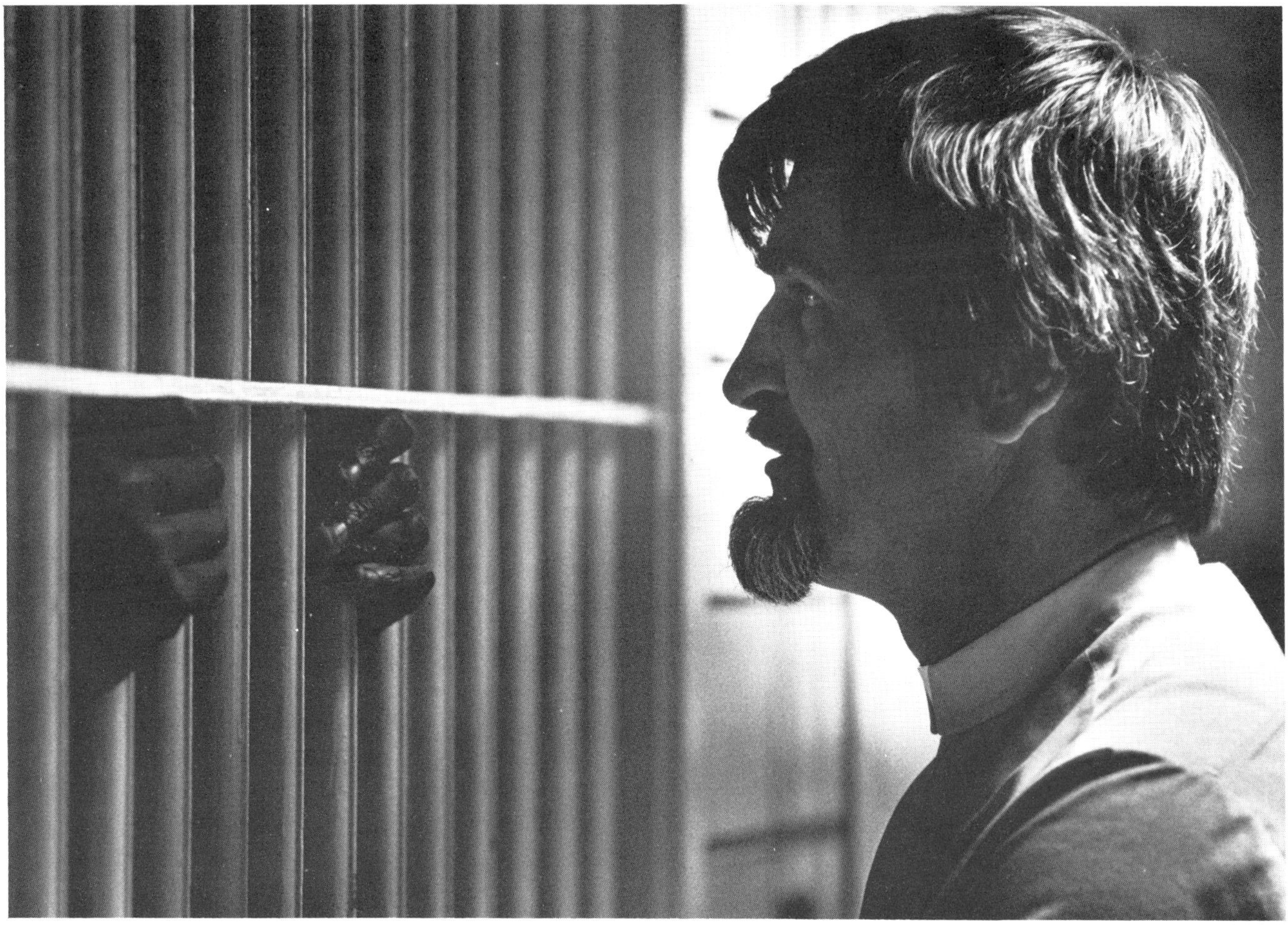

Kicking the habit

Dave Denemark, publications coordinator
Medical College of Wisconsin
Milwaukee, Wisconsin

Sometimes, photojournalism, in its true sense, will not solve a visual problem for a publication. But there are other valid approaches. Photo-illustration, the thematic interpretation of carefully controlled subject matter, may provide an answer, as it did for Dave Denemark's story on the struggle to stop smoking.

We call this a "concept" illustration, and concept illustrations are based largely upon incongruity. They are usually pictures that are created entirely out of the imagination. The reader knows they are not real—but enjoys them nevertheless. While they lack the credibility and documentary validation of photojournalism, they can still make a visual point, and make it well.

Denemark forms ten hands into a thrusting circle of fingers forcing their way into a hideous mass of crushed cigarette butts. Viewers can viscerally feel the revulsion Denemark wants to express. By coming in close and using the picture's edges to limit what we see of the anonymous smokers, Denemark focuses our attention on the *result*—the butts themselves—instead of the hands actually holding the butts.

Never in the course of human events have so many smokers quit at one time and in one place. But that is what conceptual illustration does so well. It relies on incongruous contrivance to juxtapose the real against the imagined, thereby making the point.

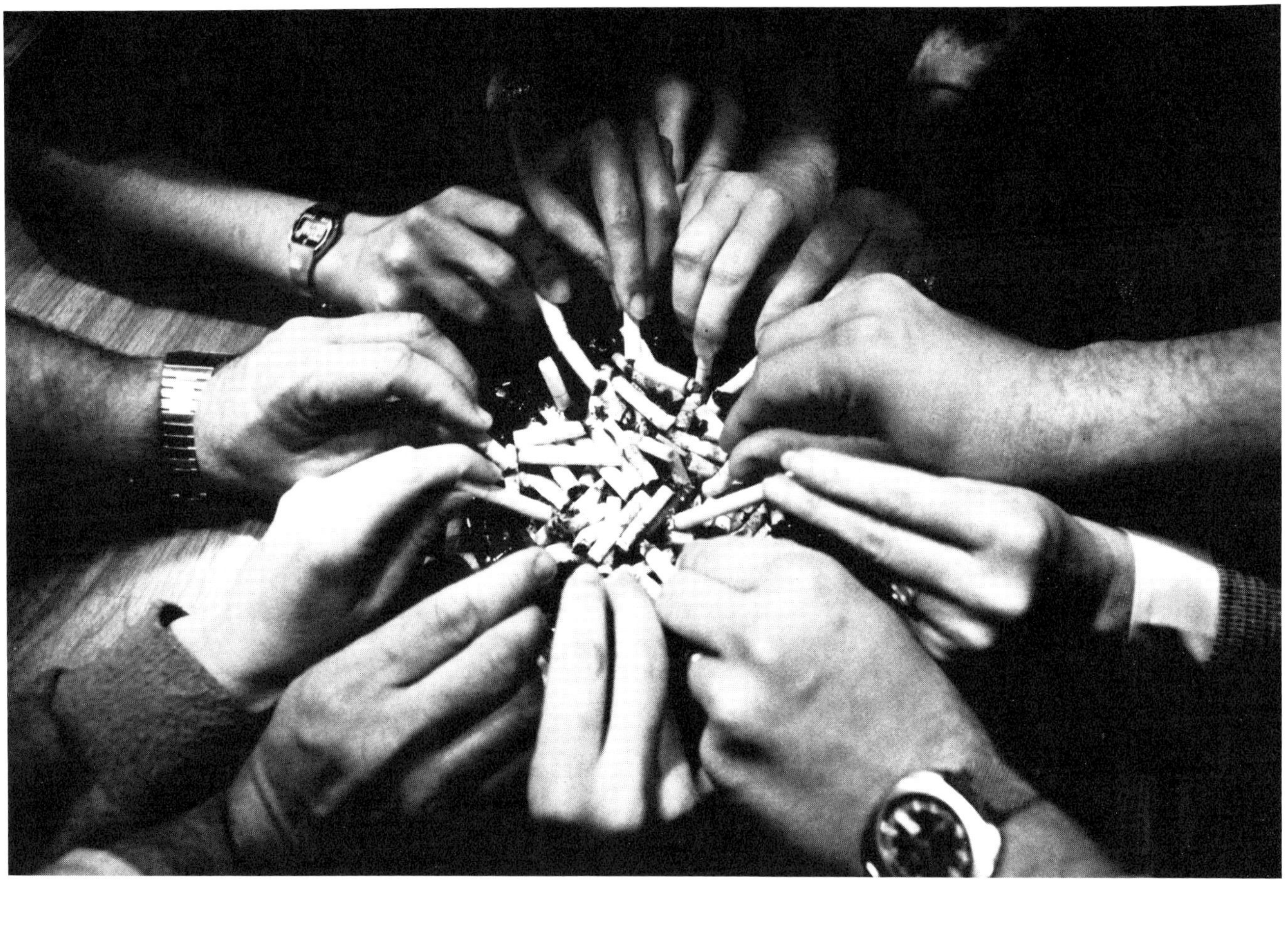

Chapter 2

Spontaneous responses: the moment picture

Of all the means of expression, photography is the only one that fixes forever the transitory instant. There is no better example of this capability than the "moment" picture.

No matter how ordinary the circumstances, people are continually responding to each other in spontaneous bursts. The meeting of eyes, movement of bodies, and gesture, supplemented by the presence of symbolic environment, can go far beyond the nature of the event itself.

Such encounters can stand for the larger forces that bond an organization into a humane enterprise. Photography can penetrate to the core of human relationships, thereby interpreting our institutions—and the people who serve them—to our readers so that ultimately the institutions themselves can be better understood.

Organizational photojournalists anticipate such encounters. They make sure they are in a position to coherently record the moments on film.

Through such moments as these, the few come to symbolize the many. These small yet precious relationships can be used in print to validate the conflicts and kinships, problems and solutions, that ultimately fuel the workings of the organization itself.

An eye for art and artist

Kurt Foss, photojournalist
Hennepin County Public Affairs
Minneapolis, Minnesota

"Moment pictures" are elusive. We never know when they will happen. But somehow the best of the organizational photojournalists get them consistently. Kurt Foss got this one because he did not pack up his camera and go home after being asked to make a ceremonial picture of a county commissioner posing with a group of handicapped artists visiting an exhibit of their own work. Foss made the photographs of the smiling commissioner and dutifully posing artists, as requested. But he knows that such pictures are not photojournalism. They will have value only to the people who appear in them, not to the readers of any publication. He must somehow go beyond the ceremonial cliche and say something about the event that will touch the emotions and the imaginations of his readers.

Foss hangs around to shoot scenes of the visitors studying the exhibit. For the exhibit itself is the story. It then occurs to Foss that the readers of his publication deserve a unique insight into the experience of attending the exhibit. For that is the great gift of editorial photography—to be able to take the reader places, showing them things and interpreting them in ways that the reader would not otherwise be able to enjoy.

After a while, Foss notices a handicapped artist wheeling herself through the exhibit and decides to concentrate on her reactions to the work of her fellow artists. As he focuses on her viewing the paintings, Foss sees a mother and her young son enter his viewfinder. Lowering himself out of sight, he imagines in his mind's eye a fantasy image. If only the mother would look at the artwork and the boy would turn around and look at the artist in the wheelchair, everything would come together. Foss holds his breath. The mother reaches the limits of the frame. The boy turns and gives the artist a look that only a child could give. Foss squeezes the shutter, exhaling at last.

"It is a strange and wonderful feeling," he says, "to get an image in your mind's eye, watch it take place, and use the camera to freeze the moment forever."

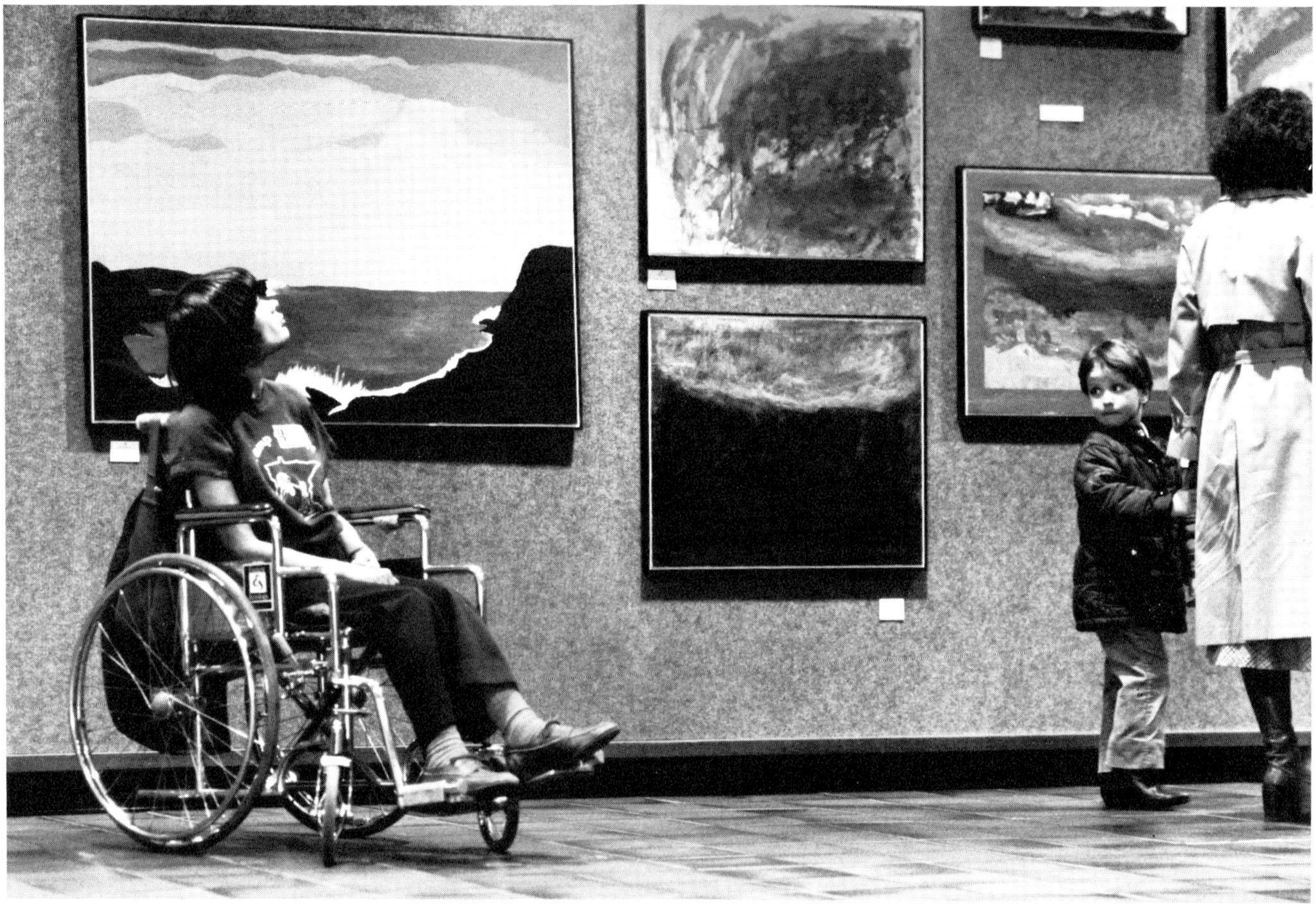

Mother's farewell

Robb Mitchell, editor, *Living*
Methodist Hospitals Foundation
Memphis, Tennessee

When Robb Mitchell needed a cover shot to reach out and pull readers into an issue devoted solely to neonatal intensive care, he had this one ready to go. A wise choice. On the surface, it is a woman and her newborn baby. Yet on another level, it is a study of a mother saying goodbye. The baby must remain behind in the hospital for medical treatment.

It is a personal moment, one that could not be effectively staged. Mitchell had to be there when it happened, and that takes planning and patience on the part of the photographer and cooperation from the subject.

Mitchell followed the story of the care and treatment of little Merrye-Marie Meeks for six months, spending a part of almost every working day interpreting her progress. He was ubiquitous, always there but rarely noticed. When it came time for the mother to say farewell, it was no accident that Mitchell was on hand to record the moment.

Mitchell can take various approaches to this picture. Should he photograph the mother full face so we can see her eyes? Should he move around to feature the full face of the baby? Should he back away and get in more of the hospital environment? All of these options are open to him. But for this purpose, none would have produced an image as strong as this one.

Selecting the right moment, the right position, the right play of light and darkness, the right expression —all occurring simultaneously— makes what seems to be the simple act of taking a picture inordinately complex. Photographers must acquire, through extensive experience, the instinctive ability to sort out these choices, selecting the most appropriate one in the blink of an eye.

The incongruity of a tiny hand held in huge fingers. A mother's kiss, not yet completed. A tender expression, framed in a cascade of hair. They all flow together to produce a cover photograph that works. It is a rare reader that will not open this publication on the spot to read—and see—more.

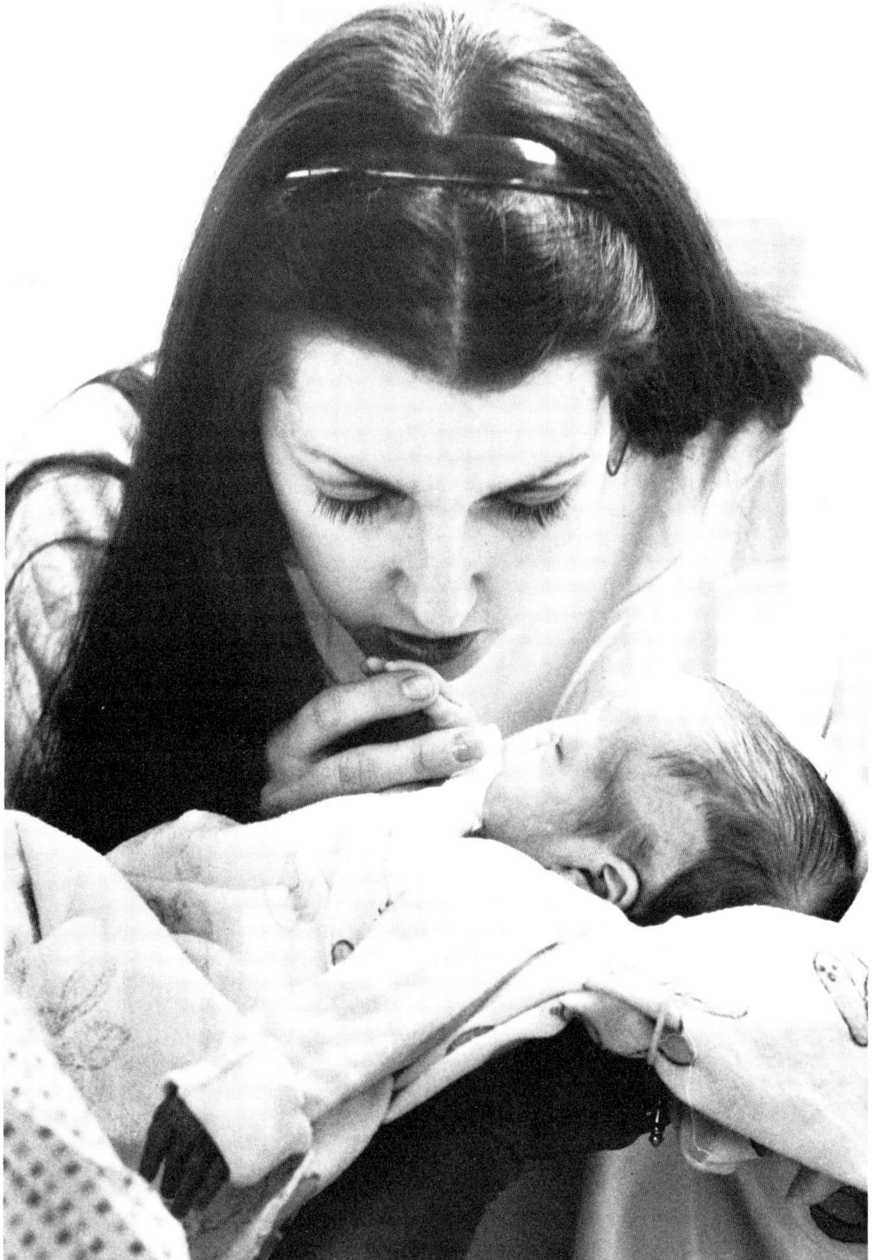

Boot camp for restaurant managers

Mike Jenkins, communications manager
Burger Chefs Systems, Inc.
Indianapolis, Indiana

To find spontaneous moments, it is often important to get out of the office, plant, hospital, or campus, and go out into the larger world. For it is often outside of the confines of the job that people become relaxed enough to spontaneously reveal themselves. For this reason, many organizations hold training programs away from the place of work. They go to great lengths to change the conditions under which people relate to each other—breaking down inhibitions, encouraging communication, healthy conflict.

Organizational photographers should get out from behind those four walls, too. When they do, they often bring back on film moments such as the one Mike Jenkins reveals to us here.

Burger Chef sends its vice presidents to a "boot camp" for restaurant managers, simulating a competition complete with military costume and customs. Jenkins goes into "combat" with them. Here, in an arena where jackets and ties are exchanged for fatigues and berets, a "four star general" shares a spontaneous laugh with his bivouac buddies. We can sense his bluff and swagger—he is a veritable Patton, cigar at the ready, sunglasses perched under the jaunty beret. Behind him his colleagues appear less confident, making his gesture all the more vivid through incongruous contrast. Jenkins makes a better picture of these mock warriors in company war games than many military publications would make of the real thing.

The readers of Jenkins' publication have never seen these managers looking quite like this. The moment of exuberance shared by the pair in conversation becomes all the more intriguing because of the costumes. Using selective focus to suggest the background and stress the featured players, Jenkins simplifies what would otherwise be a cluttered image. He emphasizes hands as well as expressions to drive home the moment. Two of the men smoke cigars, another holds what may be a can of beer. At the heart of the scene is the general's universal gesture—suggesting, perhaps, that war, though hell, can have its lighter moments.

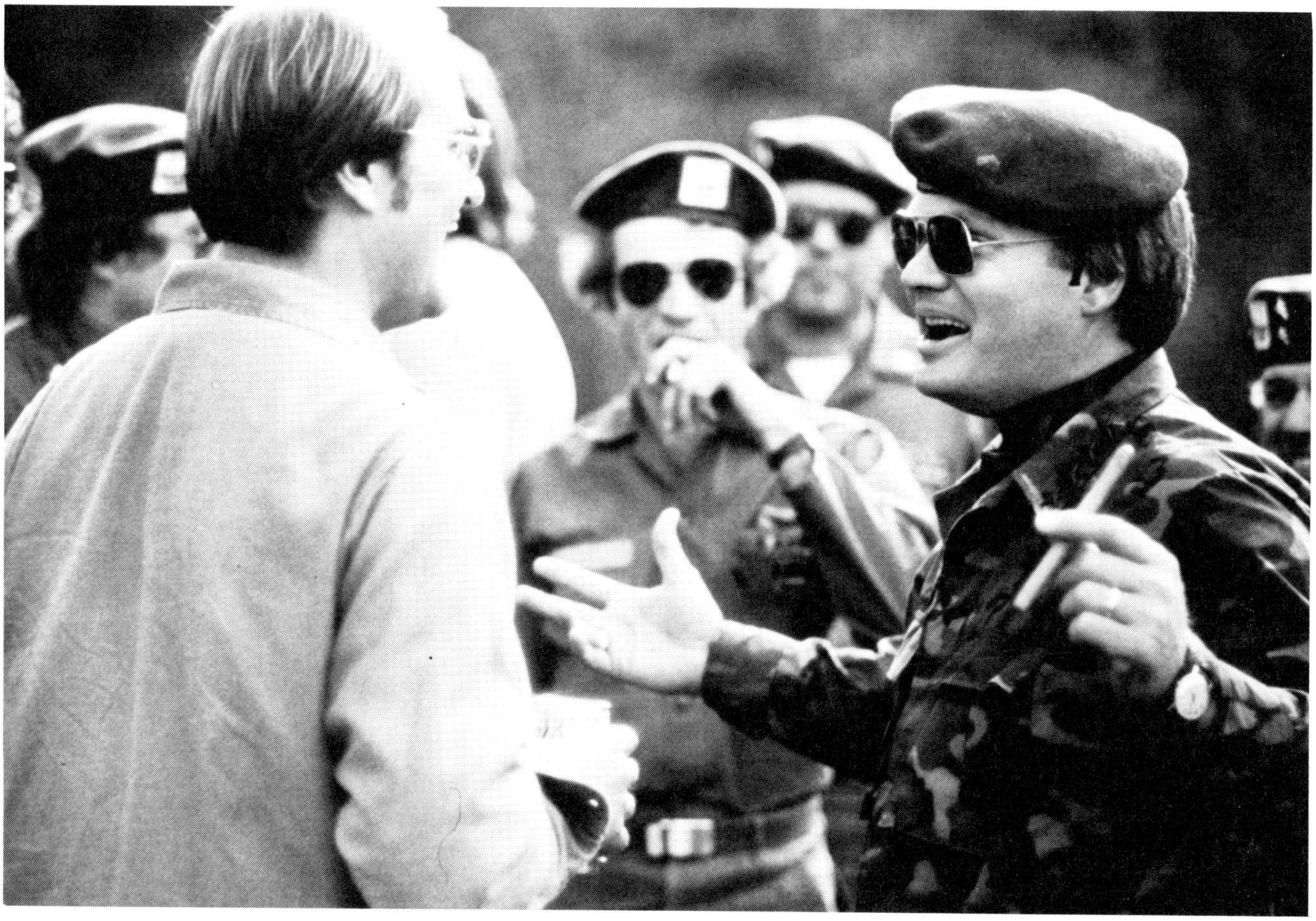

Hospice checker game

Tom Treuter, supervisor, publication photography and design
William Beaumont Hospital
Royal Oak, Michigan

Organizational publications span the cycle of life, yet few dare to visually explore the nature of the problems surrounding death and dying. The final stage of life remains the great taboo. Among the finest attempts to break this taboo is a picture feature on a hospice program in *Beaumonitor*, the publication of Beaumont Hospital, near Detroit.

A hospice gives comfort at the end of life. Marge Mollica, RN, is asked to become, in effect, an extension of friend and family for her patients. In playing checkers with one of them, nurse Mollica teaches him how to live even as he is dying. Tom Treuter manages to find those moments in the checker game when Mollica's spontaneous responses visually define the purpose and the value of the hospice. It is as tough an assignment as any photojournalist could assume.

In this pairing, selected from among the six photographs that ran with the story, Treuter's images suggest that three games are actually going on at once. Game one is simply a depiction of a checkers match between nurse Mollica and a dying patient. Game two is Mollica's own intensity—she takes the game as seriously as she takes her job. She hates to lose a move, and when she does, she displays the chagrin of a good sport. Game three is the end game itself. The quality of what little is left to this man's life rests largely in small victories won upon a checkerboard.

Treuter tells us that this man always wins these games. Nobody can beat him, although Mollica is trying her best to do so. She responds with a range of emotion to his moves. The patient is seen only as a softly focused presence in the foreground. Although Mollica and the viewer know this man will lose the ultimate game, we can't help but feel that his last days are being spent in living life to the fullest. That is the goal of the hospice program, and these pictures convey it well. Through the metaphor of the checker game, these pictures strike at the great taboo and make short work of it.

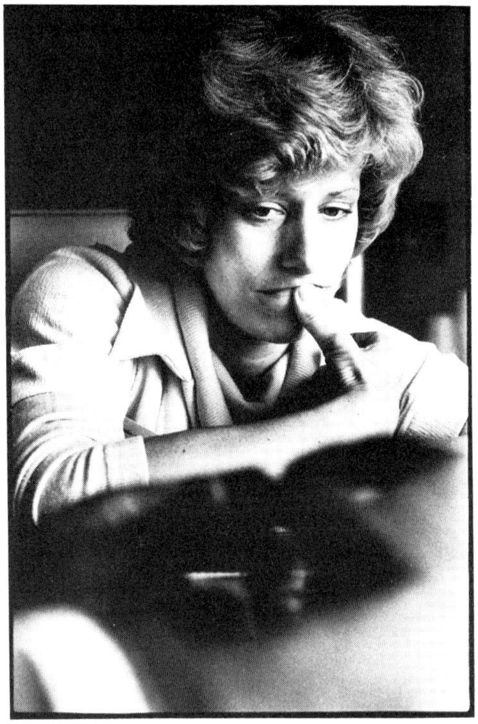

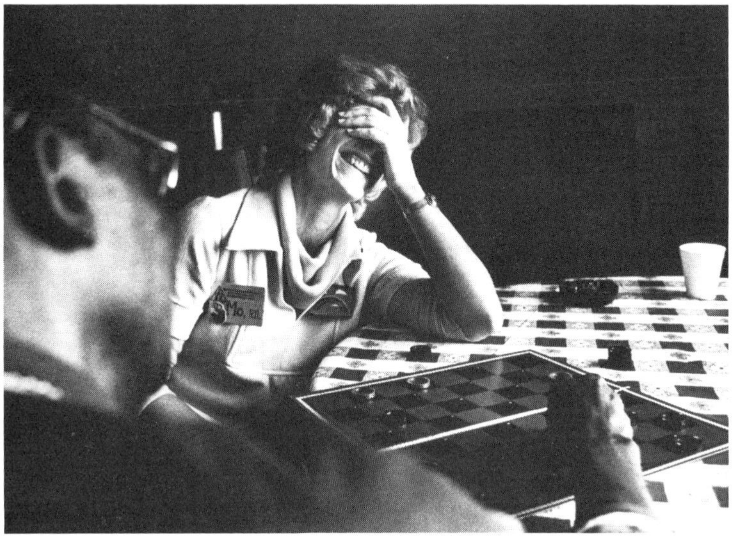

Liberated!

Paul Obregon, senior photographer
Home Mission Board, Southern Baptist Convention
Atlanta, Georgia

The liberation of thousands of Cuban political prisoners was a major news event, drawing worldwide photo coverage. Many organizational publications featured stories on the event but few with the emotional intensity of *Missions USA*, publication of the Southern Baptist Convention's Home Mission Board.

Perhaps the most striking photograph in Paul Obregon's coverage of the event is this shot of a reunified family in an empty parking garage under a Miami stadium. The Miami area Hispanic Baptist churches had chartered a plane to bring the prisoners from Cuba, and as they disperse from the processing area, Obregon follows a family taking those first steps into a new life together.

He uses a valuable technique to capture the spontaneity of the moment—working from behind instead of in front of the subject. Photographing people from behind, in order to relate them to each other and to their environment, gives photographers a unique advantage: They can't be seen by their subjects. People photographed from such vantage points are less inhibited and behave as if no photographer were present.

The rear vantage point also offers us, as viewers, a privileged perspective. We are eavesdroppers, experiencing the event as observers. It is not necessary to see the faces of these people. We are given a context for their actions by the story. We know why they are there, and now we know how they feel about the event and each other.

Obregon tells us that he believes the reader can imagine any person in their place; the emotional experience we observe here is universal. The viewer walks in their footsteps.

Spontaneous responses invite the viewer to share emotions with people they will never know. By vicariously experiencing the intimate moments of others, we will remember what they looked and felt like, long after we have forgotten the events they represent.

TROPICAL STADIUM DIRECTORY
STADIUM OFFICE
RESTROOMS
FIRST AID ROOM
CONCESSION STAND AND OFFICE #1
CONCESSION STAND AND OFFICE #2
CONCESSION STAND #3
RAMP TO SEATING
STEPS TO SEATING

Miss Polly and child

Dave Denemark, publications coordinator
Medical College of Wisconsin
Milwaukee, Wisconsin

Children make such good photographic subjects because they are uninhibited. They respond intuitively and will not hide those responses. So wide is the range of these responses that pictures of kids are almost always appealing.

And organizational photographers feast on them. Coverage of company picnics, for example, almost always include a healthy dose of happy children hamming it up for the camera. Hospital publications draw heavily on sympathetic photographs involving children as patients. No matter how ordinary the photographic technique, pictures of children are so natural and human that they can't miss drawing strong reader reaction.

The best photographic interpretations of children manage to avoid stereotypical cliches. They capture moments that are unique, that offer insights into the wonderfully open mental processes of childhood. They draw on incongruous juxtaposition, spontaneous explorations into fantasy that only a child can engineer.

Dave Denemark has found such a moment in this encounter. While shooting a story on the child/parent intervention program at the Milwaukee County Mental Health Complex, he is able to sum up in one image the fragile beauty of a mother/daughter relationship.

Denemark is invisible. He is trusted. He works quietly and carefully so as not to distract the child and break the mood. The click of his shutter is ignored as he allows this scene to unfold before us.

We never see the face of the child herself. But in the face of the mother we are treated to a sublime moment. By incongruously placing a strand of the mother's long hair across her nose, the child is doing more than playing. She is learning where things go, how they work, and, ultimately, what they mean. The mother's obvious patience and pleasure comes through. We view a private moment which says more about love and learning than hundreds of words on the subject.

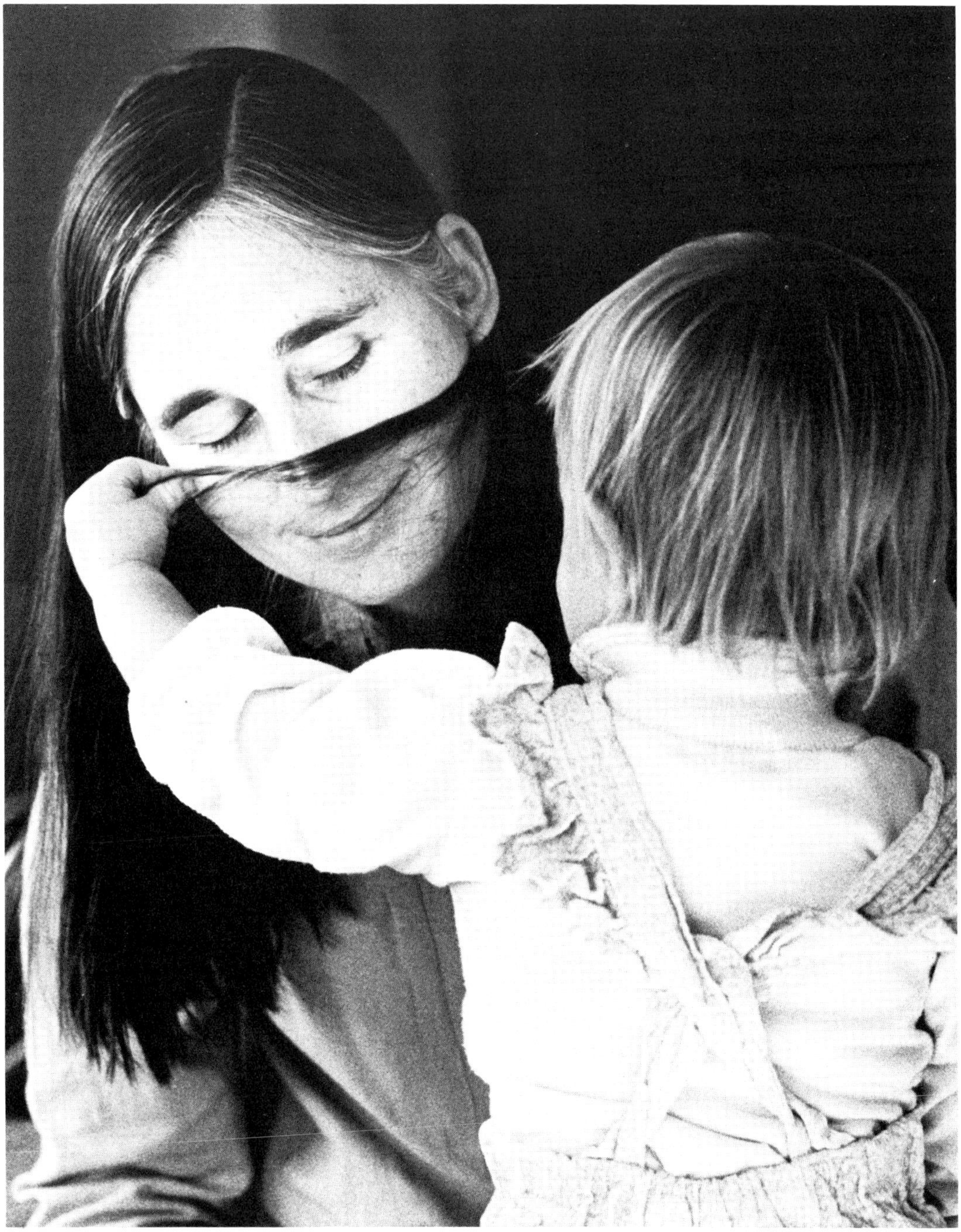

Laughter in the afternoon

Ed Eckstein, freelance photographer
Clients: Church Pension Fund, American Medical Affiliates
Philadelphia, Pennsylvania

Of all the photographs in this book, this one, probably more than any other, reveals the role of the creative audience.

For it is the viewer who must finish the process this picture begins. The facts within the photograph provide only our starting point.

The image is deceptively simple. A 104-year-old woman is rolled out onto the lawn of the retirement home for a photo session with Ed Eckstein. The woman laughs at something he says. And, incredibly, a white dog next to her is laughing, too. But to a perceptive viewer, the picture offers more than that. It is a delicious image, the kind of picture that stimulates ideas and, for some, tickles the funny bone. It is poetry, social commentary, and a visual pun.

It was originally made as an illustration on retirement for the Church Pension Fund and later used in a promotional brochure by American Medical Affiliates, an operator of health care centers. Both used it to symbolize the pleasures of old age. But the picture can take us elsewhere, if we wish.

We are looking at something we do not normally see, the incongruity of animal and human apparently sharing the same emotion at the same time in the same place. The woman is obviously infirm, yet still enjoys herself to the utmost, adding another note of incongruity. The photograph is bizarre—a depiction of spontaneous and simultaneous outbursts of joy from a most unlikely couple.

Eckstein's careful rendering of the subject enhances it. He moves in closely to make the subjects large and rich in detail. Yet the wideangle lens embraces both woman and dog and still reveals the rolling lawns beyond. The subjects are white, contrasting sharply to the grey and black tones of the landscape, making the woman and dog stand out. The tree explodes from behind the woman, rhythmically repeating the explosion of laughter from both parties. While they may laugh at Eckstein, they are also laughing at us.

And we can laugh back at them. Our own imaginations can take over at this point, and we can supply our own reasons for their laughter—and ours. We bring our own context to bear on the photograph, making of it what we wish. One viewer might see this picture differently from another. In its multiple meanings, is its strength.

Its construction reminds us of the wonderful visual harmony of Cartier-Bresson's surrealistic photojournalism. Or the ironic commentaries on dogs as human surrogates in the photos of Elliott Erwitt and Garry Winogrand. We can feast on this picture, looking at it for a long time, fascinated by the forces of chance which brought these elements together for Eckstein to bring to us.

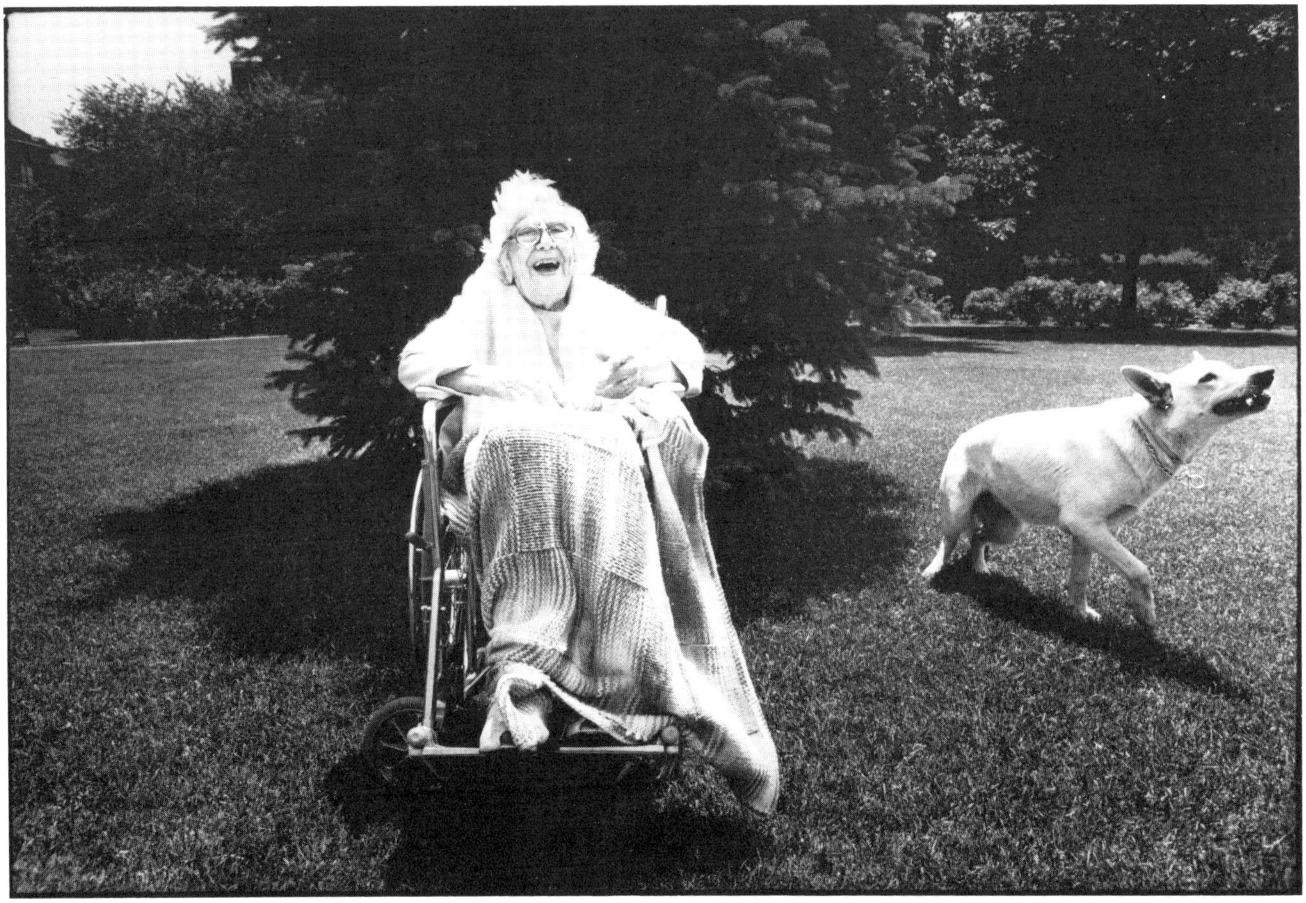

Chapter 3

Machines and equipment: beyond the thing itself

Management is usually proud of new machines and equipment. Photographers are blindly asked to record them on film, in order to convey to the viewer the fact that such machines and equipment actually "exist."

Photos such as these belong in catalogs and manuals, not in newspapers, magazines, and newsletters. How do we make pictures of such things "interesting" or "different"? We don't. If we make pictures solely for graphic or aesthetic qualities, we call attention to form at the expense of content.

The answer rests in the ability of the photographer to *say* something about the machine to the viewer. To relate it somehow to human beings. To imply how such a machine works, what is special about it, how people feel about it, and how they benefit from it.

Interpretive photographers will relate the machine or equipment to a context, often incongruous. They will draw on scale relationships, light, vantage point, and frame to stress its size, its function, its ultimate meaning. They will often bore in on the details. Instead of showing the whole machine, they may only show a fragment of it and, through such abstraction, somehow symbolize its value to its creators and users.

Automated clutch part line

Wm. Franklin McMahon, freelance photographer
Client: Borg-Warner Corporation
Chicago, Illinois

High-technology pictures are fixtures in today's industrial publications. The future is now, say such pictures, and readers have come to take them for granted. But Borg-Warner can't afford to take its technology for granted.

The company splashed this shot of a four-million-dollar computerized machine, which spits out 3,000 clutch parts a day, across a spread of its management tabloid *Perspective* to stun its audience. We learn from the caption that this machine will be obsolete at the end of a five-year run. The company, says the article, needs technological innovation to survive in the modern world. The story, along with this picture, is intended to help managers understand the urgency of "going hi-tech."

Using a lift-truck to gain a high vantage point, McMahon isolates the operator in a sea of complex machinery. His back is to the production line; the machine presumably tells him how things are going. The subordinate operator, the rhythmic progression of clutch parts, the twisting conveyer, all work to express the point at hand. Borg-Warner is technologically advanced; but in a competitive world even a four-million-dollar machine has a limited life span. Given such a context, the picture, for all of its gee-whiz aspects, asks the reader to ponder the problems ahead.

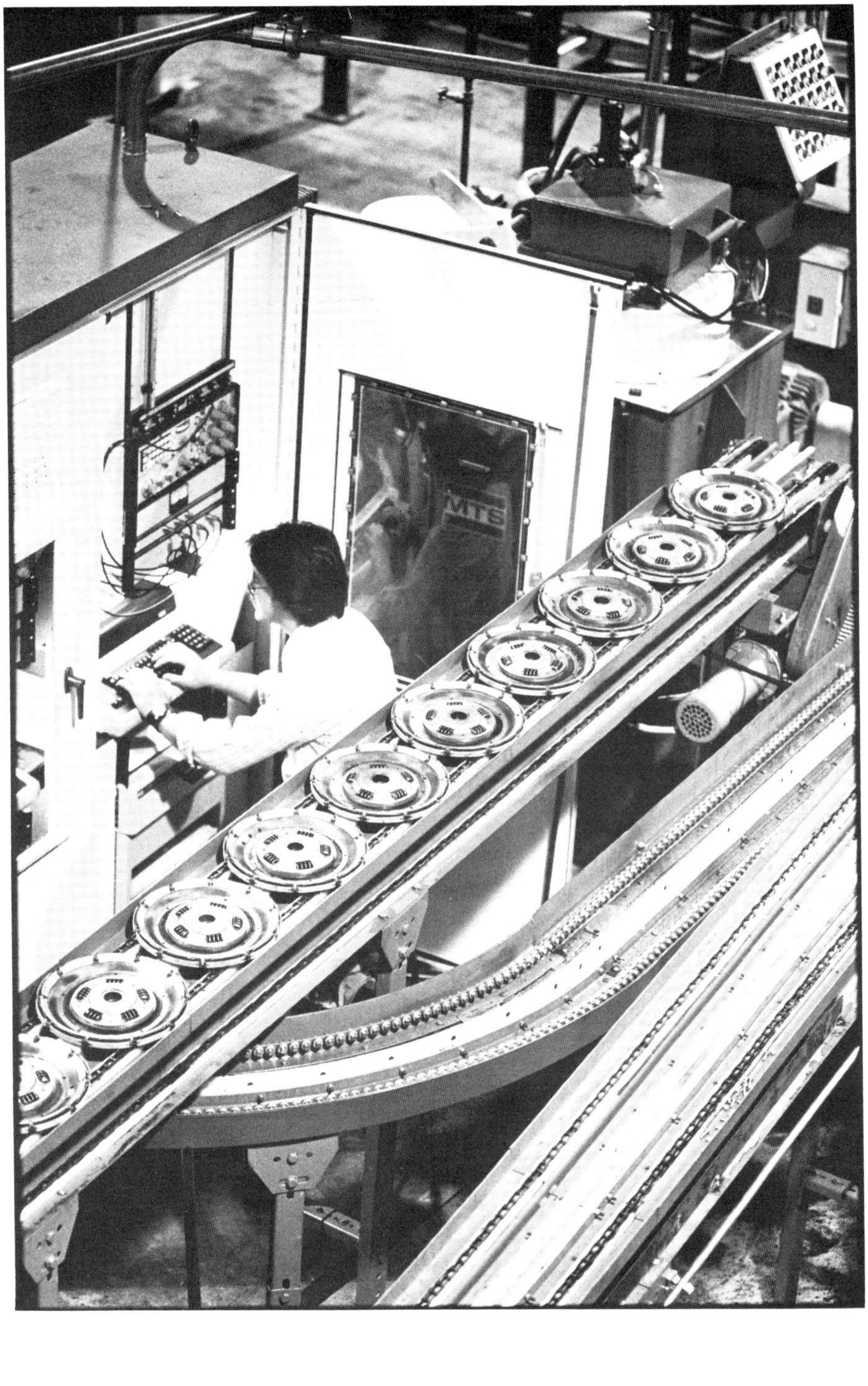
MTS

Merrye-Marie faces the CAT

Robb Mitchell, editor, *Living*
Methodist Hospitals Foundation
Memphis, Tennessee

Hospitals are naturally proud of their equipment, particularly the new generation of medical technology such as CAT scanners, the most sophisticated (and expensive) x-ray machines now in use. But when such equipment appears in pictures, it is rarely of interest to the lay audience. A machine is a machine, and usually such pictures are cheapened with the presence of "let's pretend" models, often stunningly attractive, either operating the machine or about to be rolled into it.

Robb Mitchell features this incongruous photograph of tiny Merrye-Marie Meeks undergoing a CAT scan as part of an issue-long photo-essay on neonatal intensive care. We can believe this picture. It is, to an extent, somewhat horrifying and yet comforting at the same time. To submit this helpless baby to the monstrous yawn of the machine seems almost barbaric. Yet we recognize that ultimately this technology will help, not harm, the child. It places technology in its proper perspective: on one side the risks, dangers, costs; on the other, the obvious benefits. And Mitchell uses a real person, not a model, to create a sense of identity, thereby making the picture of this machine credible to the publication's audience.

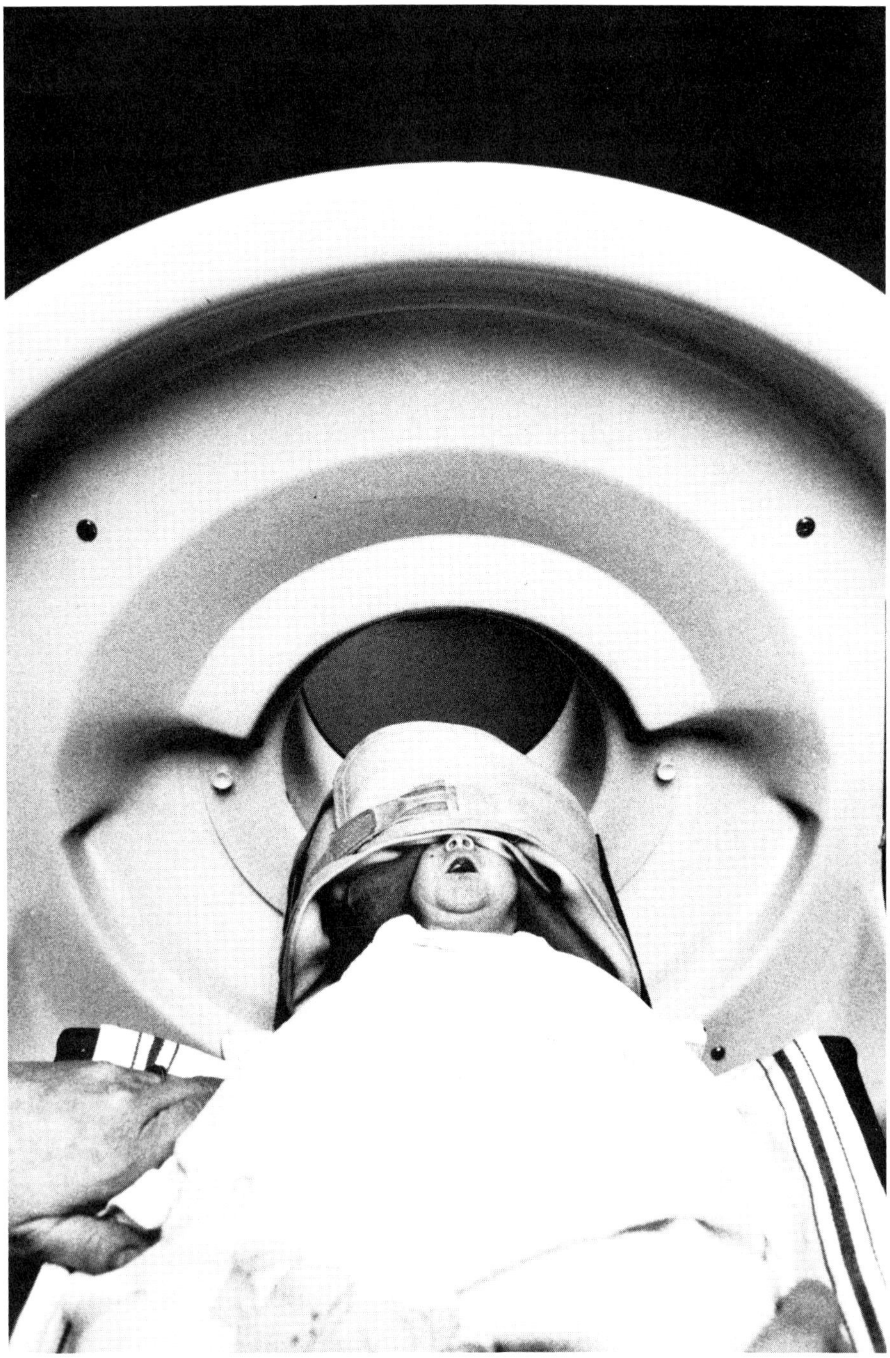

Computer printout

Bob Reznik, assistant director of public relations
Comshare, Incorporated
Ann Arbor, Michigan

Bob Reznik, editor/photographer of Comshare's employee newsletter, has managed to bring meaning to a subject that is often photographed but rarely interpreted. Nearly all attempts at photographing computer operators are made from a side view, with the camera shoulder high. Such photographs invariably merge both the operator and the computer into a busy background, destroying any potential meaning.

By taking a high vantage point and shooting down on operator and machine, Reznik organizes it coherently, emphasizing the vast trail of printout paper pouring from the computer. The operator is placed in the shadows. This is a picture of her work and its meaning, not a portrait. He stresses the nature of the machine and the operator's task, which is to somehow make sense of all that paper.

To Reznik, this machine means frustration, solitude, and effort. He claims that this picture by itself could tell someone a lot about his company and its people. By exposing his film for the highlighted paper, and letting the rest of the picture fade into the shadows, Reznik is able to place emphasis on the machine's function, rather than on its appearance—a key to photographic interpretation.

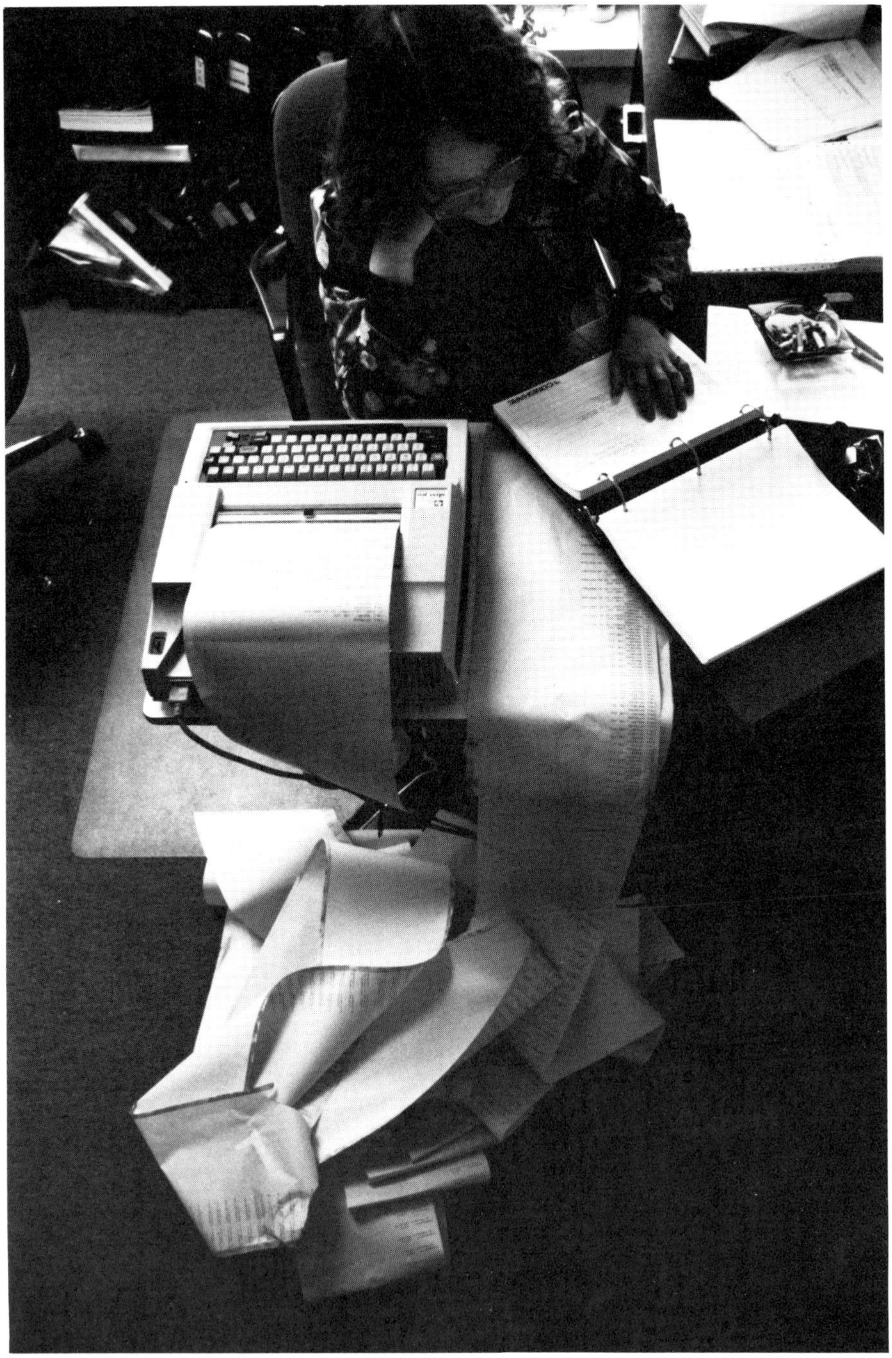

Child's eye exam

Bruce Stromberg, freelance photographer
Client: Philadelphia College of Optometry
Philadelphia, Pennsylvania

Machines come in all sizes. But to work as communication, size is not necessarily the most important consideration. The ultimate value of any machine picture to an audience depends upon the ability of the photographer to add important context for meaning. Bruce Stromberg enhances the meaning of this optometric equipment by relating it to a child's face. He uses a dark background, the rhythms of the lenses, and a close vantage point to bring cohesion and clarity to the image.

A lesser photographer would have backed away to also include the doctor, wall, floor, ceiling, chair in the picture. The point of the picture—the testing of a child's ability to see—would have been negated. But Stromberg edits his picture in the viewfinder, abstracting it by moving in, as well as by underexposing so that darkness emphasizes the array of glass upon the face of the child.

Less is more, particularly when the machine is small to begin with. Add a measure of abstraction, some incongruity, a touch of human values, and just another machine picture becomes a message with meaning.

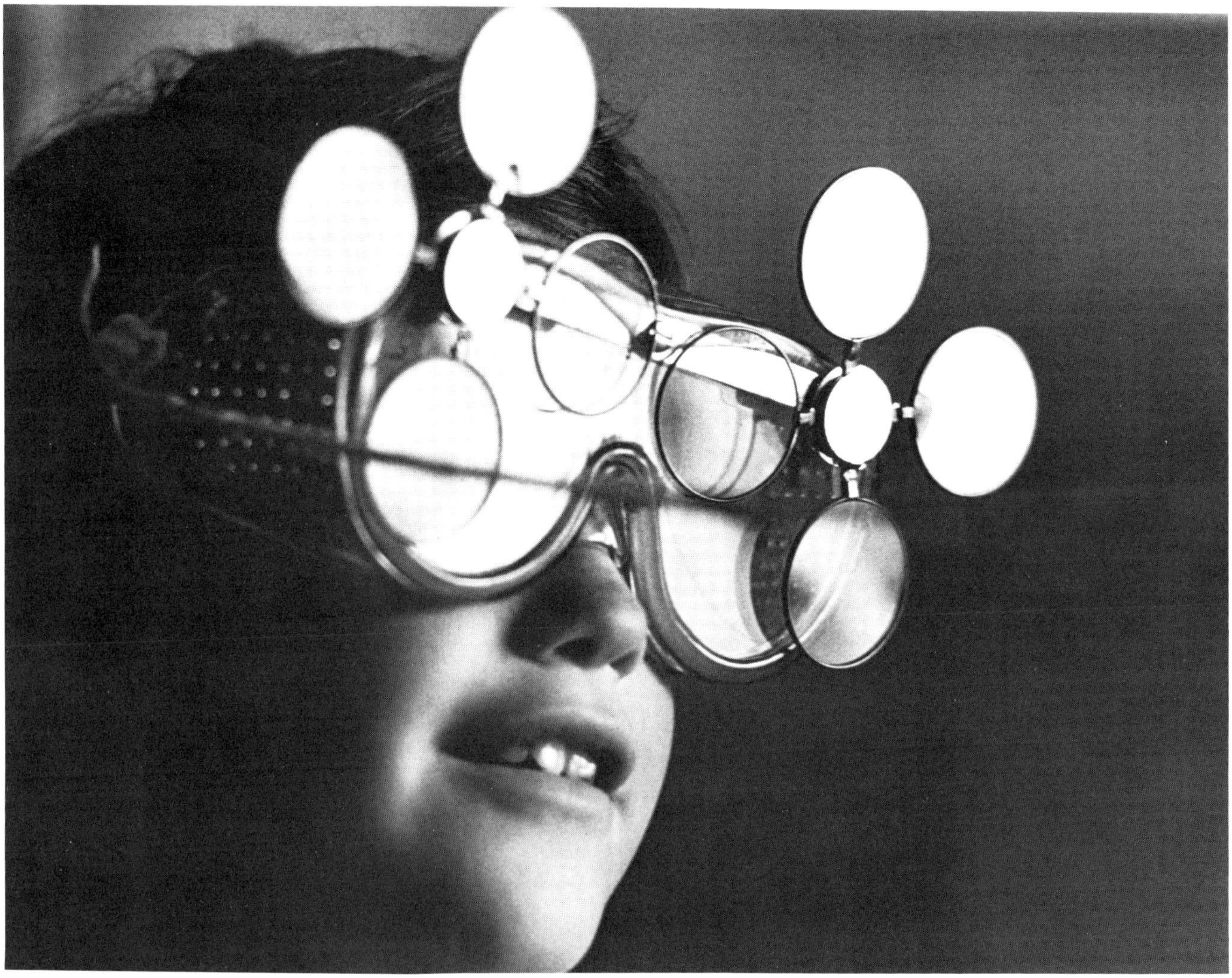

Energy Museum, Oak Ridge, Tennessee

Paul Obregon, senior photographer
Home Mission Board, Southern Baptist Convention
Atlanta, Georgia

It is difficult to make simple pictures of complex equipment. But for a photographer with the eye of Paul Obregon, it is not so difficult. Obregon has an instinctive feel for patterns, rhythms, and shapes, and he is able to move them within his frame until they make sense.

In this photograph of a theologian pondering nontheological matters, Obregon allows the man to become part of the design of the complex scientific display. By moving back, Obregon dwarfs the human figure with the design of the lighted futuristic exhibit. The man's bowed head adds a note of symbolism.

By waiting until the man moved away and turned his back on the lighted control panels, Obregon is able to merge the theologian into the surrealistic flow of patterns to the rear. The result is a photo that makes a comment on man, technology, and, in this case, theology as well.

The photo appeared in the SBC book, *Your God, My God.*

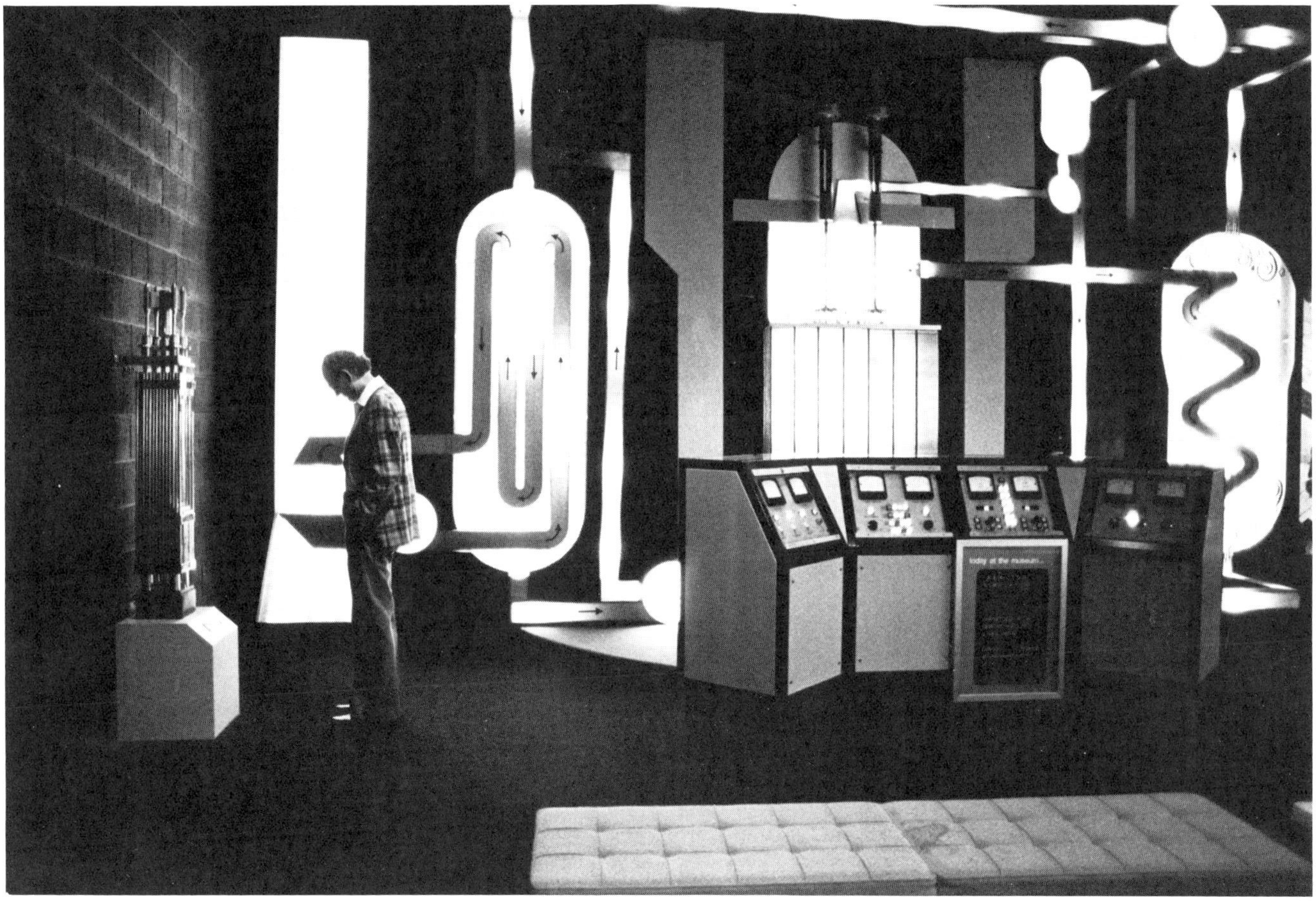

Quarry, Tampa

Ed Eckstein, freelance photojournalist
Client: Moore McCormack
Tampa, Florida

The "machine at work" picture is a fixture in many corporate annual reports. This one, shot by Ed Eckstein for the Moore McCormack annual report, attempts to give the reader some idea of what that machine is doing. But Eckstein also is using the principles of photographic emphasis, scale relationships, texture, and incongruity to make what would otherwise be a boring, literal picture into a powerfully organized statement on machine and mission.

Eckstein does not shoot the hole in the ground. He does not really shoot the big crane, either. Both are context for the prime subject: the fascinating texture of the huge pile of stones before us. Eckstein obviously enjoyed the incongruously textured stones, looking very much like a giant pile of popcorn. He strives to activate the tactile sensations of the viewer. Using his wideangle lens turned vertically, Eckstein emphasizes those stones, filling half the picture with them. Framing them to create a diagonal crest, he rhythmically repeats the diagonal with the crane, which moves the other way against the sky.

Eckstein also realizes that what we don't see in a picture is as important as what we see. He crouches to obscure the lower half of the crane. It pokes up over the brow of the hill, like a dinosaur on the prowl. Its claws hang motionless in the sky. Eckstein makes it seem less menacing by reducing it in scale instead of stressing its size, bulk, and impact on the environment.

Eckstein puts together a striking landscape for us. The crane becomes just another part of this landscape. It does not seem to intrude because Eckstein has integrated it into the picture. Note how the tip of the crane points to the upper-left-hand corner, and how Eckstein contrasts that open upper-left-hand corner with the stone-filled lower-right-hand corner? This is done on purpose. Eckstein carefully studies his edges, his corners, and the directional lines of his subject matter, integrating them into a coherent, cohesive whole.

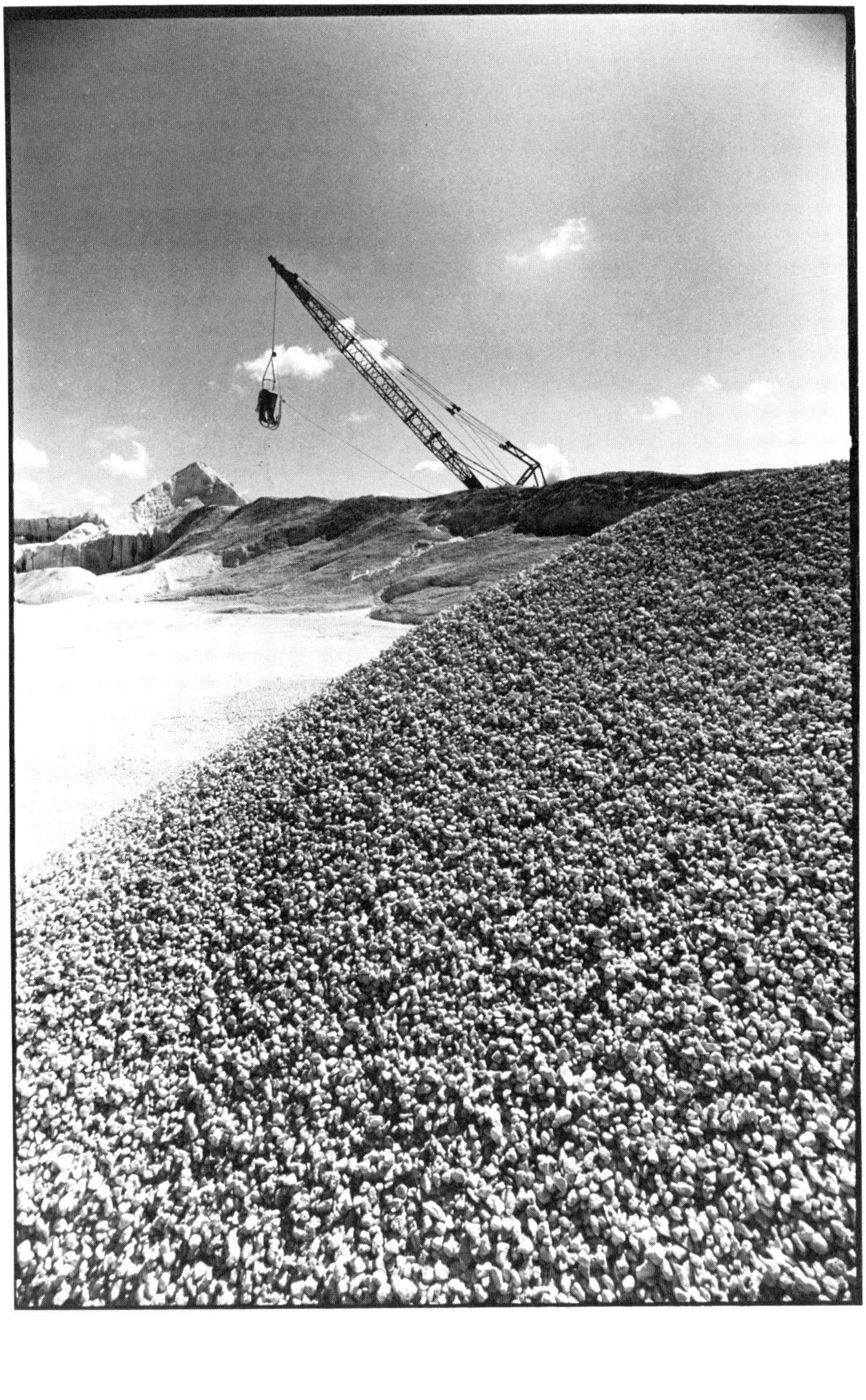

Great Lakes ship, Milwaukee

Dave Denemark, publications coordinator
Medical College of Wisconsin
Milwaukee, Wisconsin

The point of this picture, made a number of years ago for *Pulse*, a magazine published by St. Francis Hospital in Milwaukee, rests in the function of the ropes securing the ship to the dock. Dave Denemark made the picture to symbolize the struggle of its captain, a patient at the hospital's Diabetes Control Center, to control his disease as effectively as those ropes controlled his ship.

Moving beyond its role as a metaphor for diabetes control, the photograph also represents an effective way of interpreting the ship as a machine. Denemark uses a wideangle lens turned vertically to stress a single aspect of the subject: the need to make it stay put. He moves in very close to the ropes, emphasizing them through distortion. They appear larger than the ship itself. Without such strong emphasis, achieved through close vantage point, wideangles will clutter the frame and make subject matter vanish in confusion.

Denemark is actually making a picture of ropes, using the ship itself as context, not prime subject matter. The rhythms of the ropes echo the receding dock and the soaring crane. Every element leads the eye to the ship. The readers are left holding the ropes, and thereby the ship, in their own hands.

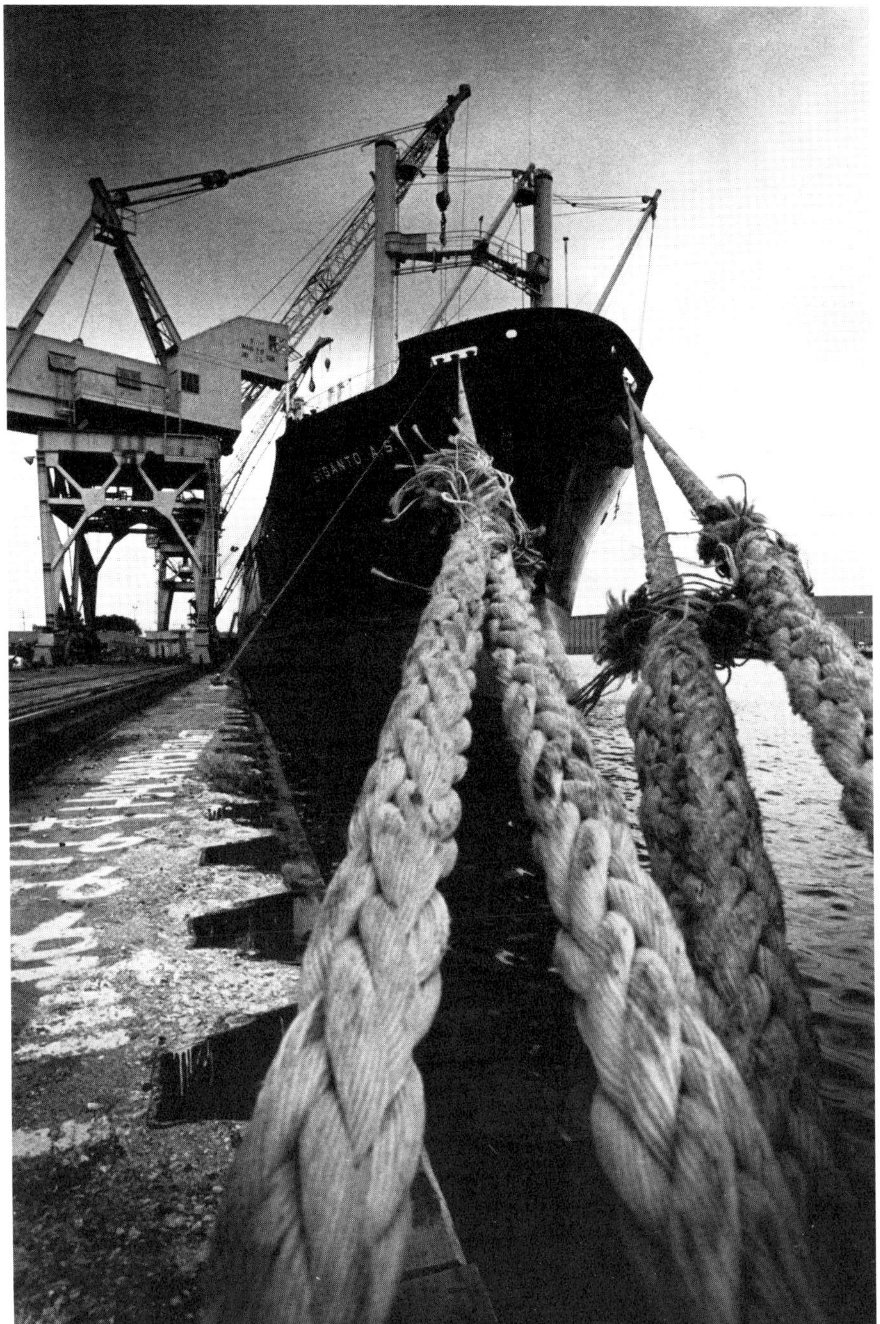

Farm Progress Show, Nevada, Iowa

**John Gerstner, editor, *JD Journal*
Deere & Co.
Moline, Illinois**

To the employees of a tractor company, nothing is more ordinary than a picture of a tractor. For John Gerstner, the task is to turn the ordinary into the extraordinary. He must somehow tell the story of his company's machines in human terms. Here, he interprets the largest agribusiness show in the country as a stampede to view a John Deere tractor in action.

Used in an article called "Struttin' our stuff," this color picture is really a study of how people feel about this company's machinery, rather than a description of the machine itself. It is an exercise in space—deep space. Only the top of the machine can be seen; the masses of people are dwarfed by the trampled brown corn and the soaring blue sky.

Gerstner compresses the crowd and the tractor within a sandwich of husks and feathery clouds by using a wideangle lens. We are left in the wake of all the excitement, and somehow feel left out. We almost wish we could *see* what all the excitement is about. And that is how Gerstner wants us to feel about the machine and its performance. Sometimes, the best pictures imply, rather than reveal, what is actually happening. This is one of them.

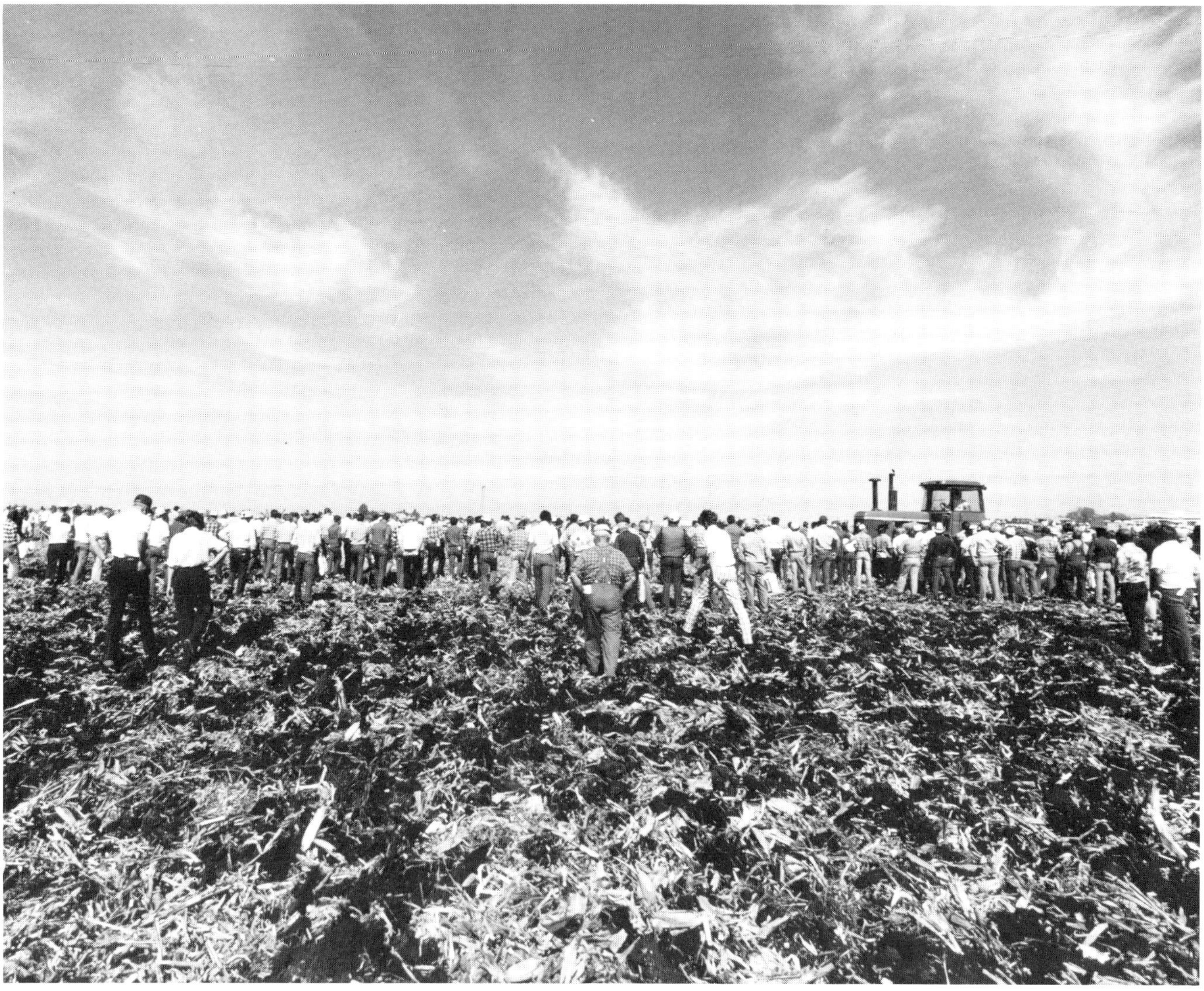

Chapter 4

Pictures of buildings: What makes them special?

Like most organizational photographic subject matter, buildings are usually depicted for their own sake. Such photos show the surface appearance of the building but rarely define the nature, purpose, or unique qualities of the structure itself.

We do not have to be skilled architectural photographers to make effective pictures of our offices, plants, schools, churches, and installations. But we do have to understand the function of the building and show those special qualities that make it work as an organizational asset. Once we define this function, we can isolate the point we want to make about the structure and bring the camera to bear upon those aspects of the building that make this point.

One of the biggest mistakes building photographers can make is to show the "whole thing." That approach only works when the immensity or scale of the structure is the point at hand. And that point, in turn, can only be made by contrasting the size of the building to its surrounding environment.

Most effective building shots, whether interior or exterior views, involve abstraction: using details, vantage point, and incongruities to symbolize the function and the value of the structure. This means letting the parts stand for the whole.

Before you photograph it, ask yourself not what the building merely looks like. Instead, ask what it does, and what it means to those who work in it.

Reading between the lines

**Kurt Foss, photojournalist
Hennepin County Public Affairs
Minneapolis, Minnesota**

Scale relationships are extremely important in making sense out of buildings. How large are they? How tall? How much space do they occupy? How do they relate to their surroundings? All these questions and more can be answered by the camera's ability to express contrasts in scale.

After seeing this picture, we have no doubts about the size of Hennepin County's Government Center. It's a vast, inhumanly sized structure. Yet Kurt Foss has made it far less formidable by contrasting it in scale to but one person. The photo is strikingly incongruous: That person is using the massive concrete structure as a personal back support.

Foss uses the lines upon the facade of the building to lead us to the lunch-hour reader. The editor of the county's employee newspaper ran this picture very large; otherwise the tiny figure would be difficult to see.

Foss got the shot because he was experimenting with an ancient square format camera he found around the office. Like all effective photojournalists, Foss uses the 35mm format exclusively; his are Nikon single lens reflexes. But, like many photographers, Foss enjoys experimenting with bizarre equipment in order to see what he can learn from it. The only reason Foss was on the scene at all was to see how this clumsy, archaic camera worked. And this is what he got. The picture drew more favorable comments than any picture in the publication's history. Says Foss, "It pays to experiment."

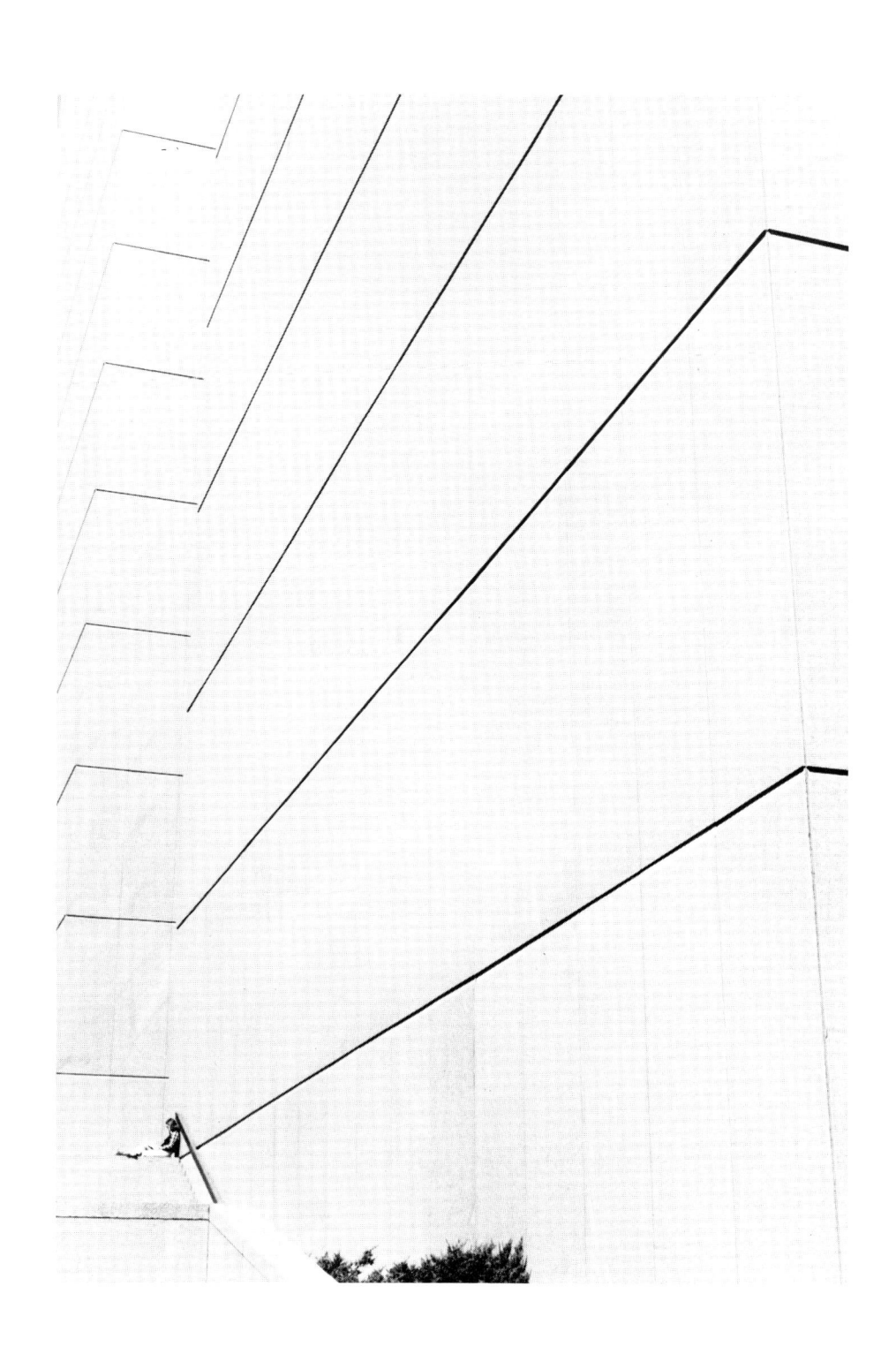

Campus landscape

Bruce Stromberg, freelance photographer
Client: University of Pennsylvania
Philadelphia, Pennsylvania

A common cliche in college recruiting brochures is the "view of the campus." Admissions officers always want to show prospective students what their campus "looks like." Their brochures invariably depict a cluster of buildings looking just like any other buildings, fronted by the typical view of the campus itself, usually featuring students trudging along intersecting sidewalks. Rarely do admissions officers insist that pictures of the campus give readers insights into the nature of the institution itself.

Such is not the case in the University of Pennsylvania's 1980 recruitment brochure. Penn asks freelancer Bruce Stromberg to *interpret* the view of the campus, bringing to it the flavor of the university, its style and tradition.

Yes, Stromberg shoots the buildings and the sidewalks. He even includes students walking the snow-covered campus. But the difference between Stromberg's view and the typical view is that Stromberg selects an ornate window as the actual subject. He makes a picture of the window, using the campus and its buildings as context.

The window *is* the university. Ivy League all the way. Gothic, historic, traditional. It is a work of art. We find ourselves looking through it, warm and dry, enjoying the view. We experience the campus, but it is secondary. The mundane buildings are downplayed. Instead, the character of the institution itself is expressed.

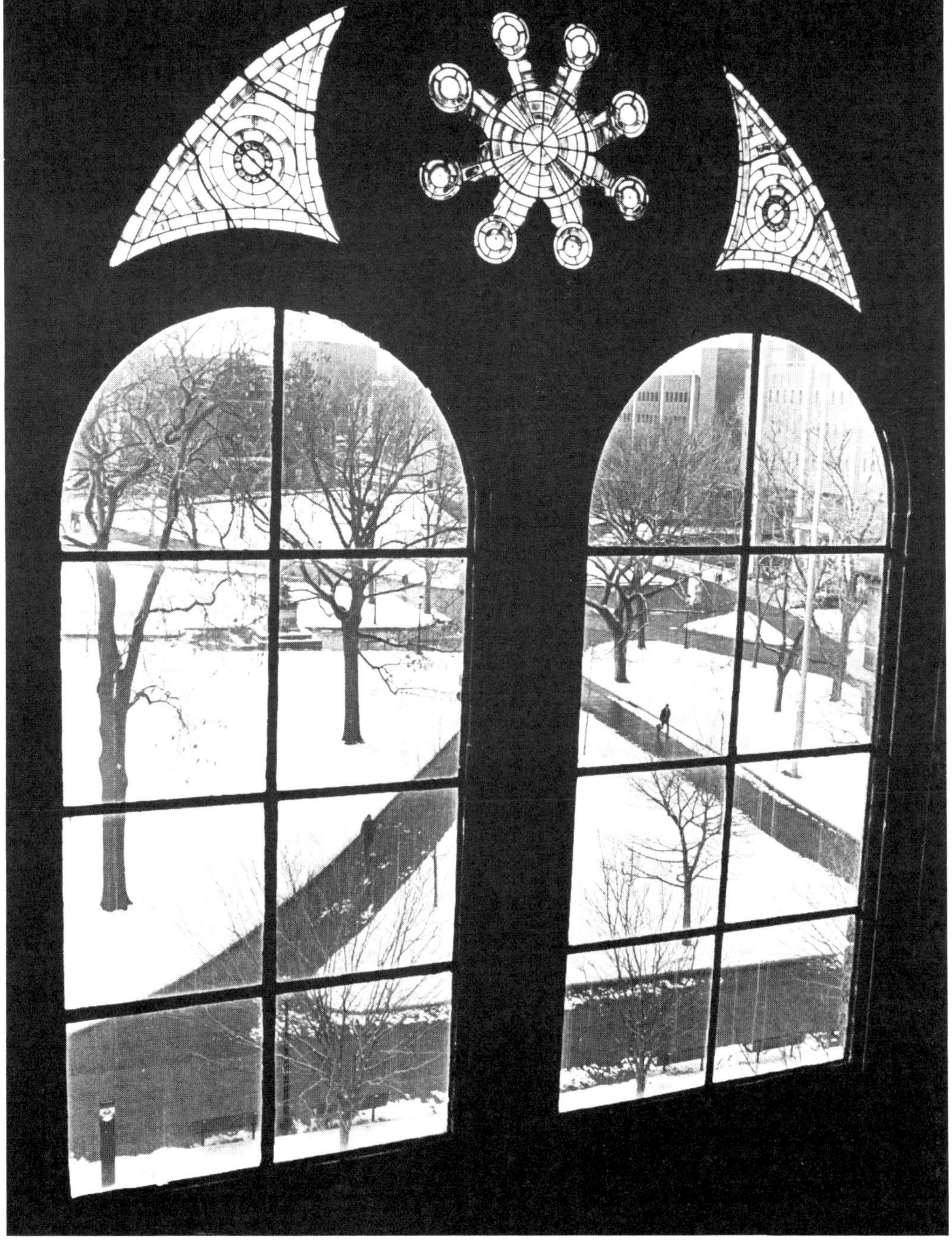

The library

Dave Denemark, publications coordinator
Medical College of Wisconsin
Milwaukee, Wisconsin

Photographers attempting to make interior or exterior pictures of buildings for editorial purposes must always ask themselves what they are trying to say about that particular structure before releasing the shutter. Otherwise they will make just another literal view, superficially describing the appearance of the structure but saying little else to the reader.

On one level, Dave Denemark shows us what his college's library looks like. We can see that it is modern, large, and simultaneously stores books and allows people to read them on site. But Denemark takes us further by relating the structure to its use. He notices two students studying, and uses the one in a prone position as an incongruous focal point. By choosing the wideangle lens, Denemark concentrates on the student yet adds context and scale by including the sweep of the ceiling, floor, stacks, pillars, and study carrels.

Denemark shoots quite close to the recumbent student. The couch serving as a resting place takes up almost half the picture. Yet the wideangle lens also includes much more. The big book resting on the floor adds still another incongruous touch to the photo, stressing the informality of the facility.

Denemark humanizes the setting, making it seem just like home. He gives the building a purpose, making a point about the structure to the viewer.

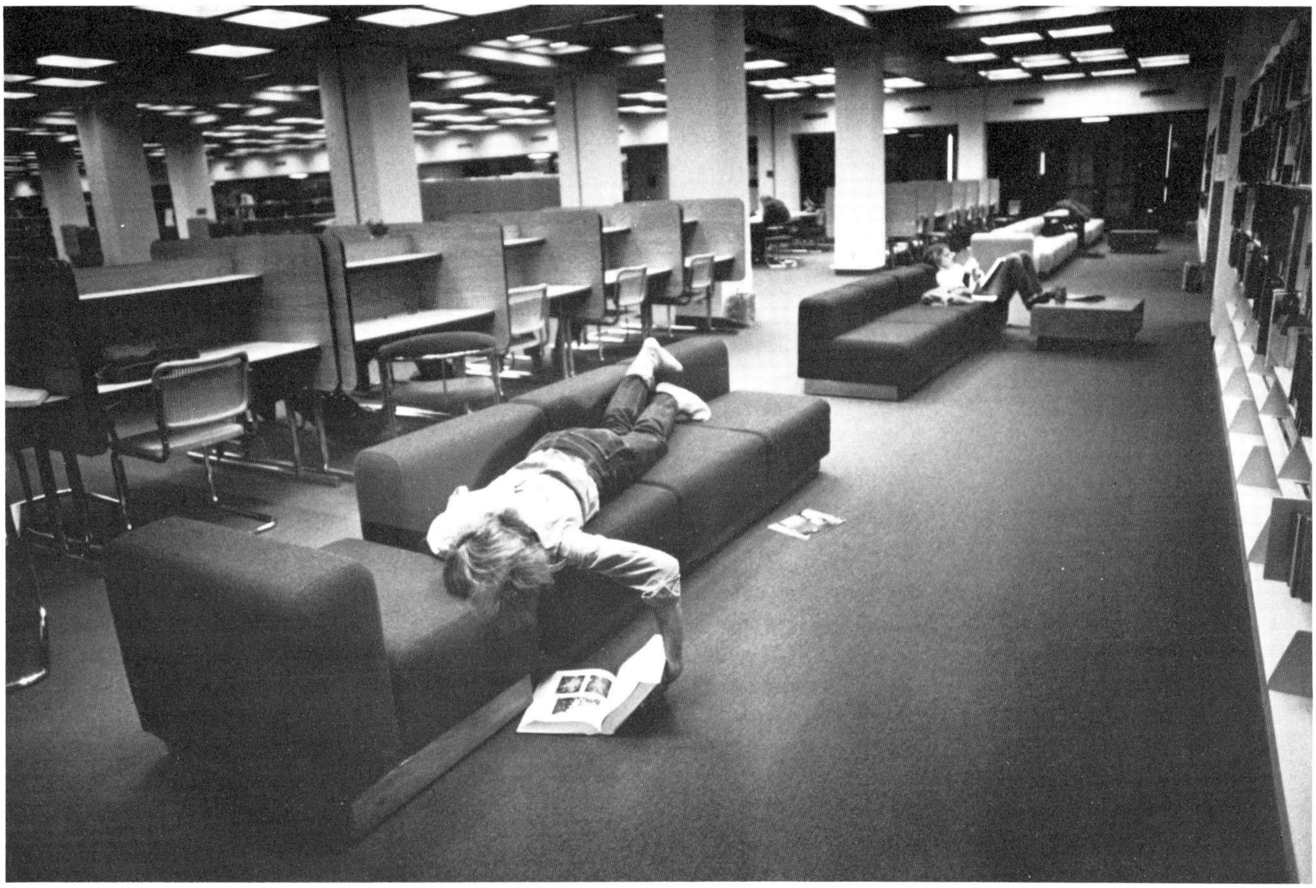

Up the downtown staircase

Mike Jenkins, communications manager
Burger Chefs Systems, Inc.
Indianapolis, Indiana

Mike Jenkins is one of those editors who has no photojournalists and no designers working for him. He does everything himself and does a remarkable job at it. Typical of his efforts is his interpretation of the world's newest, largest, and most spectacular Burger Chef restaurant, which opened in 1980 in downtown Detroit.

The restaurant offers a special architectural feature: a gracefully curving wood staircase leading to a second-level eating area. For Burger Chef, the design departure was startling. Jenkins makes it more so through his bizarre vantage point, turning the staircase and its railing into a rhythmic curve. A shiny wall to the right becomes an abstraction in converging lines. Both elements lead us to the salad bar directly below.

Jenkins shoots only when diners enter the frame, helping themselves at the salad bar. Their arms echo the thrust of the staircase, and their forms add scale to the scene.

Jenkins ran the picture as a full bleed, double truck, in his magazine. He uses additional photos of the restaurant in his article, but none could be as coherent, compelling, or communicative as this one. It does more than show us what the new restaurant looks like. It tells us what makes it so special.

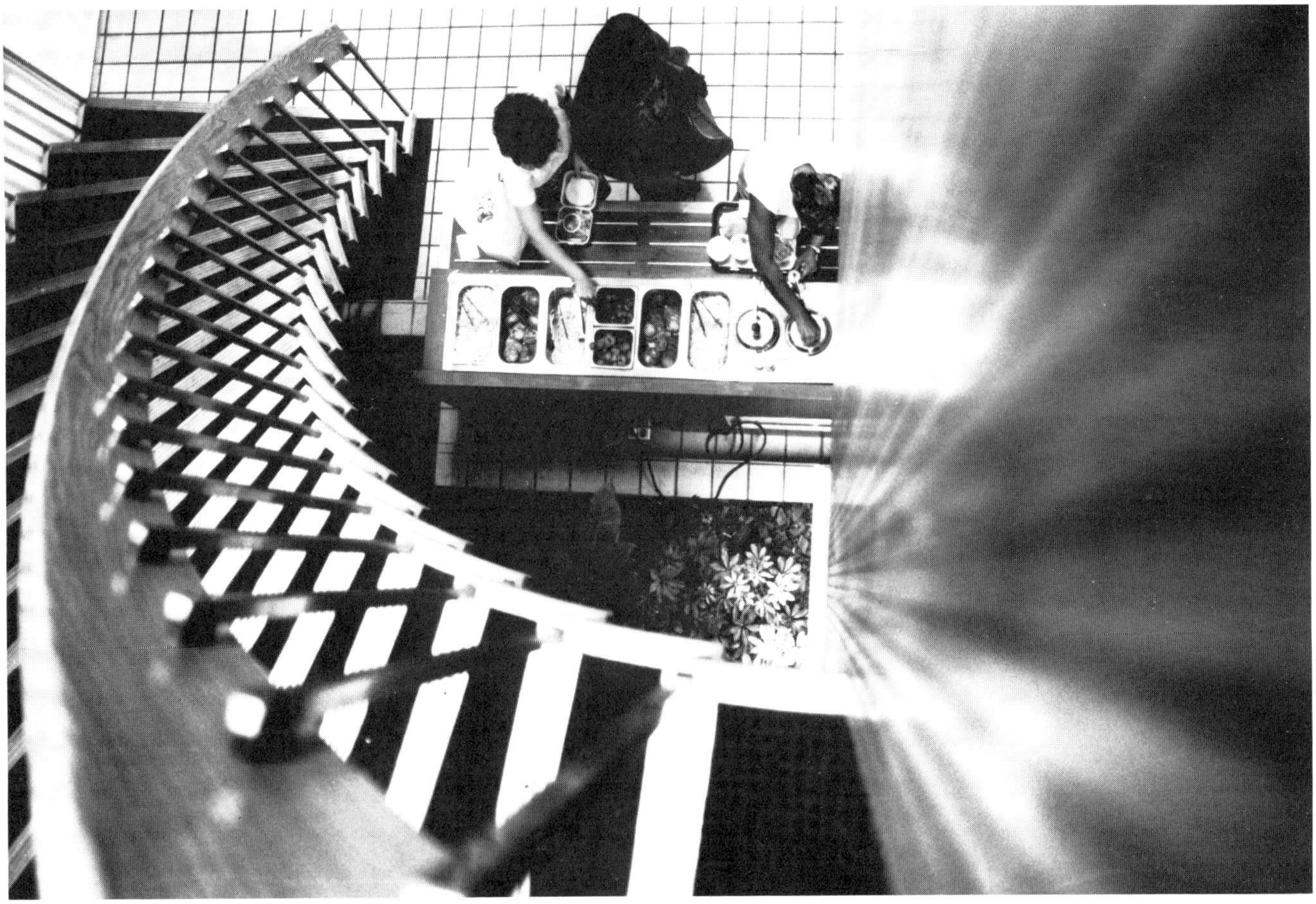

Alone

Dave Denemark, publications coordinator
Medical College of Wisconsin
Milwaukee, Wisconsin

Sometimes a building shot can convey a mood which tells the entire story in itself. This is such a picture. Dave Denemark is preparing a story on the demolition of the old Milwaukee County Infirmary, once termed the "poor house." It housed many elderly ill and mentally incompetent persons in the 1920s and 30s.

Instead of shooting the whole building or waiting until the wreckers' ball smashed into its walls, Denemark decides to tell the story from inside out, before the wreckers start to work. He shoots just one room, an old dormitory which no doubt once echoed to the sounds of suffering and disorientation. It is the classic archaic hospital ward, and Denemark uses light to create a grim, melancholy mood.

Distorting slightly with a wide-angle lens, and underexposing his film, Denemark allows darkness to take over the scene. The light that does come through is far away, barely illuminating the floor and ceiling. To give the picture its scale and to add a touch of human values, he includes a distant figure in the scene. The woman's hand rests on a window; she appears to be reflecting on those who once passed this way.

It is a lonely scene. No doubt the room has known its share of loneliness. With such impressions, Denemark tells the story of a building that soon will be no more.

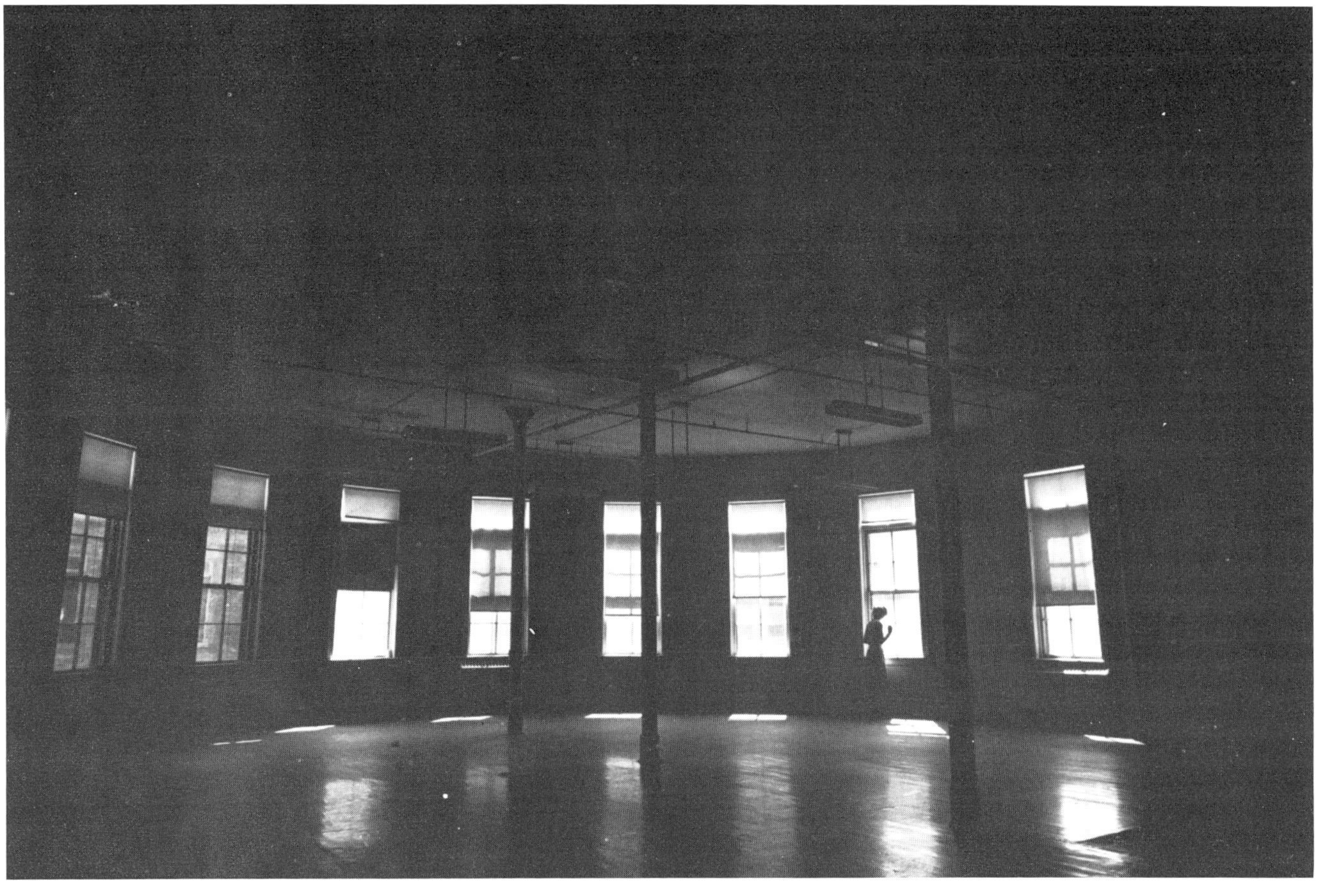

Refinery

Ed Eckstein, freelance photographer
Client: Atlantic Richfield
Philadelphia, Pennsylvania

Lighting masks a variety of problems. It abstracts the subject, simplifying it so that it becomes symbolic instead of literal. It creates mood and feeling. And light, with its counterpoint, darkness, is always there for us to work with.

Today's photojournalists generally prefer to work with available light. Those who use flash often destroy the very quality of light that would have given their pictures meaning. The available-light photographer uses the quality of the light and the nature of darkness as part of the message itself.

So it is with Ed Eckstein's photograph of this refinery, which was made for ARCO's annual report. It is the play of light against darkness that focuses our attention on the man and his shadow in the foreground. If flooded with frontal light, the picture would just be a man and some pipes, instead of an abstract human shape finding its way through a glittering jungle of high technology.

Perhaps this structure is unsightly. A lot of buildings used by industry are not photogenic. That is another good reason to use lighting to mask such flaws, activating the reader's imagination instead of revealing unnecessary problems.

How do we get lighting effects like this? Skilled photographers usually "bracket" exposure attempts. When they shoot at two or three lens openings on each side of the "correct" reading, they get astounding effects. Details vanish in light or darkness, abstracting the subject and changing its meaning. Later, they will make sure their photographic prints retain the effect of this deliberate over- or underexposure.

Another way of abstracting through lighting is to shoot directly into the light source itself, as Eckstein does here. This puts foreground subject matter into silhouette and also causes striking halo effects, rim lighting, and the glowing sunburst effect Eckstein is getting.

Photojournalists such as Eckstein use their lighting approach to stress meaning. They avoid using lighting effects for the sake of the effects themselves. They keep in mind that shadows and darkness are not "wrong"—instead they regard them as part of the picture's meaning. Today's lenses, films, and developers can be made to work together to record and interpret existing light in any way the photographer desires.

This shot may be called a building picture or a machine picture. It doesn't matter. What does matter is that Eckstein is using the light he finds on the scene, through exposure control and vantage point, to create an interpretation that offers more to our imagination than would a normal, frontally lighted subject.

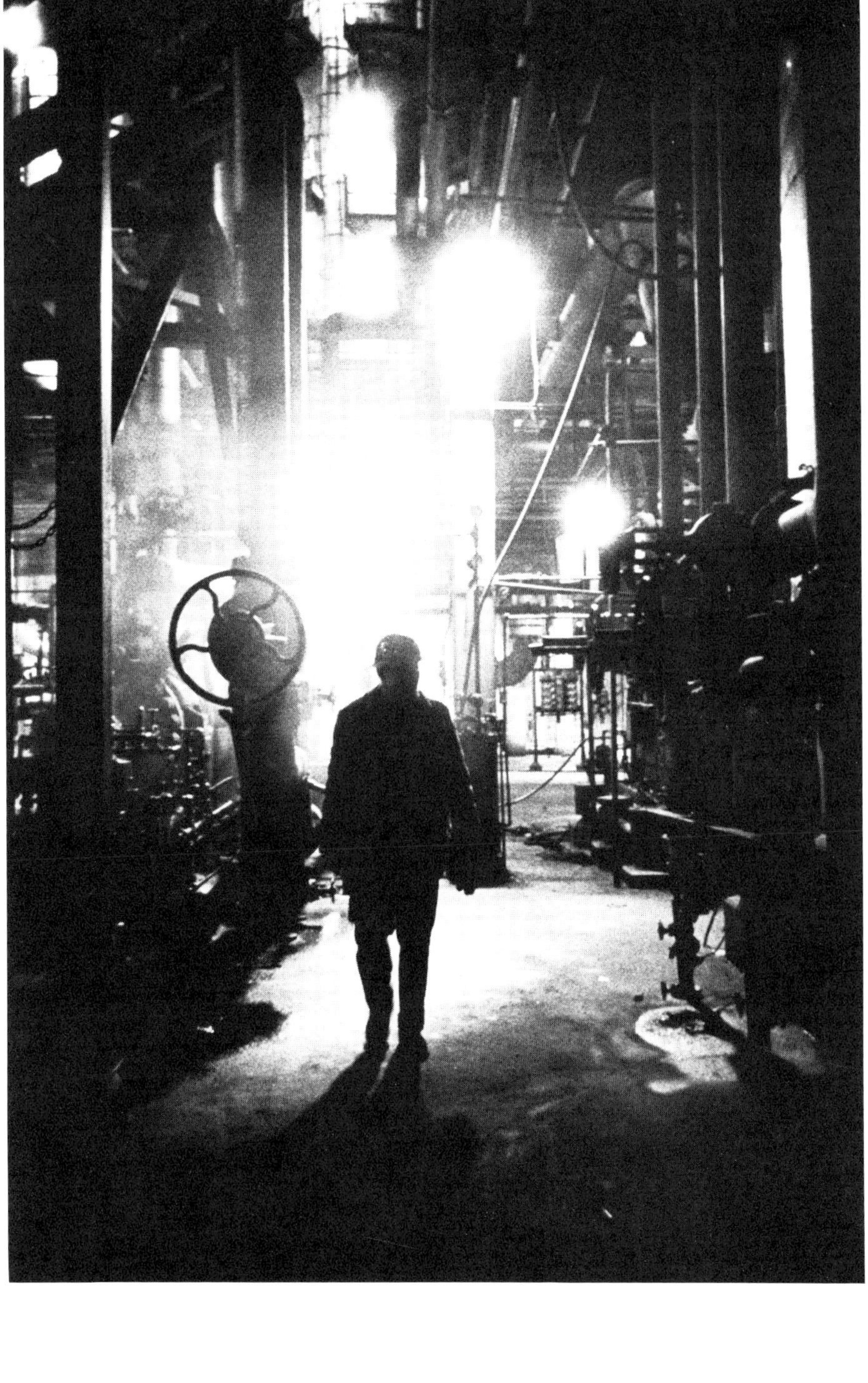

A leg up on the new wing

Tom Treuter, supervisor,
  publication photography and
  design
William Beaumont Hospital
Royal Oak, Michigan

Construction pictures are also building pictures. They usually include too much—confusing masses of beams and bricks, concrete and cranes. And they are often literal in the extreme. Good construction pictures are rare. Even the better ones sometimes border on cliches. We've all seen those shots of the sun flaring behind the silhouetted worker on the open beam or the wideangle shot through the big pipe. And we will, no doubt, see them again.

The best construction pictures are usually very simple in organization. They often use incongruity, as does this one. Shooting a hospital wing under construction, Treuter notices that from a particular angle, the worker all but vanishes, leaving only his lower leg in view. He also sees that the configuration of the leg resembles the angular construction of the building framework.

Using a telephoto lens to reach up and isolate this juxtaposition of man and steel, Treuter is asking us to ponder an illusion: Where is the rest of him? That is for him to know and for us to find out.

Our imaginations become actively involved. We may well smile, even laugh, at the ironies Treuter offers us. He gives us a blend of whimsy and geometry in equal parts. Such original compositions are usually all around us, says Treuter, but only if we spend the time to look for them.

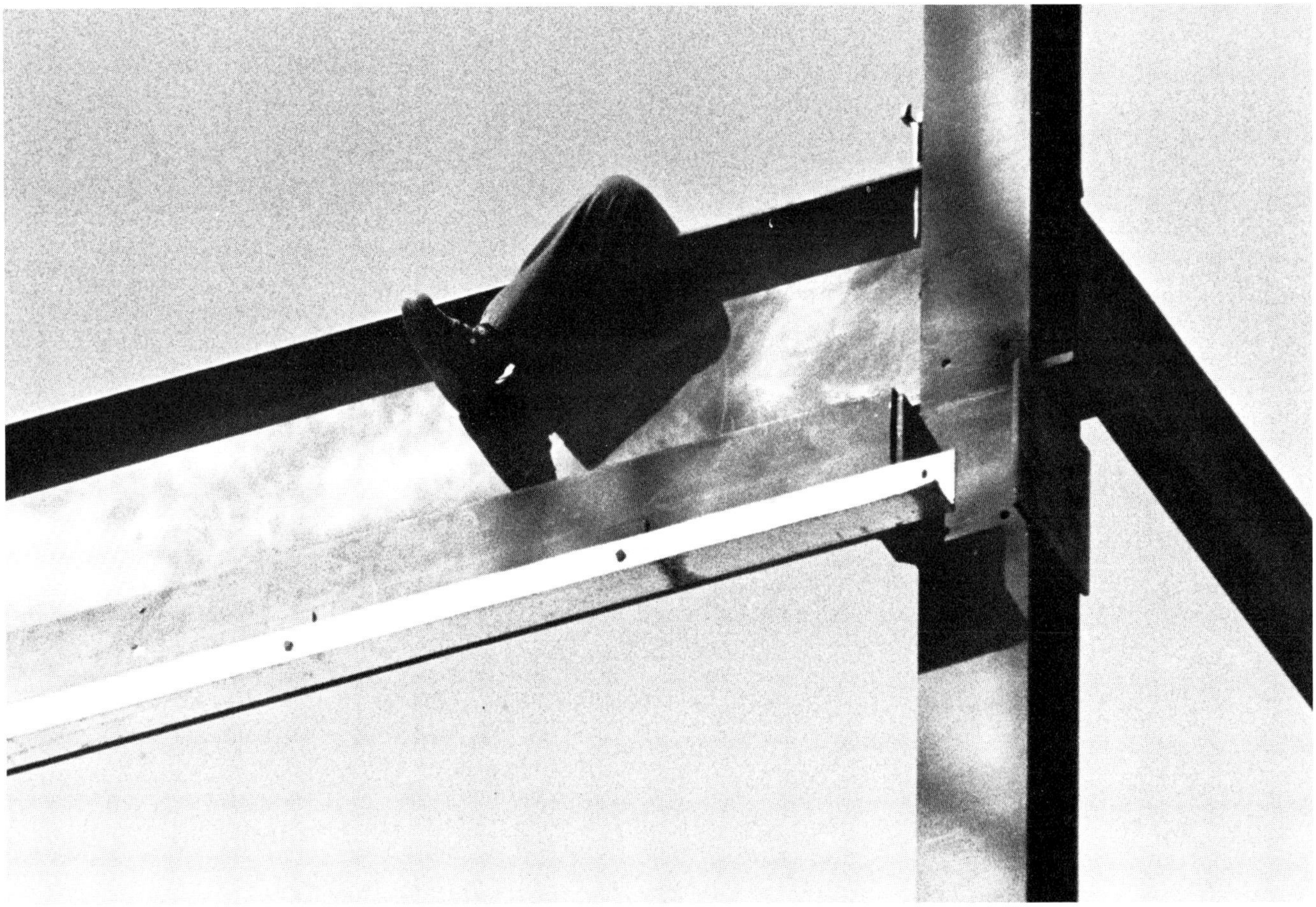

Chapter 5

At work in the office: more than papers and desks

Over the past quarter century, the bulk of the work force has moved from assembly lines to offices. Our institutions, no matter what their missions, invariably are managed from rooms filled with desks, computers, telephones, and papers. And—let us not forget—people.

Often the alibi is heard: "It's one thing to photograph people in such dramatic settings as hospitals or out in the streets, but what about photographers who have to make pictures over and over in plain, ordinary offices?"

What such complainants fail to see is the fact that offices are not ordinary at all. It is the job of communicative photographers to find the extraordinary within the ordinary, and the office is no better or worse a setting for this adventure than anyplace else.

The key to successful office shooting invariably involves the nature of the people who work in them—their problems, solutions, feelings, moods, struggles, and triumphs.

Using a telephoto lens, an office photojournalist can reach across distance to unobtrusively capture responses, relationships, symbols, and details. He or she can turn to the wideangle to create strong emphasis on a part of the office environment which embodies meaning, and relate it to the surrounding context to bring the message home to their viewers.

Problem solver

Bob Reznik, assistant director of public relations
Comshare, Incorporated
Ann Arbor, Michigan

"Let's face it," says photographer Bob Reznik, who is also editor of his company's employee publication. "To the untrained eye, business offices seem to be places where people sit around working with paper, talking with others, maybe sharpening a pencil now and then. But wait a minute! Business offices do offer much in the way of drama and excitement. These people are tremendously involved in what they are working on. That feeling of involvement, of the excitement that these workers are experiencing, is what I try to communicate visually."

Very few office photographers match Reznik for turning mundane desks, papers, business machines, and people into palpable drama. In this shot of a man struggling with a computer problem, Reznik shoots into the light source itself, abstracting the subject through a silhouette. The eye goes to his fingers playing over the keyboard. The printout on the wall behind him adds context. The key, of course, is the hunched body language of the standing silhouetted form. With no time to sit and type, the man must either be in a big hurry, or else he is so preoccupied with problem-solving that he doesn't even think of using a chair.

Reznik has obviously blended into the woodwork. This man is so lost in his work that he has long forgotten the presence of the camera. He responds naturally, spontaneously, unselfconsciously. Such responses are critical in effective office photography.

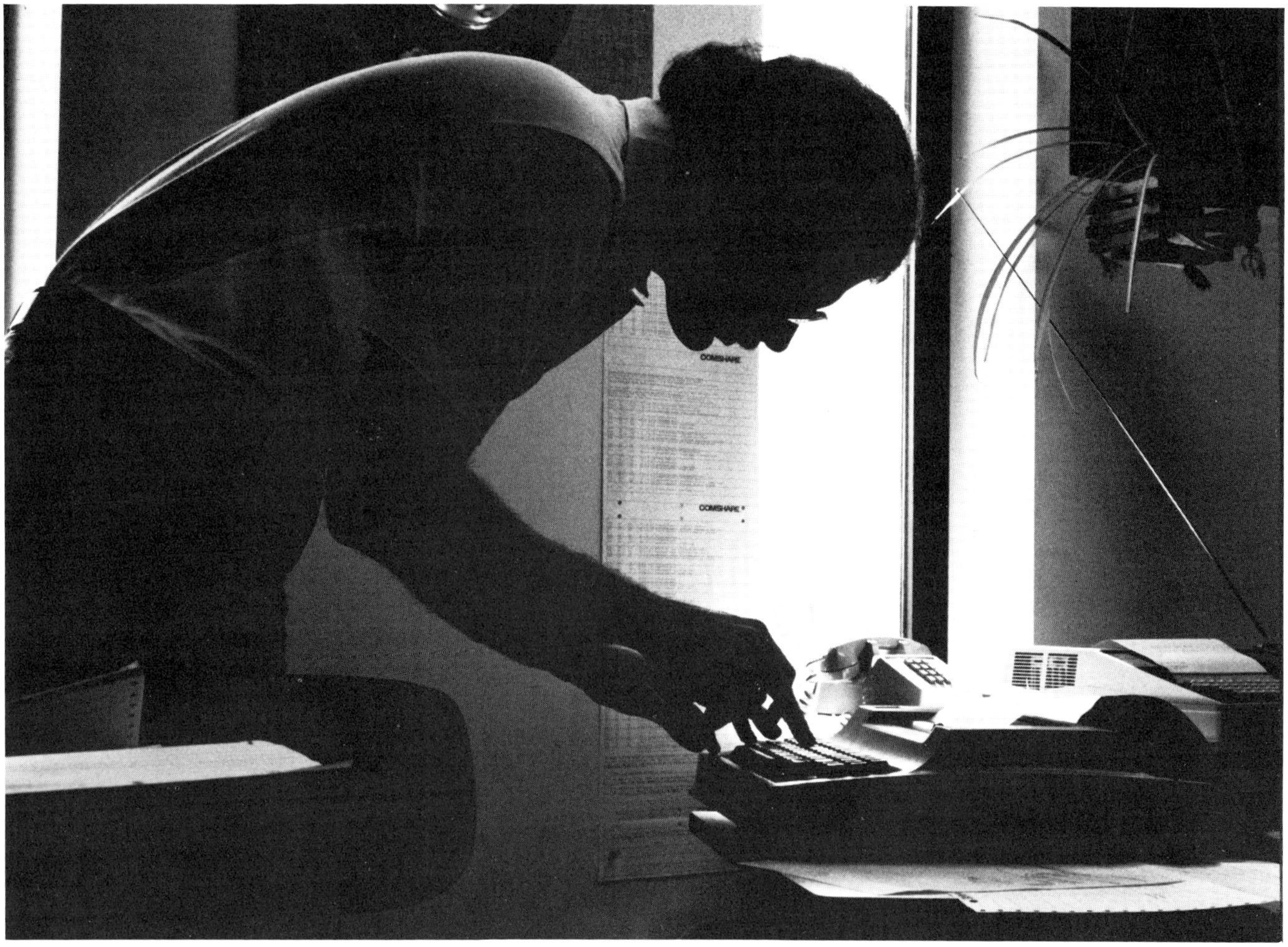
COMSHARE
COMSHARE

Tax time

Bob Reznik, assistant director of public relations
Comshare, Incorporated
Ann Arbor, Michigan

Bob Reznik is aware that good office photographs can emphasize certain aspects of work in order to make a particular point about that office or job. In this case, he photographs Comshare's tax services operation. He tells us that in the course of two or three months, this office handles about 80% of its yearly volume. About half of its yearly volume is squeezed into a mere three weeks. Such is the nature of tax time.

A hectic scene greets Reznik. He brings order out of chaos by using a wideangle from a low vantage point. He moves close to the piles of tax forms to create a landscape of paper, framing two workers. We get that buried-under feeling. And if we feel like that, what about the workers?

That's the purpose of office photography: to give the reader a sense of what is happening, what the problems are, how the people in those offices feel about those problems.

If employees elsewhere in the company can come to sense the nature and depth of the problems their fellow employees are facing, the entire institution benefits. Credible, interpretive photographs such as Reznik's go a long way towards bringing an organization together through visual communication.

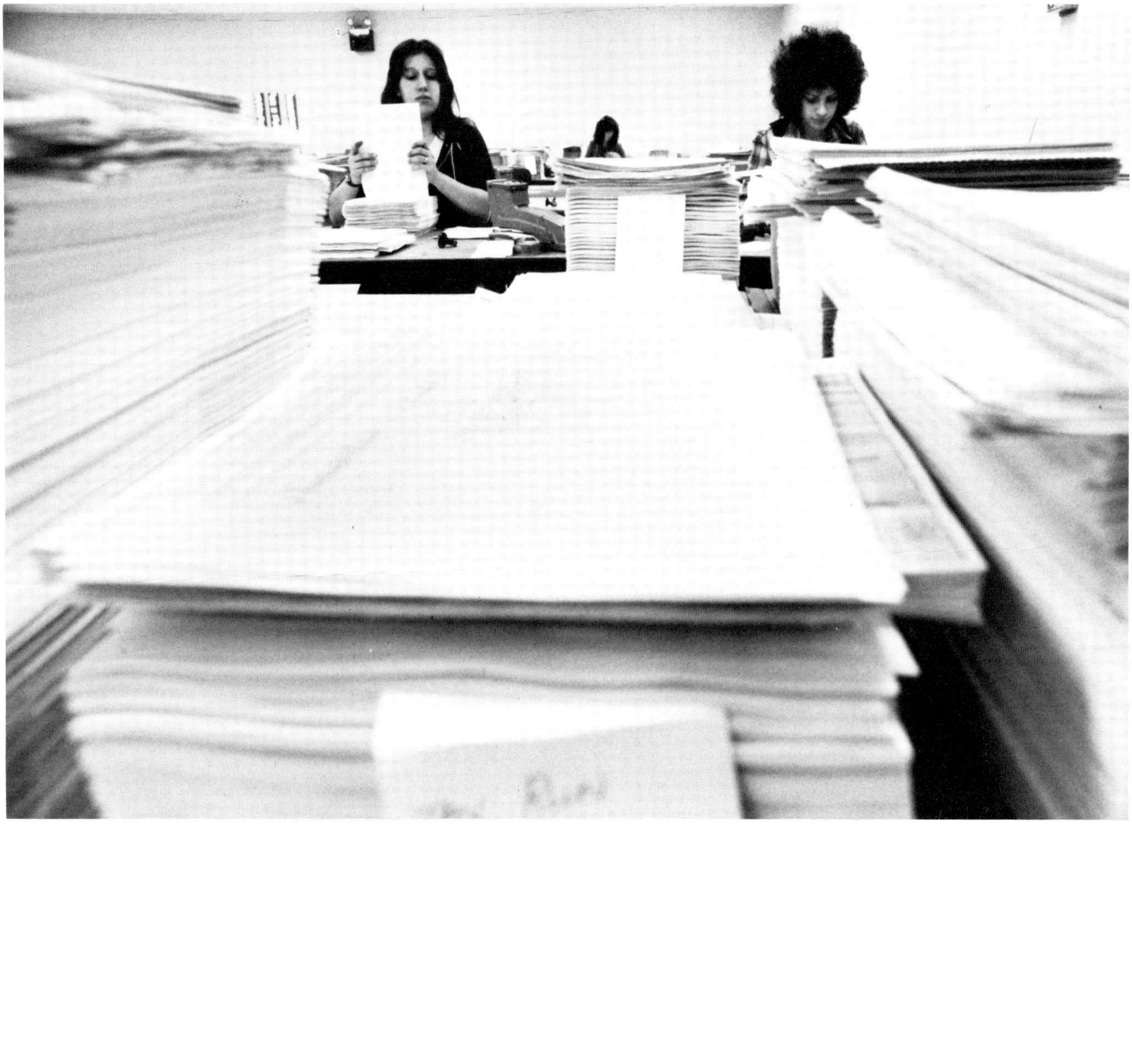

Take a letter? How about P for productivity?

Bob Reznik, assistant director of public relations
Comshare, Incorporated
Ann Arbor, Michigan

In this, the third Reznik photograph in this chapter, we see how he organizes the various sections of his photographs so that they take the viewer on a coherent trip through the image. Most organizational pictures are disorganized, randomly put together. But in editorial photography we must move beyond the snapshot level. We must very carefully select our position, choose our lens, and manipulate exposure and time controls in order to make sense of the random information before us.

Some call this process "composition." But that word implies that a given set of rules exist, which simply is not the case. The word "organization" is far better, because a photograph reflects, in essence, the recognition of an order. The organization of a photograph follows a set of priorities that are established according to the photographer's intentions.

Here, for example, Reznik says he wants to imply that this secretary is increasing the productivity of her boss. The trays on the right are intended to launch us into the photo. The lines started by these trays carry us past the secretary who is, as Reznik observes, "deep into what she is doing." Those same directional lines, aided by the secretary's left arm, push us through the open door behind her and eventually lead us to her boss at work behind that door. Reznik says this photo is one of his favorites. We can see why.

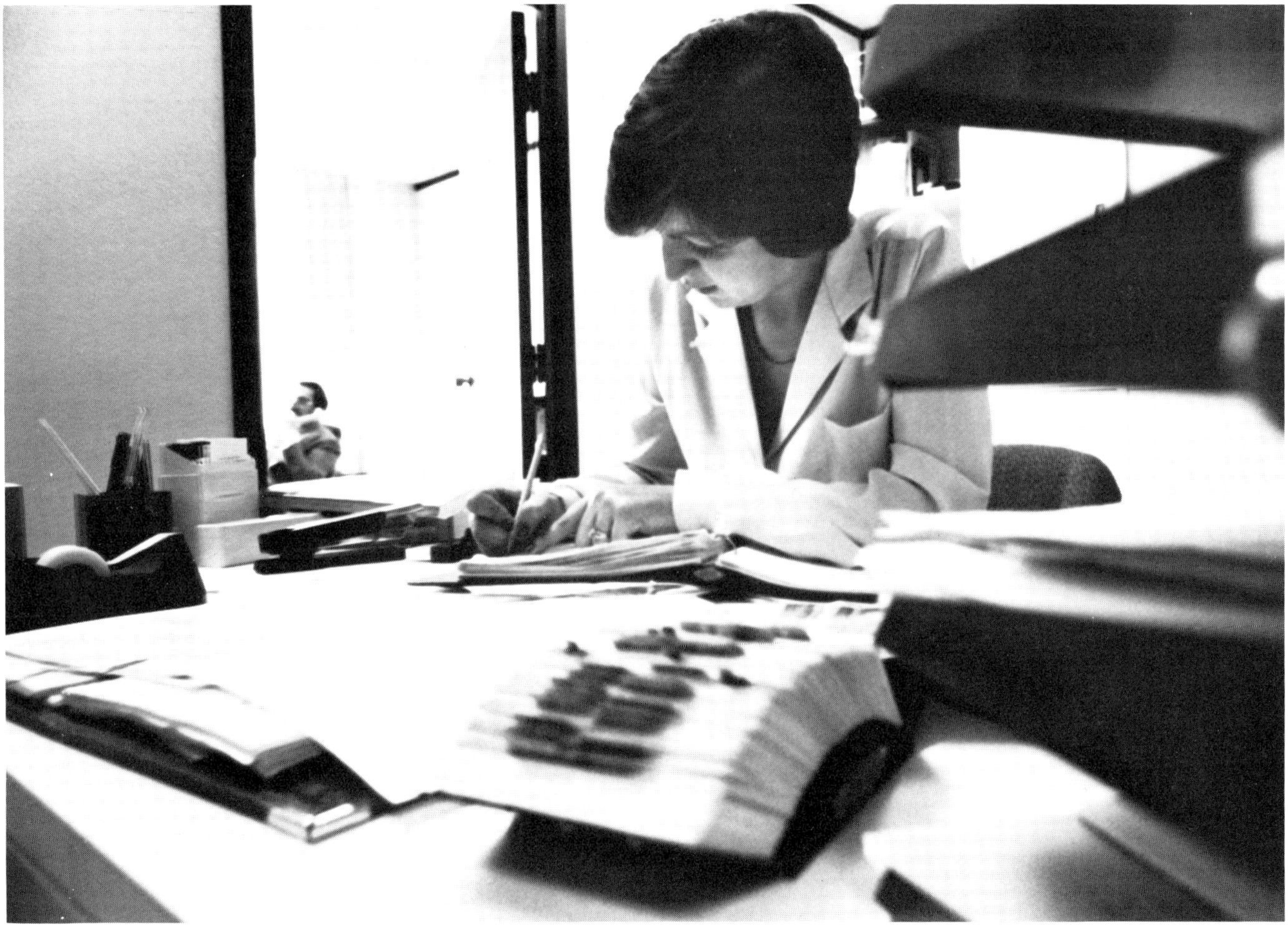

Indochinese interpreter: Hennepin County, Minnesota

Kurt Foss, photojournalist
Hennepin County Public Affairs
Minneapolis, Minnesota

Some office photographs can be deceptively simple, little more than a person sitting at a desk, filling out a form. But even such a basic subject can, if handled properly, have a lot to say to the viewer.

Kurt Foss was asked to make a portrait of the county's new Indochinese interpreter to accompany a story in the employee newspaper explaining how the county was handling the influx of Indochinese refugees. Foss wants more than a mugshot. He wants to somehow capture the meaning of what this man does for the people he serves.

He asks to attend a counseling session. Once admitted, he finds a deserted corner of the room, puts on a long lens, and works from the floor. He photographs the interpreter as he helps refugees fill out the many required government forms. From this vantage point, Foss is soon forgotten. He shoots an entire roll—36 frames—of the interpreter helping the man sitting beside him. This shot was selected for use in the publication. Look closely at the faces. The interpreter must know his stuff; he seems to be doing the job with his eyes closed. Meanwhile, in soft focus, so as not to steal the scene from the interpreter, the refugee gazes at him in appreciation, not to mention dependency.

A simple subject, a simple solution, a memorable message.

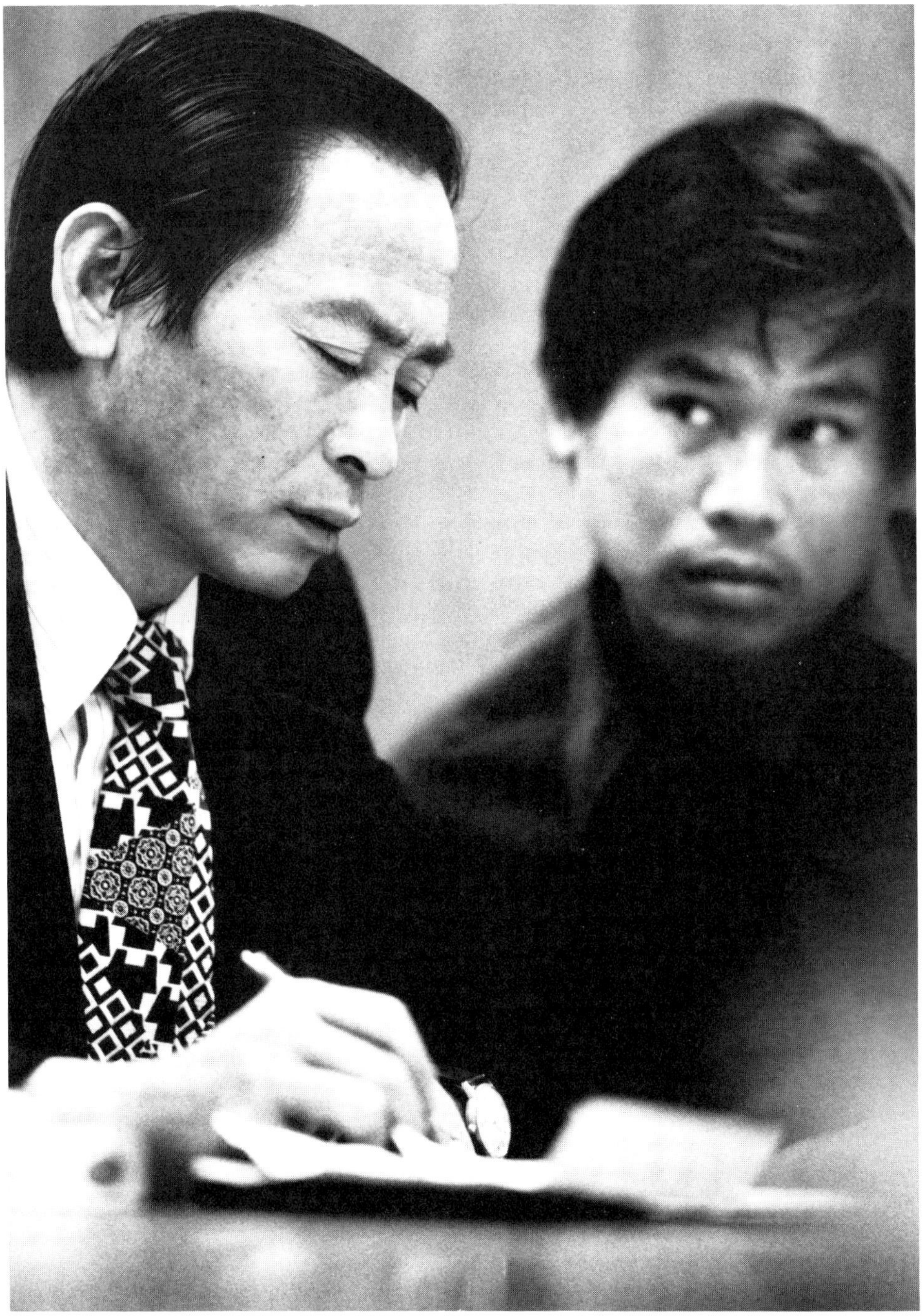

Man on the spot

Gordon Baer, freelance photojournalist
Client: Procter & Gamble
Cincinnati, Ohio

The great office cliche is the shot of the person talking on the phone. If a photographer asks somebody to pick up a phone and pretend to talk, we can be assured that an embarrassingly self-conscious photo will follow.

The phone can work in a photograph as a symbol for communication, but it must be believable. Gordon Baer does it with this photo of Procter & Gamble's Gordon Edwards on the job. The difference between this photo and the phone cliche is that Edwards really is using the phone. From the attention he is getting from the men behind him, the conversation is probably important.

The photograph is credible. It reflects a moment in office life when everything seems to hang in the balance. Edwards is seated, wears a jacket, and is surrounded by four phones, placing him in what seems to be a communications hub. The men behind him wear no jackets. They stand, their body language indicating anxiety. Edwards's face is animated. He seems to be both talking and listening at the same time.

The reader needs to know one more fact that will add important context and still another dimension to this picture. Gordon Edwards is blind. Yet his sense of hearing and touch is so acute that he is probably more skilled at doing this job than those who can see. What appears to be a handicap becomes, in the end, an asset.

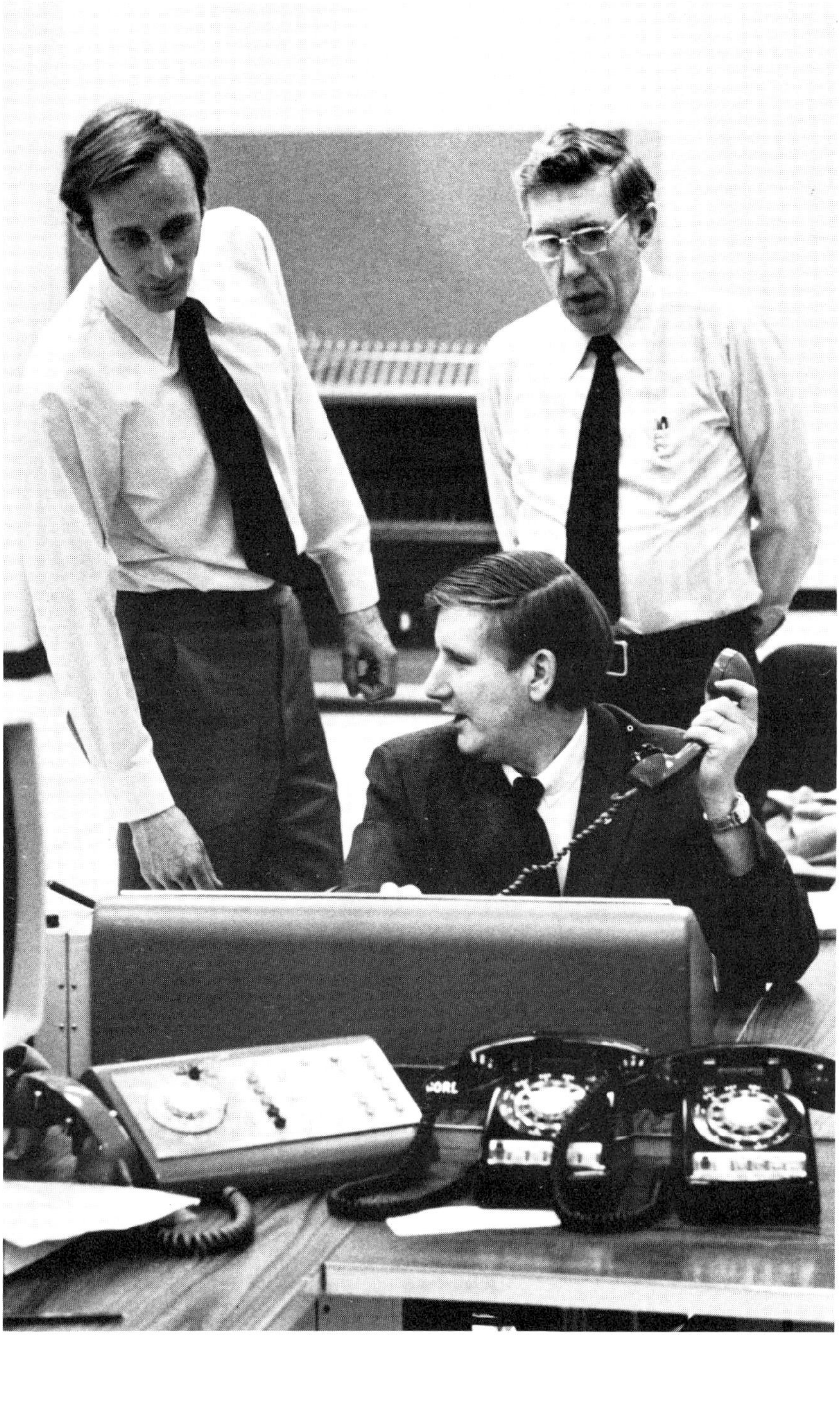

Joanne Jones, Transco receptionist, Linden, N.J.

Beverly Freeman, senior editor
Transco Companies Inc.
Houston, Texas

While this photograph certainly qualifies as a portrait of Joanne Jones, it also is an excellent example of an office picture. For Beverly Freeman has given her readers the experience of walking into the Transco Companies reception area and actually being greeted.

Jones is looking right at us, pencil in hand, light glowing around her. The photograph becomes an eyeball-to-eyeball confrontation of the most pleasant sort. Note how the body language complements the softness of the light. The hands, at rest naturally; the rythmic flow of the shirt; the informal hair style—all add to the experience of meeting this receptionist at the entrance to the Transco office.

Freeman uses her lens wide open, overexposing slightly, and takes advantage of a very shallow focusing field. This makes the background soft, only suggested, avoiding confusion and competition.

Joanne Jones may be a receptionist in Linden, New Jersey, but through this photograph she becomes a symbolic office worker, the representative of an entire company and the embodiment of its style.

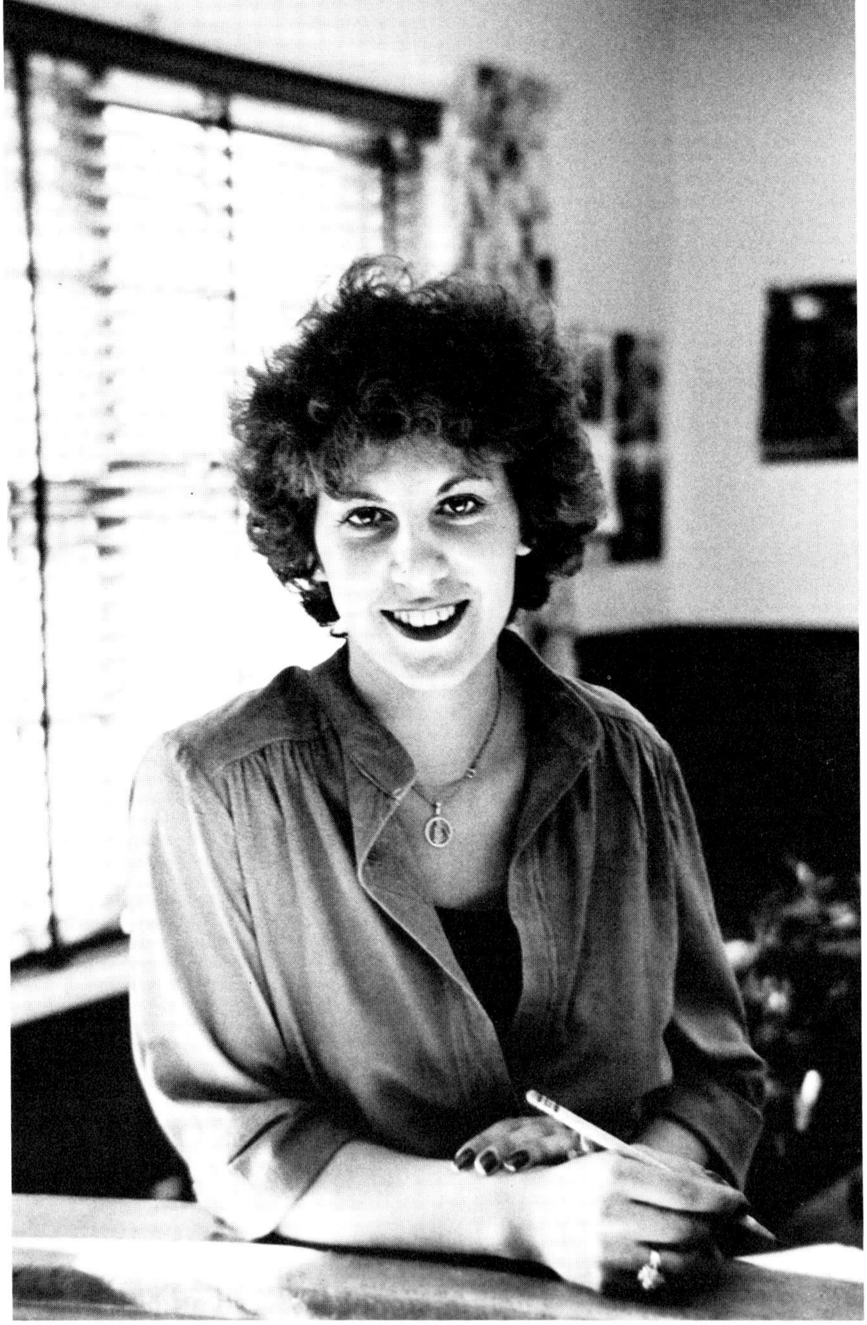

Banker at work

Ed Eckstein, freelance photographer
Client: Girard Bank
Philadelphia, Pennsylvania

One of the biggest problems photographers face when shooting executives at work is the preconditioned demand: "Make it quick. I only have a few minutes for pictures."

It is only natural that busy executives respond this way. Generations of hack photographers have indeed usurped precious executive time by demanding clean desks and arduous posing, bringing in hot lights and cumbersome studio cameras for the traditional "shooting session."

But photojournalists such as Ed Eckstein tell their subjects they will take "no" time at all. For the subject is expected to go on working. Eckstein will become an observer, an eavesdropper. If the nature of the conversation turns confidential, Eckstein will leave, returning later. Such an approach produced this picture for Philadelphia's Girard Bank.

The banker's desk is anything but clean. The clutter is part of the man's job, and he is obviously at home with it. His job also calls for many reference books. One wonders how he finds the time to read them. Thus Eckstein constructs his message: an executive who reads, reads, reads, and must act on the information he gathers. A story-telling office shot if there ever was one.

Eckstein violates a cardinal rule of photographic organization here, but does it for a good purpose. We usually avoid placing the subject in the exact middle of the frame, because it makes the picture static. But Eckstein places his banker dead center. He even divides the picture across the middle into two strikingly different worlds. On top, a world of clutter. Below, a dark and quiet hideout for the legs of the chair and the man's gleaming shoe.

Sometimes it is good to break the traditional rules of photographic composition. By centering the man, he becomes "surrounded" by the chaotic office. By dividing the picture horizontally across the middle, we get a better look at the contrast between the turbulence above and the peace below.

The photo was made for the Girard Bank's annual report. It would be interesting to find out if the picture editor of that report cropped out any of this picture. To do so would alter the meaning Eckstein brings us.

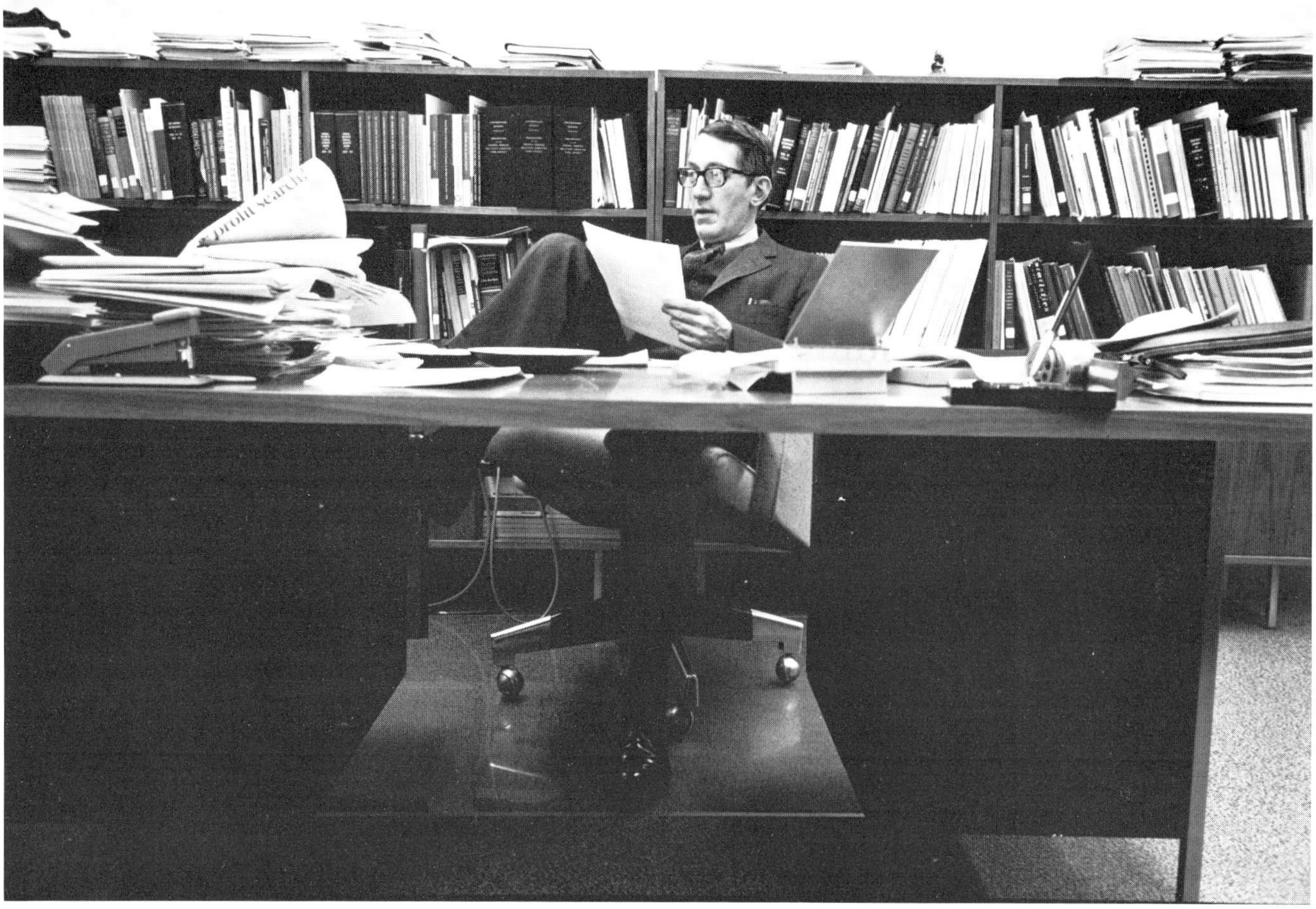

Chapter 6

Hospital scenes, symbols: human beings in crisis

Health care is one of the country's largest economic enterprises. It touches everyone, from birth to death. There is no avoiding the organizations that dispense it. Nearly all of them publish thousands of photographs to prove to their employees, patients, neighbors, government, and professional colleagues that their institutions are special. Yet most of these images fail to do so.

The vast majority of photographs published by health care institutions are empty, sterile, patently phony. Everyone smiles. Hospitals routinely ignore such basics as pain, suffering, and even death. But there is a minority of health care institutions that have, in recent years, broken barrier after barrier. In the early 80s, one hospital editor even managed to make—and print—explicit photographs of a baby being born, complete to the mother's scream.

Outside pressures, generated by television, film, and classroom audio-visuals, have forced at least a handful of hospitals to render their institutions in realistic terms. The best of them produce images that are as strong a testament to the human spirit as can be found in the entire field of organizational communication.

Yet it takes more than simply realism to make memorably communicative images of health care. It takes an understanding of special problems, such as the rights of privacy granted to every patient. Aware of such sensitive issues, effective hospital photographers enlist the enthusiastic cooperation of patients, when possible, to create such images as we see on the following pages.

The hospital room

Tom Treuter, supervisor,
 publication photography and
 design
William Beaumont Hospital
Royal Oak, Michigan

Hospital environments are unique. They are designed with but one purpose in mind—to help people get well. Yet by and large, hospitals terrify us. We see pain, complexity, and high costs. Even the people who work in them often do not really understand them. It is up to hospital publications to make sense out of this special world, to provide visual explanations that not only reassure us but educate us as to the purpose and benefit of all this scary exotica.

The *Beaumonitor*, published by William Beaumont Hospital in Royal Oak, Michigan, has been consistently able to do this since its publication program acquired the eye of Tom Treuter in the late 1970s. This picture tells us why.

On the surface we see a seemingly simple subject. A man in bed in a hospital room. Yet Treuter is able to bring vantage point, detail, light, and organization into play to interpret the scene, making it a metaphor for the special services and range of equipment this hospital provides its patients.

Look again. The room suggests a theatre: A proscenium arch gracefully sweeps across the right-hand side of the picture. The lighting is striking, flowing through the window at rear to bathe the room in sculpted dimension, turning shapes into form. Treuter is able to imply depth, offering us a three-dimensional effect. We become the audience, and this unknowing patient is the star.

Study the detail. It seems as if everything known to modern science is here to help this fellow get better. Cables and special lifts support his injured leg. A trapeze hangs overhead, offering him a handhold should he need it, as well as exercise. The bed raises and lowers its ends at his command. Various drinks and medications are within his reach. He even has companionship; a shadowed figure sits just outside the arch at the right edge of the picture. A final touch of incongruity: He is encouraged to hang his sporting cap irreverently on the apparatus overhead.

What all of this tells us is that Beaumont spares no effort to make him comfortable and help him recover. The diffused light lends a restful quality to his recuperation. We sense the passage of time. We feel he is not hurting, just comfortably drifting. The bed itself seems to be floating, lifted off the glowing floor by its delicate struts.

Lesser photographers might have closed the curtains at the rear, then flooded the room with overhead light, in order to "show everything clearly," thereby destroying the mood and meaning that Treuter's mastery of light and space has provided.

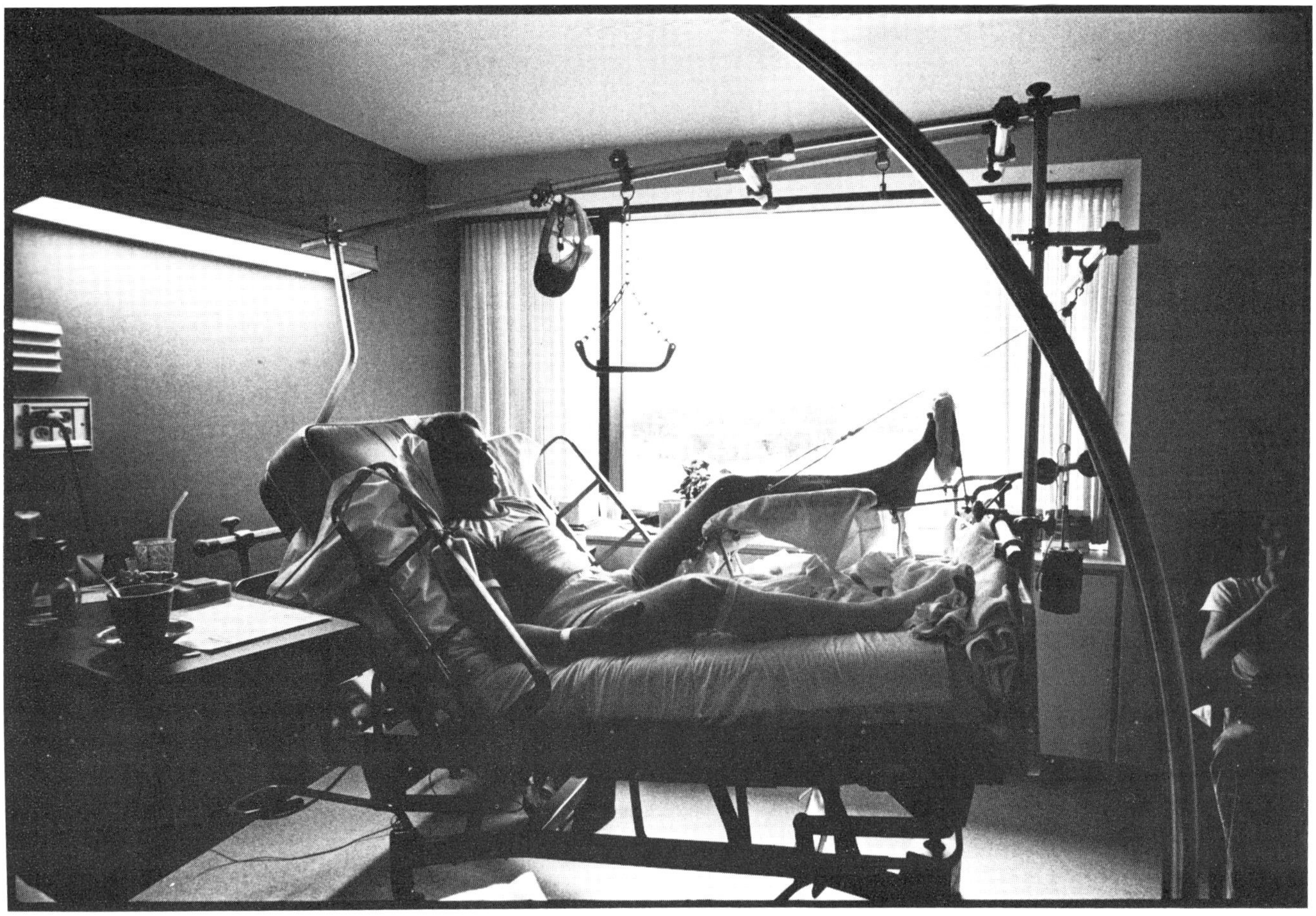

Birth of a baby

Chris Craft, freelance photographer
Client: Albany General Hospital
Albany, Oregon

These photographs, part of a six-picture essay on the birth of a baby at Albany General Hospital, represent a major breakthrough, a landmark for organizational communicators. If we can present, within an appropriate context, information as open, explicit, and honest as this, we should be able to cover *any* appropriate subject matter.

The essay won a Gold Quill award from the International Association of Business Communicators as the best photo-story to appear in an organizational publication in 1980. It won the Sandoz award for medical photojournalism. And it also brought upon editor/photographer Chris Craft—and her client—accolades and attacks from readers of the publication.

At the heart of the controversy surrounding the essay is the question of *context*. To some readers, who had never seen the birth of a baby presented in such painful, explicit terms, the photos were a revelation, a valuable insight into the realities of one of the two most basic events of human life. This is how it begins for all of us, and Craft does not spare us a detail. For many readers, these images of husband and wife, sharing the most wondrous moment of life together, offered an experience they will never forget.

Others saw it differently. Some felt the mother's privacy had been violated. (Even though the family encouraged Craft's essay, and to this day cherishes these photographs and the knowledge that they were shared with a larger audience.) Other readers told Craft these were things we just didn't need to see. A few self-appointed censors called the essay obscene and demanded that the hospital apologize to the readers and retract the entire issue. One woman even demanded that all copies be burned and that Craft be punished.

The hospital administration stood by Craft's contention that by establishing a climate of honesty and credibility, Albany General would be perceived by employees and community as a more concerned, humane enterprise. It was willing to take the knocks from readers who felt threatened, embarrassed, or angered by the photographs.

It is important that we also look at these photographs in the context of each other. The most explicit photo, which caused the furor, cannot be viewed in a vacuum. It must be seen as part of the birth process, which Craft's essay covers in full—a step in a chain of events beginning with labor and concluding with a father's embrace. The pictures come to us from a hospital, as *medical*, and not as general, information. In this context, these pictures can be viewed quite differently than if they came to us in, say, a daily newspaper.

Craft offers the last word: "Even after fielding much of the violent reaction, I would do it again. My idea was to communicate the real stuff—the real mission and purpose of the hospital. I wanted the hospital to talk about sickness and pain, life and death. They are real. And they belong, of all places, in the publications that hospitals send out to their audiences. If these pictures make people think, talk, argue, if they move them one way or another, they are doing a job for both the hospital and the reader."

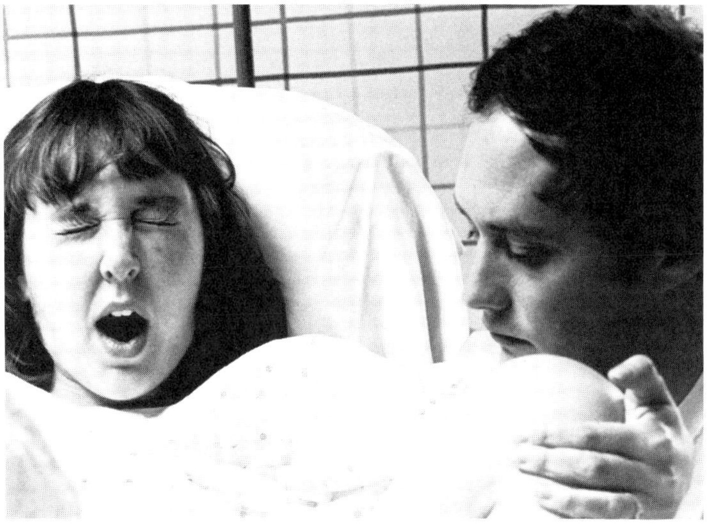

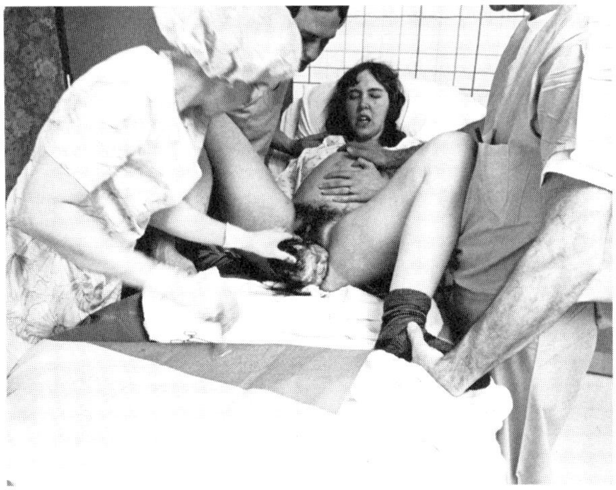

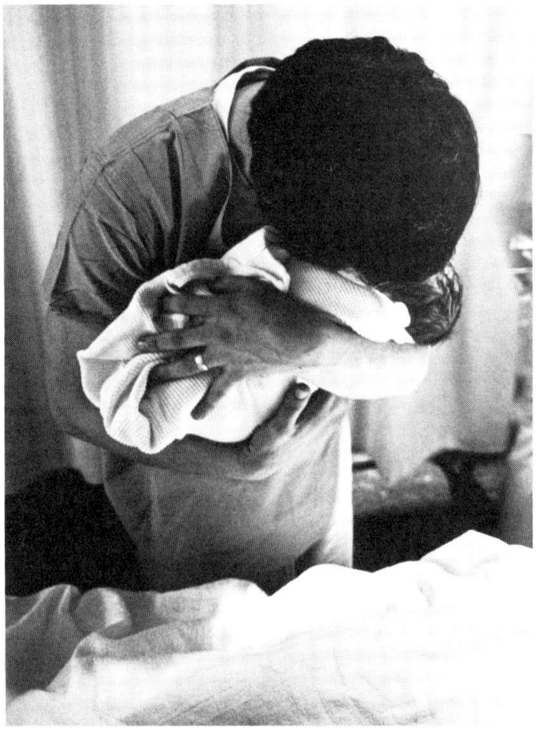

The end of a life

**Tom Treuter, supervisor,
publication photography and design
William Beaumont Hospital
Royal Oak, Michigan**

Chris Craft documents in the preceding photos the beginning of life in one hospital; Tom Treuter here visually articulates the end of life in another.

This picture was used as a cover illustration featuring Beaumont's involvement in a hospice program. As Craft uses human response to underscore the suffering and joy of birth, Treuter uses the play of light to symbolize the approach of death.

The old man waits for death to come to him with a grim certainty. There is no false bravado here, only a sense of inevitability. The blackness hovers around him, even as the burst of light from the window seems to warm and comfort him. Caught in the flow of this light are two companions—his niece in the middle and his wife at right. Both lean towards the dying family patriarch, their body language suggesting a calm acceptance of what is to come.

Treuter says he uses the window light to organize his picture and also to represent the origin of strength. For it takes strength, presumably, to meet death head-on. This man—as all patients who share the hospice he inhabits—knows he is terminally ill. Although he appears gaunt and tired, there is comfort in the presence of that light, and those he loves. And that is the mission of the hospice itself—to provide comfort to the dying.

Treuter, like Craft, is fighting a hospital taboo. Death takes place in hospitals routinely, but it is almost never discussed in print or interpreted in photographs within hospital publications. But it must be, if hospital publications are to communicate effectively *all* the issues involved in health care. For humane, professional care of the dying is just as important a function of a hospital as the care of the newborn, and of those in between. To pretend death does not happen in health care institutions is, like the proverbial ostrich, to bury our heads in the sand.

Some would say that stories on death are out of place because readers will not "like them." But communication should not be limited only to things we like. It must embrace all that concerns us, if it is to be effective.

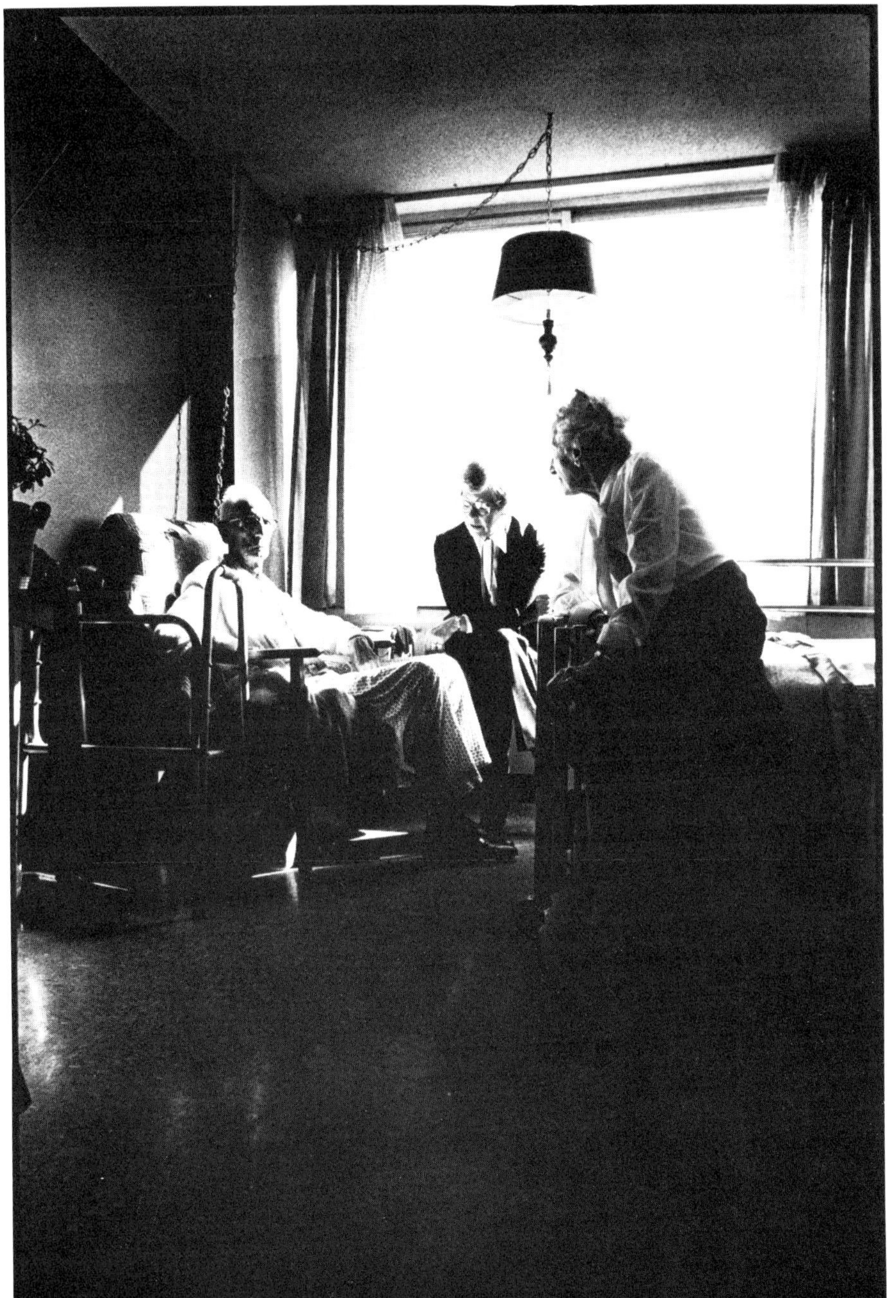

In touch

Rob Mitchell, editor, *Living*
Methodist Hospitals Foundation
Memphis, Tennessee

There is a growing sense of dissatisfaction in our society with people who control parts of our lives: doctors, lawyers, government officials, judges, law enforcement officers, teachers. They no longer get our unquestioned trust. We have become, in many respects, a nation of cynics.

Some of this criticism is justified. Much of it is probably undeserved. Meanwhile, reputations of entire groups of dedicated professionals can be tarnished. One way to restore their credibility is by effectively documenting, interpreting, and validating their contributions to society. Only through such effective communication, can we restore confidence in professions now under public criticism.

A hospital foundation, for example, must prove the value of its services and professional staff to the community. If it doesn't, funding will dry up. The public and employees must come to view the institution as a positive force, or it will not survive.

In the first issue of his new magazine, editor/photographer Robb Mitchell strives to establish credibility for the entire hospital by featuring the efforts of one typical unit—the hospital's neonatal intensive care unit. He humanizes the story by focusing on one baby, showing how an entire department mobilizes talent and resources to help her get a foothold on life. (Other examples from this photo-essay appear in this book in the chapters on machines and moment pictures.)

This key picture establishes, in symbolic terms, the vulnerability of the baby and the steady, helping hand of the health care professionals who work to make her well. We don't see the nurse who holds the tiny finger. But we feel her presence, and that is enough to make the point.

The picture acquires additional context from detail. A Mickey Mouse device in the child's crib confronts the myth of technology-worshiping, impersonal medical institutions.

The baby's eyes are shut and her mouth is open. Tape stretches across her face. She is a captive of her situation, absolutely helpless to do anything about it. But the incongruously huge hand gripping her tiny finger implies that professionally competent, humane care is quite literally at hand. This sense of personal concern, expressed and reexpressed throughout the entire essay, challenges the cynic within us and implies that there are still people serving institutions who know what to do, do it well, and care about those they do it for.

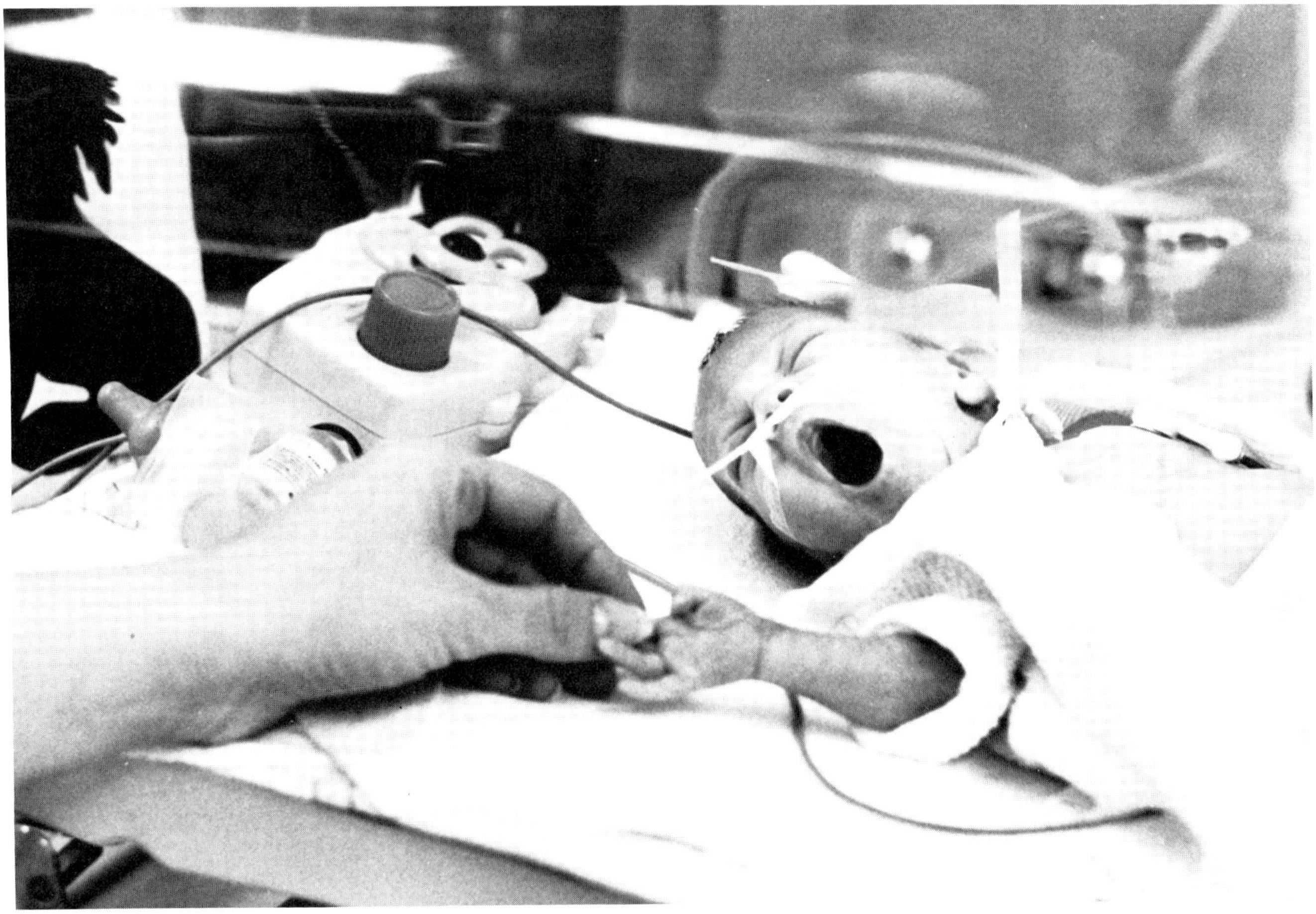

The counselor

Stormy Fitzgerald, chief photographer
Methodist Hospitals of Memphis
Memphis, Tennessee

A test of visual literacy—the ability of photographer, editor, manager, and reader alike to make, use, and read photographs as a language—is acceptance of the fact that we need not show or see *all* of a subject within a photograph. To show the "whole thing" is merely to describe it. By abstracting it, thereby working with the subject on a symbolic level, we can more effectively engage the imaginations of all who see the picture.

Margaret Page, R.N., a counselor at Methodist Hospital in Memphis, enters a patient's room. She is there to help him. It is ironic, and useful, that she sits on the bed, and the patient sits in the chair, instead of vice versa. By taking her position on the bed, Page sees things from the patient's point of view, a perspective essential to such counseling.

Stormy Fitzgerald knows that this reversal of physical positions represents the whole point of Margaret Page's job. Fitzgerald emphasizes this reversal by taking a vantage point behind Page instead of in front of her, and stresses the sweep of the bedding and the complementary textures of the back of Page's uniform by using a wideangle lens. We see this man from Page's point of view and also from a place where the hospital patient is normally seen —the bed.

Fitzgerald frames Page in the lighted window to stress her sympathetic body language. The patient is sidelighted from the same window. By moving her camera position to place Page before the window instead of the drapes, Fitzgerald avoids a disastrous merger of forms.

Some who are not as visually literate as others would protest that we can't actually see Page's face and would so claim that this picture is invalid. But we do not need to see Page's face to get the point. An accompanying story would give us enough context to appreciate the woman and her role in helping people get well. In addition, the editor always has the option of using other pictures to give us insights revealed by the face of the subject. (See portraiture chapter for another shot of Page, a photo which could be used to add important context to this picture.)

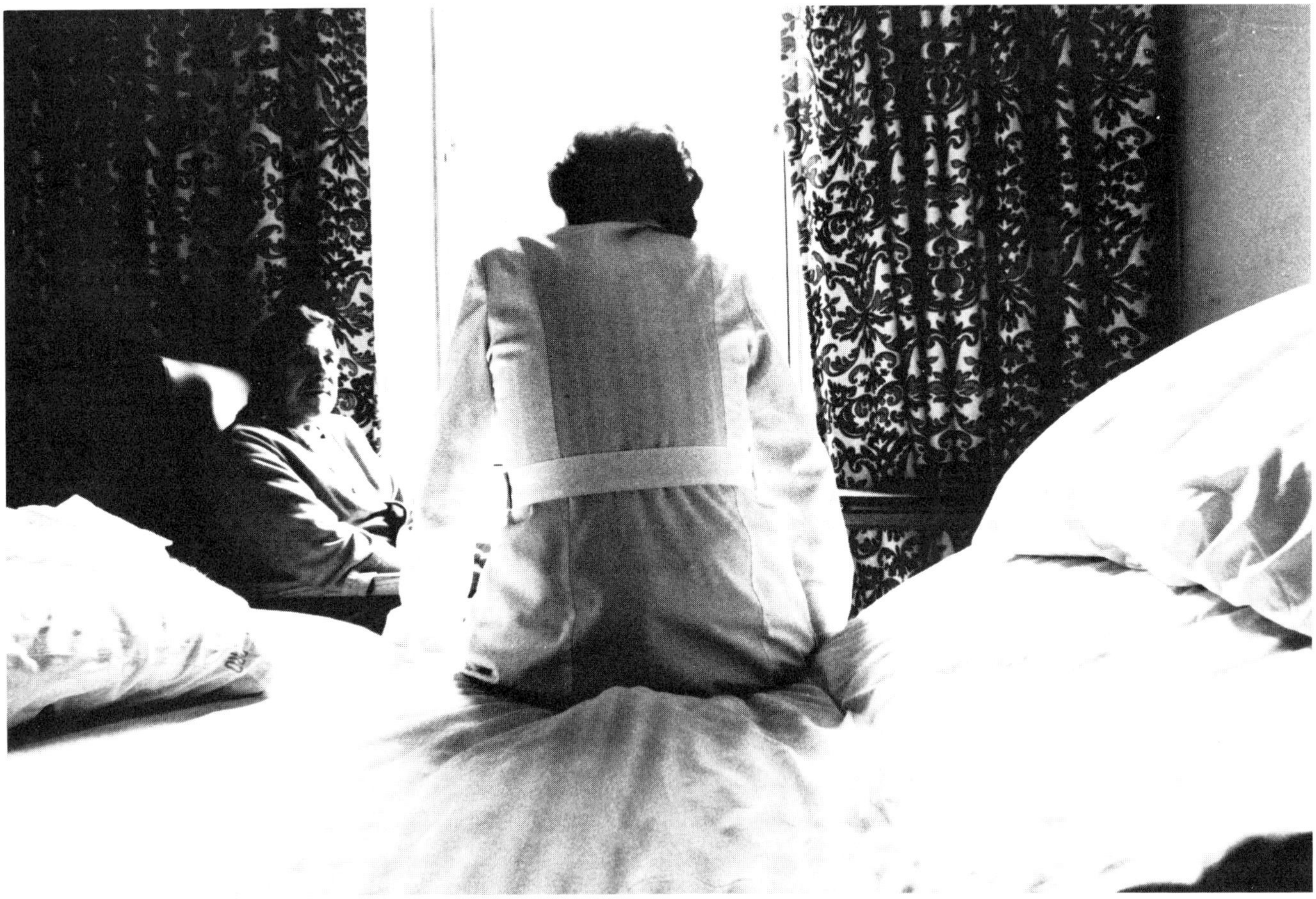

Life in the morgue

**Kurt Foss, staff photojournalist
Hennepin County Public Affairs
Minneapolis, Minnesota**

Sometimes we should not make pictures of certain subjects. If we were to actually see, for example, what these people are doing, we would be distracted from the point of the story. Kurt Foss must instead *imply* the presence of the subject, letting the caption and story add specific information on it. He is then free to offer us an interpretation of the *employees* who do this job, instead of photographically describing the details of the job itself.

These people work in a hospital morgue. They must establish, beyond a doubt, the causes of death and must document those causes. Foss concentrates on their feelings, while the environment adds a mood underscoring those feelings.

The medical examiner uses a camera to document facts important to the case. An assistant holds a light to improve the general lighting and allow the examiner to make extremely detailed photographs at small lens openings.

Through Foss's vantage point, the light comes at us, obscuring the face of the assistant and giving the picture an unworldly quality. The light dramatically intensifies the concentration of the examiner. She is serious, sympathetic, intently professional in the face of what might seem to most of us to be an unpleasant job.

Supported by a good story, this picture can take us inside that job. To these people, it is all in a day's work. To be crisply professional, yet retain sensitivity and feeling, is a goal of every hospital employee, and Foss implies this here.

The picture is an example of a solution to a problem frequently encountered by hospital photographers. Sometimes it is impossible to shoot certain things. Here, for example, it is unnecessary to show the subject of the autopsy. Likewise, it is sometimes impossible to obtain permission to photograph certain patients or situations. The solution: *Imply* the subject; concentrate instead on other things—such as expressions of people *working with* the subject or environmental details that enhance the point we are trying to get across. Implied subjects are often stronger than revealed subjects because they more directly involve our imagination and stimulate our thinking.

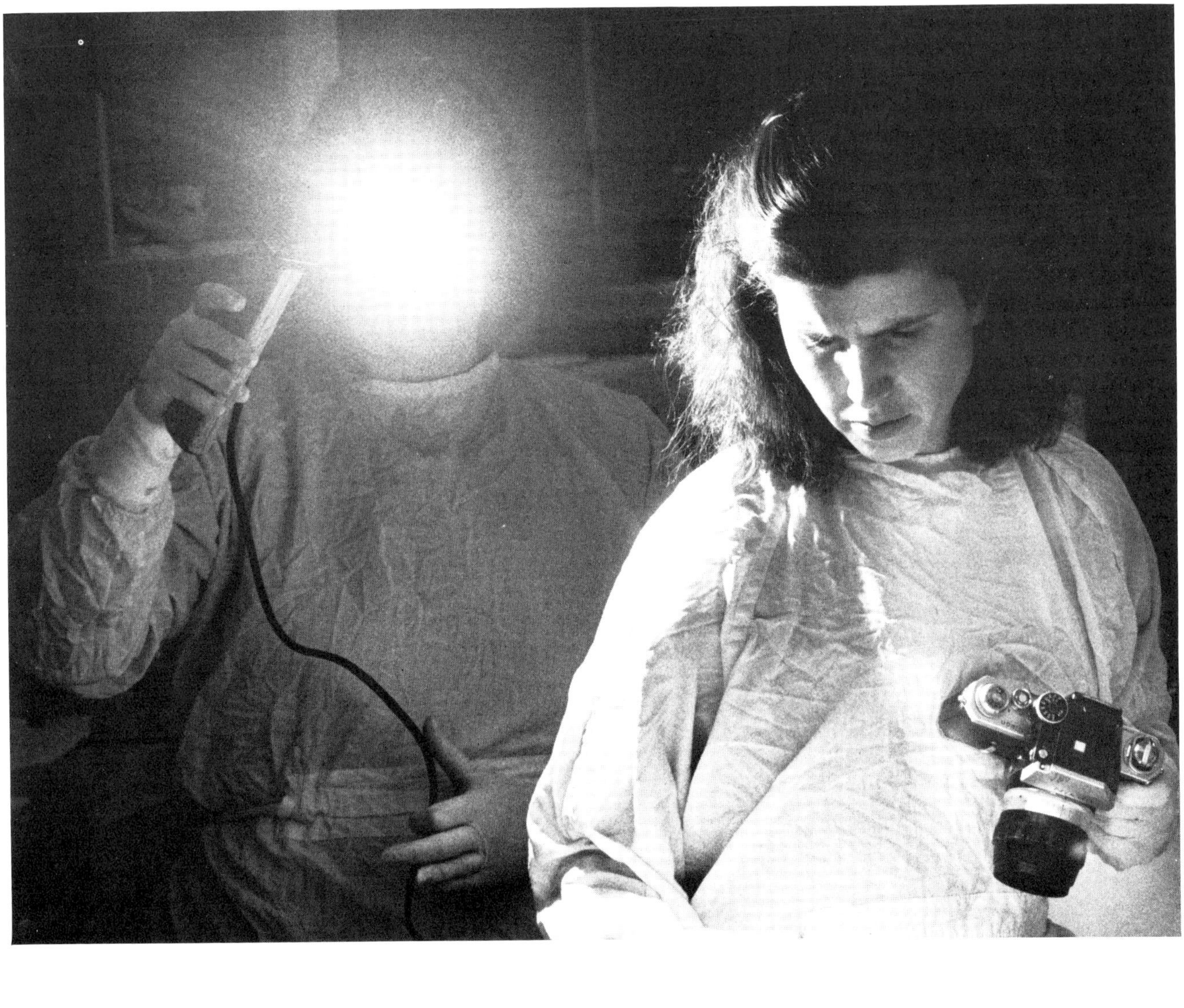

Walking wounded

**Tom Treuter, supervisor,
publication photography and
design
William Beaumont Hospital
Royal Oak, Michigan**

This enormously appealing photograph is more than a hospital picture. It comments on childhood, need, gratitude, vulnerability, and frustration. Perhaps the reader can bring still more meanings to it.

Again, Tom Treuter works with a very simple subject, a child with her arm in a brand new sling. She faces some logistical problems: We hope for her sake that she is right-handed. The photo is made even more effective by what Treuter and his designer Linda Liske will do to the picture *after* it is made.

For this is not the same picture we would see on Treuter's negative. The frame of the 35mm camera, enhanced here by a wideangle lens turned vertically, allows Treuter to shoot the child from head to toe yet still get close for strong detail. Because of this lens and vantage point, Treuter's original frame includes distracting information on both sides. Liske crops it and reshapes the picture into a strong vertical. She keeps only a sliver of space to the left of the child's dangling good arm, creating tension and emphasizing the child's helplessness. No camera makes a picture exactly like this. A picture editor or designer must do it.

This picture is improved by cropping. It is also enhanced by Treuter's darkroom manipulation. It is virtually impossible to expose film to get both detail in the face and jet black shadows on the legs. Treuter chooses to expose the *film* for facial detail. In the darkroom, he later underexposes part of the *print* to create silhouetted legs. The legs become frail symbols of youth. The picture, begun in the camera, is continued in the darkroom and finished on the artist's cropping table.

This photograph now reaches out to all of us, conveying the mission of the hospital in the most humane and positive way. Primarily because both Treuter and Liske have been able to strengthen it beyond the powers of the camera itself.

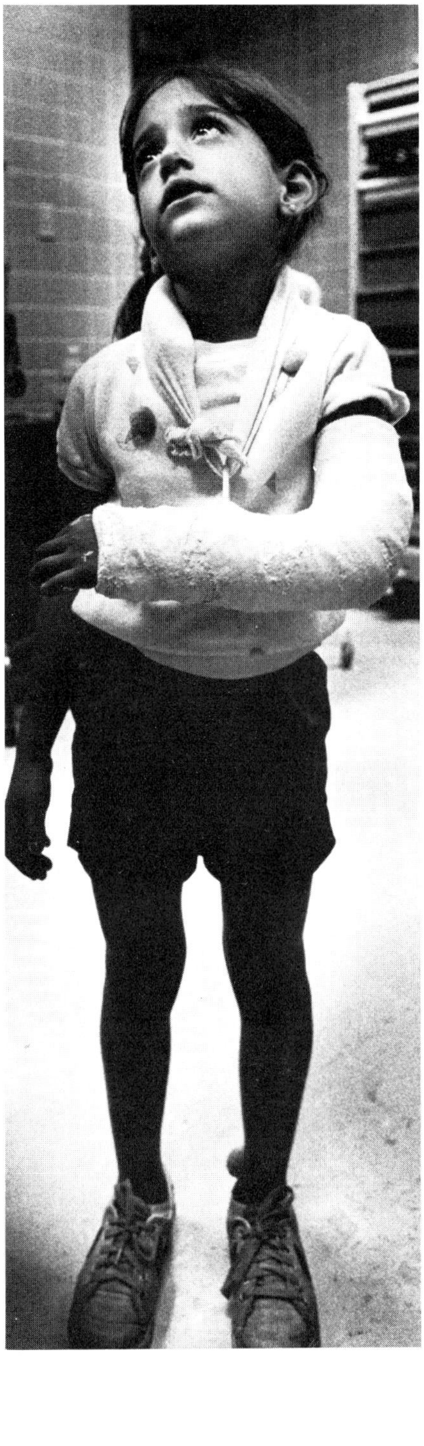

Chapter 7

Camera in the classroom: capturing the essence of education

Thousands of school districts, colleges, and universities fill the mails with publications, brochures, catalogs, and recruiting materials aimed at students, faculty, parents, and potential donors. Almost all carry photographs, and nearly all of them are basically the same: pictures of people sitting in classrooms and laboratories or walking arm in arm under the campus elms. When we've seen one, we've seen them all.

Interpretive photographers working for educational organizations know that the ultimate objective is to convey the values of learning itself. They somehow manage to insert their camera between student and teacher, capturing those rare moments when the spark of knowledge explodes in plain sight. Or they probe the nature of those who teach and those who study, making pictures that ask questions and demand answers from their viewers.

As with companies and hospitals, educational facilities provide services to people and through people. To attempt to convey the essence of those services through superficial views of buildings, gymnasiums, and chemistry labs, is futile. A more valid mission rests in the adventure of discovering who we are, how things work, what things mean.

And that is what the best of the classroom photographers try to accomplish with their pictures.

Looking for a direction

Paul Obregon, senior photographer
Home Mission Board, Southern Baptist Convention
Atlanta, Georgia

Classroom pictures must go beyond describing educational environments. They must convey a sense of the problems educators face, explore teaching innovations, and, most importantly, reveal the process of learning itself.

Paul Obregon made this picture for a story on how Baptists are improving literacy and the self-image of kids with problems. Through the expression on the face of one child, Obregon represents all who are vulnerable. For this child, a good education represents the last, best hope.

The picture contrasts a strong foreground portrait against a subordinate symbolic background. The profile of the child is placed in just the right spot—if Obregon had been a few inches to the right, the face would be blocking the most important part of the background chart. Photographers must learn how to see foreground/background relationships and must acquire the skill to position elements in space to convey a message. They must also be able to choose lens openings not only to let in enough light but to focus selectively and emphatically, creating sharp vs. soft contrasts. Until they can master these techniques, they will continue to see haphazardly, making snapshots instead of carefully organized photographs.

For Obregon, this image displays the innocence and vulnerability of the youngster. "He seems to be suspended," says Obregon. "He is looking for some direction. His future is in the background for the reader to see."

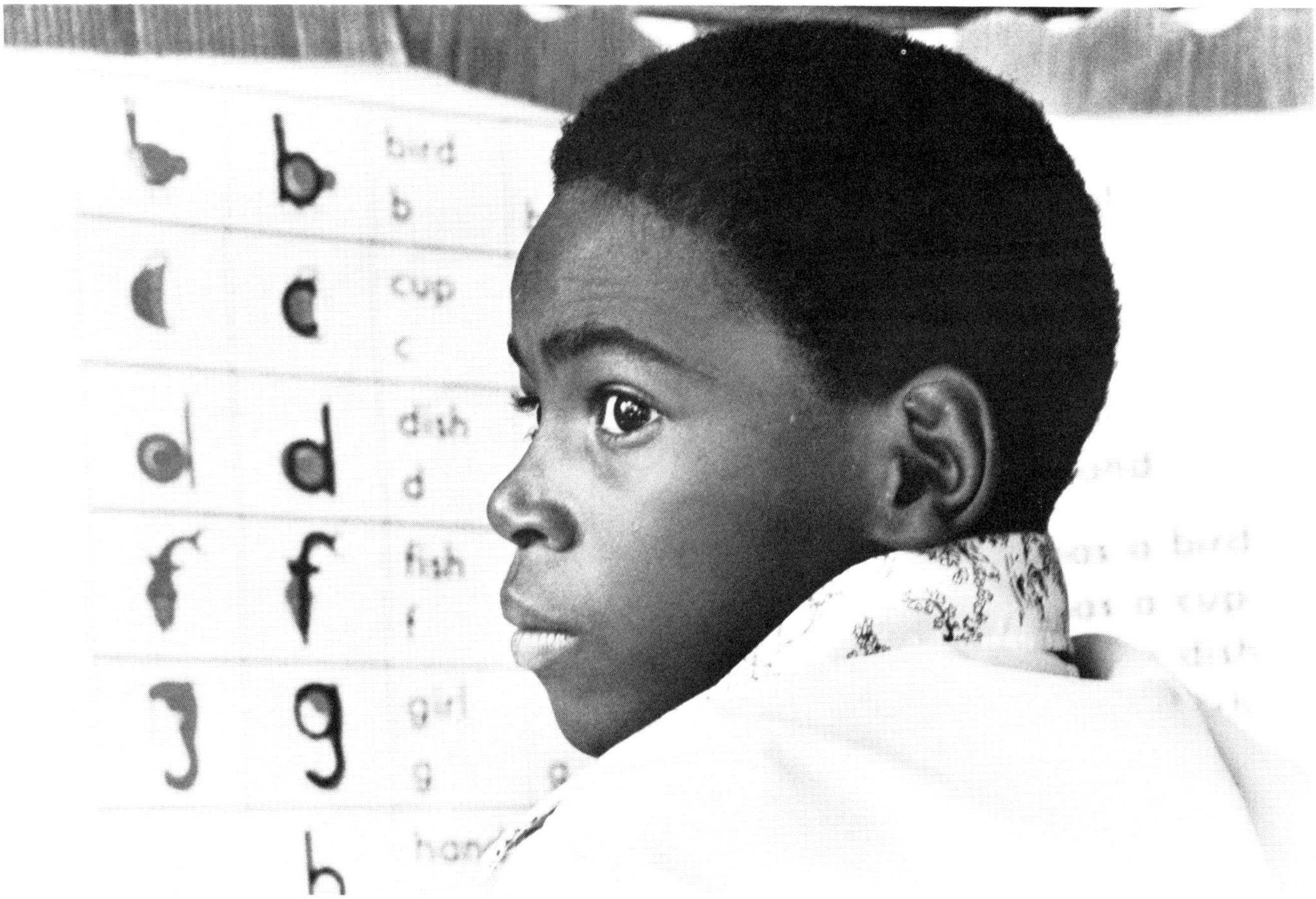
b
bird
b
c
cup
c
d
dish
d
f
fish
f
g
girl
g
h

The classroom is everywhere —and for everyone

Kay Engelsen, public
information officer
Tacoma Public Schools
Tacoma, Washington

School districts produce thousands of photos annually in an attempt to reach parents, community, and students. Most of them fail to say very much with their pictures. Amazingly, educators are often among the visually illiterate. They are usually word-people. They make and use pictures only to "show" the subject, rarely to interpret it.

The Tacoma, Washington, school district, thanks in large part to Kay Engelsen, is an exception. For Engelsen, photography is a passionate form of expression. She makes sure her district places *equal* emphasis on visual and verbal forms of communication by taking camera in hand herself—following the teaching process as it unfolds, interpreting it in humane, cogent terms.

In this photo, Engelsen makes two points. First, that under law, handicapped youngsters must have access to all educational opportunities. And second, that such opportunities exist not only within the classroom but also in the world at large.

Engelsen unfolds both messages simultaneously. The wheelchair identifies the child as handicapped. The teacher supports him close to the tree and explains the purpose of bark, giving this student an experience far more valuable than any textbook or lecture could provide. But the key to the picture rests in the intensity of the child's response. Young Patrick Schriver is learning, and he cares about what he learns. No handicap will hold him back.

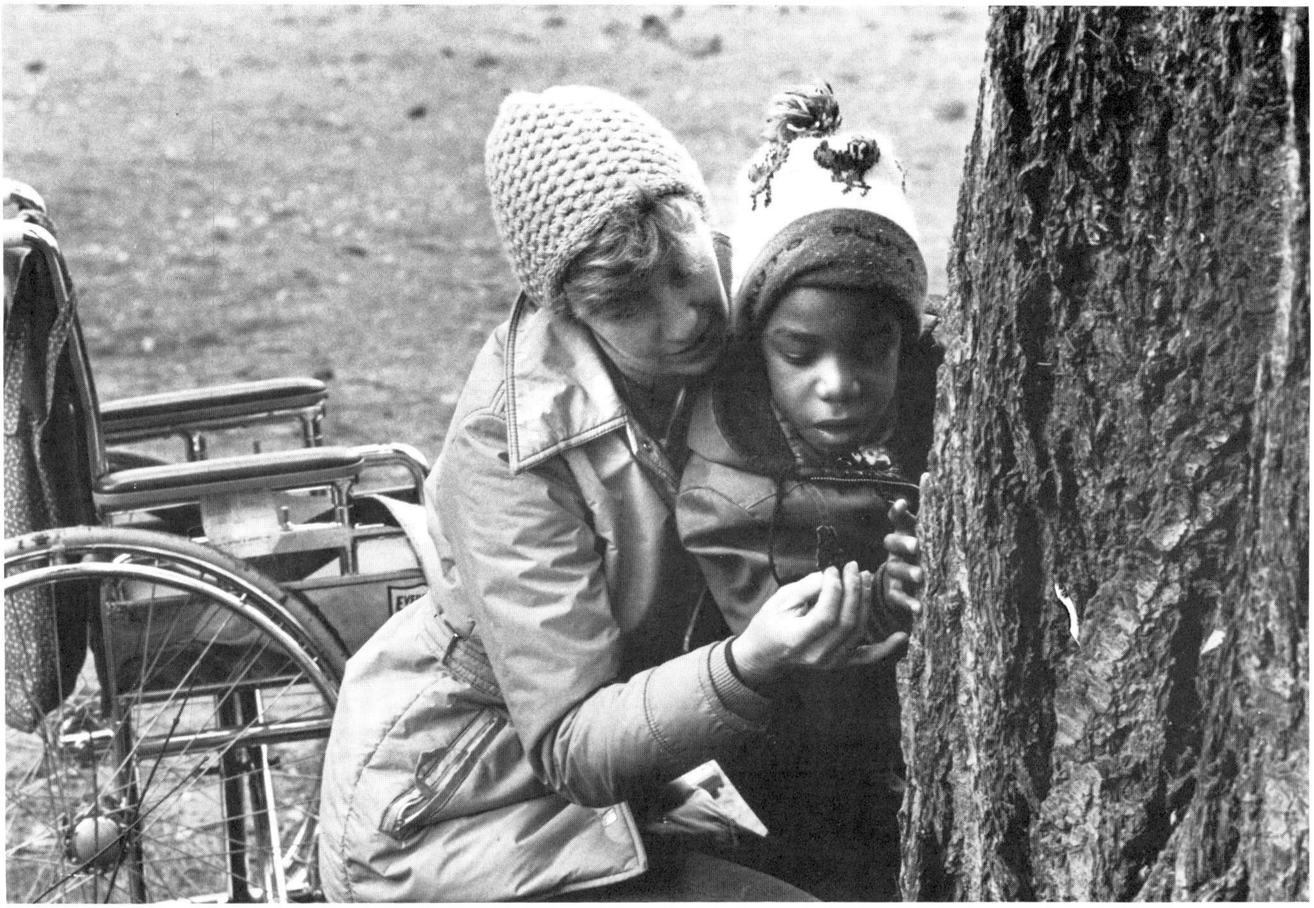

By the numbers

Don Rutledge, photojournalist
Home Mission Board, Southern Baptist Convention
Atlanta, Georgia

It is generally easier to photograph one teacher, one student, or the interaction between them than it is to photograph a teacher working with many children at once. By using fewer subjects, we can generally make our point with greater impact and meaning.

However, this photo by Don Rutledge proves an exception to the rule. He successfully interprets a teaching effort involving seven students at once by waiting for a moment when all respond simultaneously and spontaneously.

Teacher Shirley Baty is teaching "number five" to her charges at an Albuquerque neighborhood center and holds up five fingers to make the lesson visually indelible. Apparently, the lesson is working —except for the little girl at right, who seems to think that five is really three. This touch of incongruity adds an important dimension. We don't all learn at the same speed.

Rutledge is sitting at the end of the table, all but forgotten. He uses a wideangle lens, leading us in from the edges, down through the tangle of arms and hands, until we reach the teacher in the center. Behind the teacher is symbolic reinforcement: The rhythms of the numbers and figures on the wall echo the rhythms of the thrusting fingers before it.

All eight people in the picture share in the moment, and Rutledge makes of it a cohesive, undiluted statement on the thrill of learning.

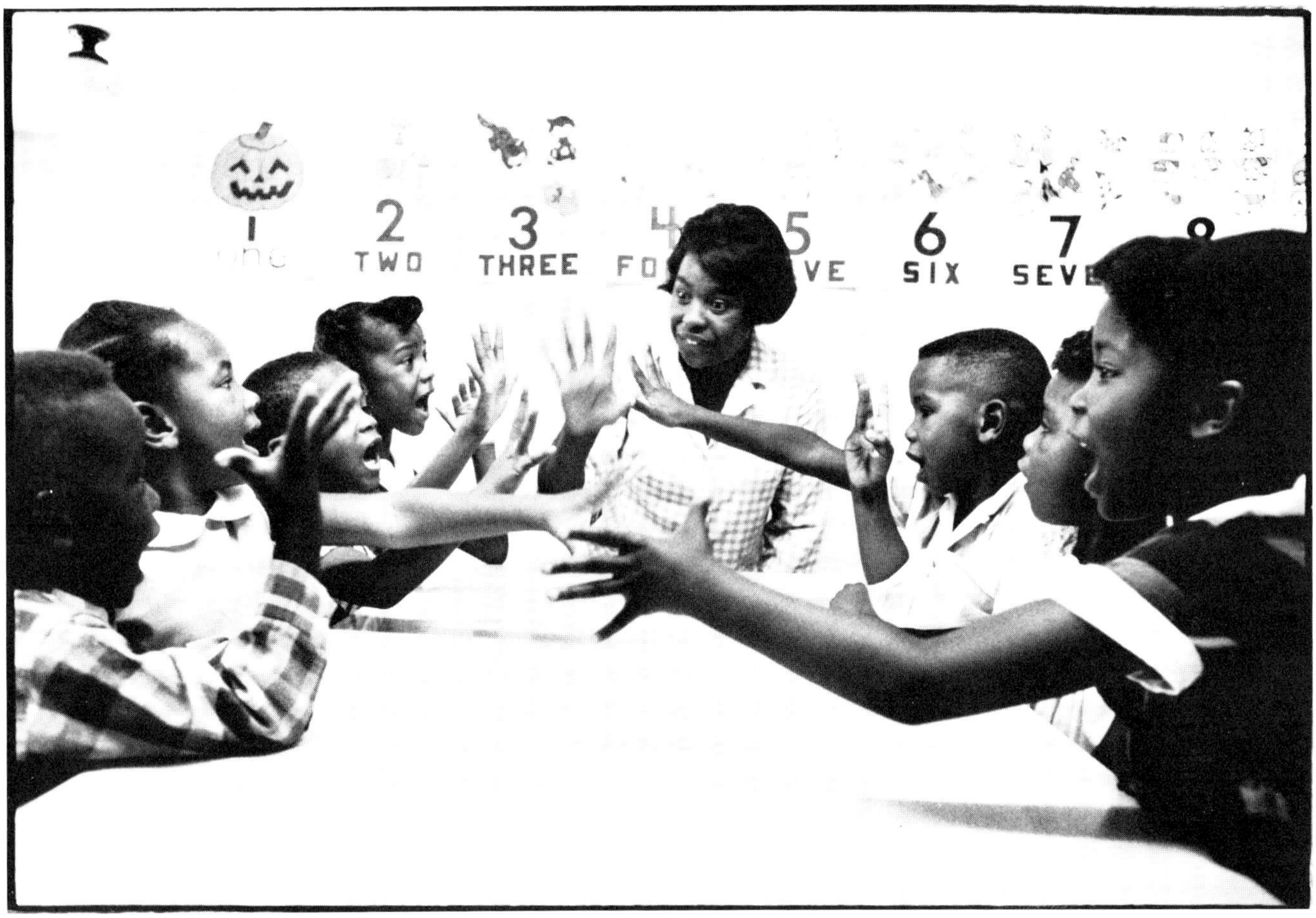
2
TWO
3
THREE
5
6
SIX
7

Letting their fingers do the talking

Kurt Foss, photojournalist
Hennepin County Public Affairs
Minneapolis, Minnesota

On the surface, this photograph of children learning with their fingers is similar in subject matter to the preceding shot by Don Rutledge. But the point of this picture —and the reason why it works—is quite different.

Rutledge chose to relate students to the teacher. Foss, on the other hand, elects to concentrate on the children alone, stressing the differences between children in their approaches to learning. The teacher is implied instead of actually seen.

Variations in learning ability offer classroom photographers a chance to contrast the expressions, body language, and feelings of students, ultimately making the point that people are individuals who learn at different rates and in different ways.

Here three children are learning the basics of sign language in a class at a Hennepin County library. The child in the middle seems to be getting it, and she is the focal point of the picture. The girl at right is not so sure of herself. And the youngster at left, out of focus, also seems hazy in her grasp of the skill. The point of the picture rests in the differences among the students, and Foss drives it home so well that the county used the picture on the cover of its 1980 annual report.

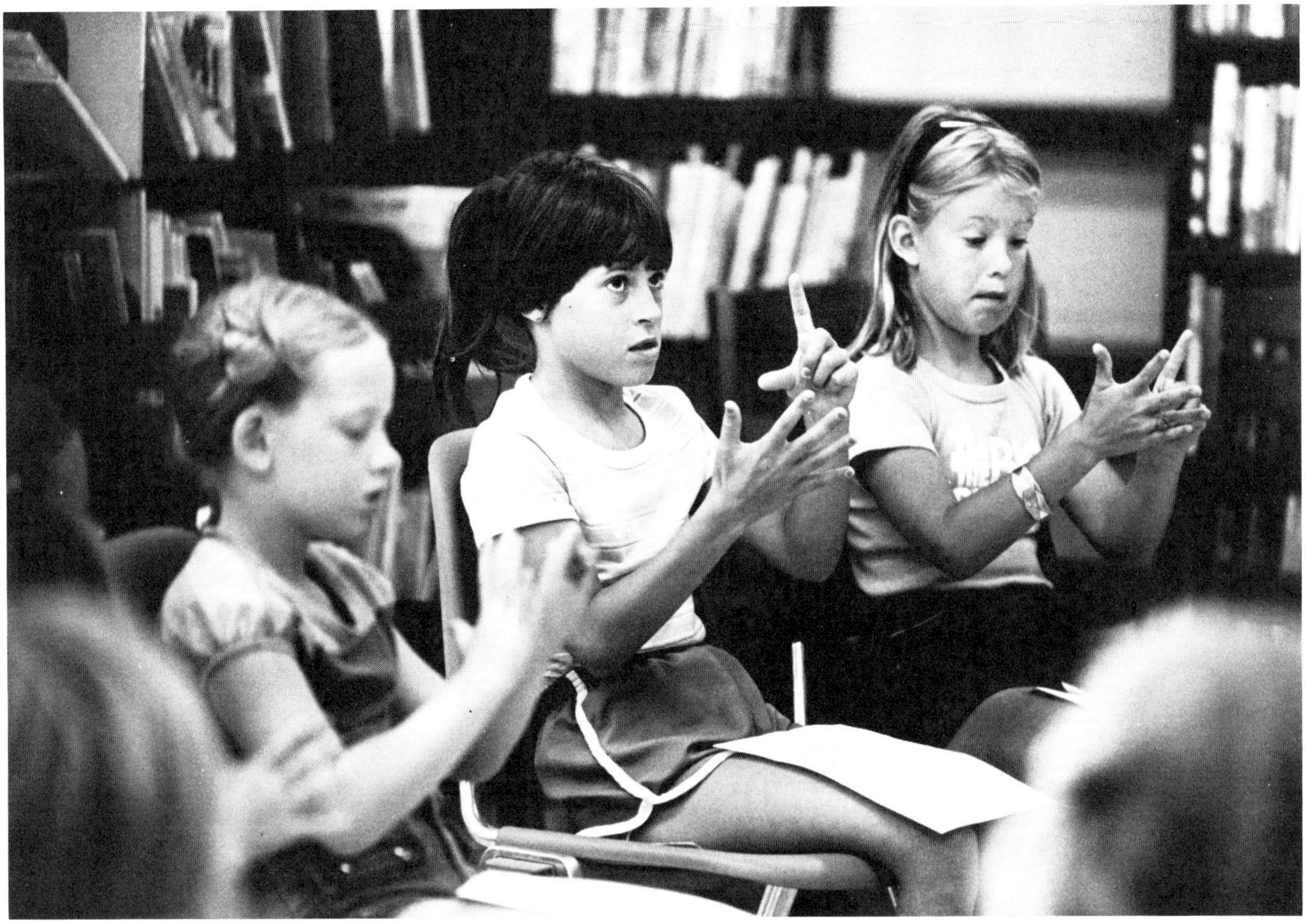

The professor

Bruce Stromberg, freelance photographer
Client: Haverford College
Bryn Mawr, Pennsylvania

It is just as important for educational institutions to communicate the skills, personalities, and assets of faculty members as it is to portray students, facilities, and extracurricular activities. Pictures of teachers must convey a sense of the inner person if we are to appreciate the values they bring to their teaching.

Bruce Stromberg does this in a professorial portrait, used in the Haverford College alumni magazine. This environmental portrait carefully matches the man to his surroundings, forcefully interpreting what he does and who he is.

Notice how Stromberg uses diagonal rhythms, light, symbols, and response to integrate the professor into his setting. To make such a portrait, Stromberg places the man just to the side of the blackboard, allowing light from a window to illuminate him from the side. Stromberg asks him to rest his right arm naturally upon the desk, making sure his notes are placed next to his hand. By doing this, Stromberg cohesively organizes his picture. The rhythms of the arms echo the rhythms of the light playing against the wall behind him. The notes repeat the rectangular shape of the blackboard behind him.

The words on the blackboard relate to the course the man is teaching. His expression, probably a response to a question Stromberg has asked him, seems thoughtful. His clothing is informal, presumably typical of a Haverford professor. Everything works to give us insights into the nature of the man and his job.

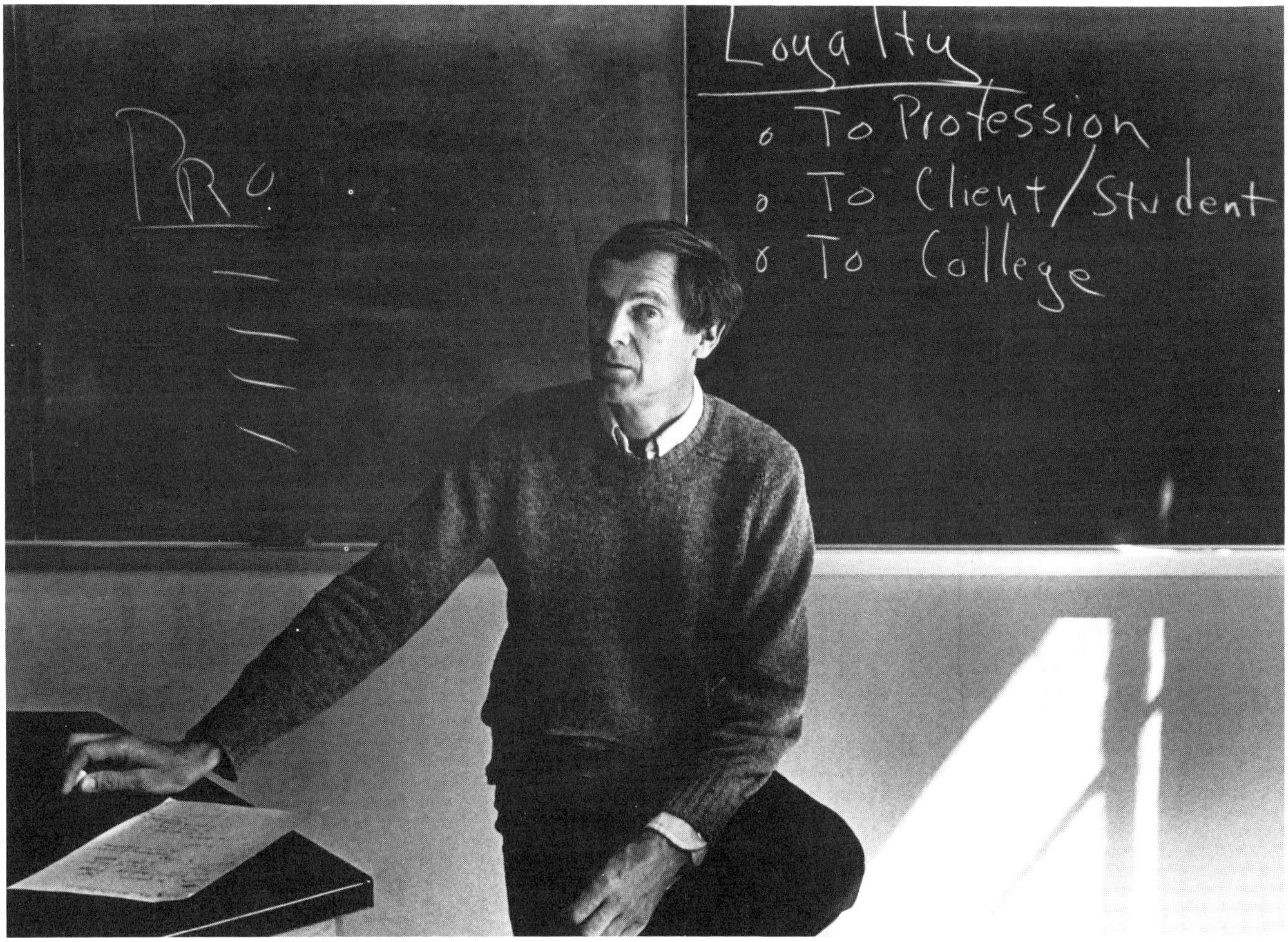
Loyalty
o To Profession
o To Client/Student
o To College

Teacher abuse

Bruce Stromberg, freelance photographer
Client: The University of Pennsylvania
Philadelphia, Pennsylvania

Creating "concept" illustrations requires technical skill and a good deal of incongruity. As in Dave Denemark's photo of smokers kicking the habit (see chapter on incongruity), Bruce Stromberg gives us a created image, one we would never see in ordinary life, to illustrate an article on teacher abuse for the University of Pennsylvania.

We know it is fantasy because of the deliberate diffusion Stromberg brings to the edges of the picture and the model. To get this effect, Stromberg applied moisture or another diffusing substance to the lens. The picture relies on verbal content, effective body language, and a symbolic classroom setting to make its point.

Concept illustrations function best in an appropriate context. They usually are reproduced large and are used on the opening spread of an article. They stand by themselves. It would be an awkward mix of photographic styles to lead with a picture such as this and then follow it up with pictures of actual teachers. Concept illustrations are best used in publications that use them regularly. To use such pictures without this context can imply that they represent real events, which is not fair to the reader.

Correctly used, this picture will be viewed by readers as a theme or symbol. It is a creation of the photographer's imagination designed to activate the imaginations of those who see it. Such photographs can effectively make a point, if the technique is competent and the concept incongruous.

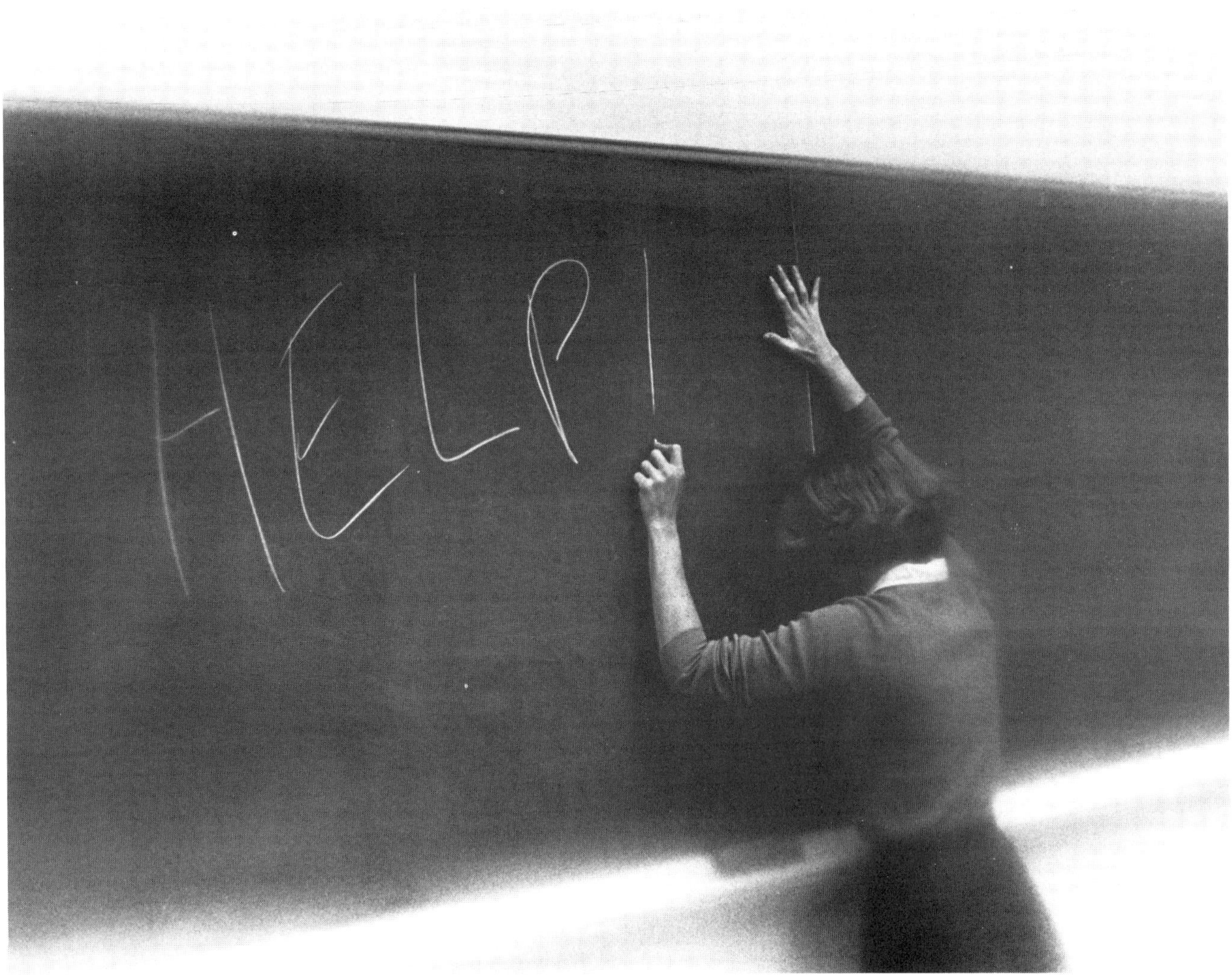
HELP!

Chapter 8

Meetings, speeches: beyond the talking head

A large percentage of organizational photography is devoted to coverage of meetings, conferences, speeches, seminars, discussions, conventions, and pep talks. Most of them are covered as literal "attendance-taking" shots. But pictures of people having their pictures taken do not succeed as organizational communication. The people who were at the meeting know they were there; few others care that they were.

The infamous "talking head" picture also fails. A picture of somebody talking into a microphone is of little value to a reader, who has probably seen hundreds just like it.

Organizational photographers must go far beyond this level if they are to capture the meaning of the meeting to the participants and ultimately convey that meaning to the reader.

Photographers who can do this are usually selective in their approach, rather than encyclopedic. Instead of "getting everyone in," they will allow the few to stand for the many who attend. Those few usually display an emotional response which can symbolize the tone or theme of the meeting itself. Often the environment plays a role in conveying the story of the event.

Meeting hard times with straight talk

Wm. Franklin McMahon, freelance photographer
Client: Borg-Warner Corporation
Chicago, Illinois

Information is exchanged and debated. Bargains are struck. Ideas are accepted or rejected. People agree—and disagree. These are the elements that make meetings work. If such things are not taking place, the meeting is not doing its job. Meetings are usually more than ceremonial gatherings. They are extensions of institutions at work. They offer organizational photographers much material for interpretation. Yet few organizational photographers are able to produce meeting pictures that do more than scratch the surface.

Frank McMahon proves an exception. His photographs of an employee/management meeting at the Springs Division of Borg-Warner strike at the heart of the event: The division's employee incentive fund had come up dry, and it was time to explain why. Materials handler Rueben Schneider rises from his seat, pen in hand, demanding the facts. He listens as the division's vice president balances bad short-term news against long-term hopes.

This is employee communication at the most basic, hard-hitting level. McMahon has captured the confrontation, the tension, the employees' demand for answers to tough questions. Although Borg-Warner's management publication *Perspective* uses this photo with three other pictures to soften the confrontational aspect, it is this adversarial relationship that carries the spread.

Borg-Warner communicators hope other divisions will consider such meetings between management and employees. They try to realistically convey both the tensions and benefits. The photos enable a vast audience to share a fascinating managerial and human experience.

McMahon uses a telephoto lens to reach across space and fill his frame with the form of Schneider. Here is the powerful symbol of a man confronting hierarchy. For the moment at least, he is participating at the level of the top brass. In his body language we see patience, a hint of skepticism. The photo of the division management team, facing Schneider from across the room is reproduced across a spread of the publication and reveals three men very much on the spot. Note the body language of the vice president at center. His expression depicts a man very much in control, his hands and his feet reveal inner tension. The division production manager on the right appears self-confident, at ease, with legs crossed and shoe pressed to the table post. But his crossed arms also indicate a guarded attitude. The industrial relations director on the left, collar unbuttoned, hands folded, is a good listener.

We can read our own interpretations into the body language. But the value of these photos to the reader is clear: They tell us that in this company, employees are given a chance to ask hard questions and hear answers to them. Face-to-face meetings are a staple of organizational life, and photographs of them must be able to extend participation, vicariously, far beyond the walls of the meeting room.

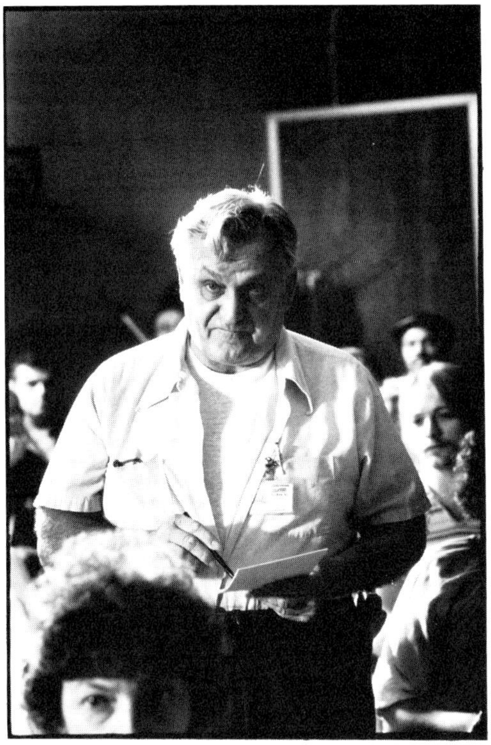

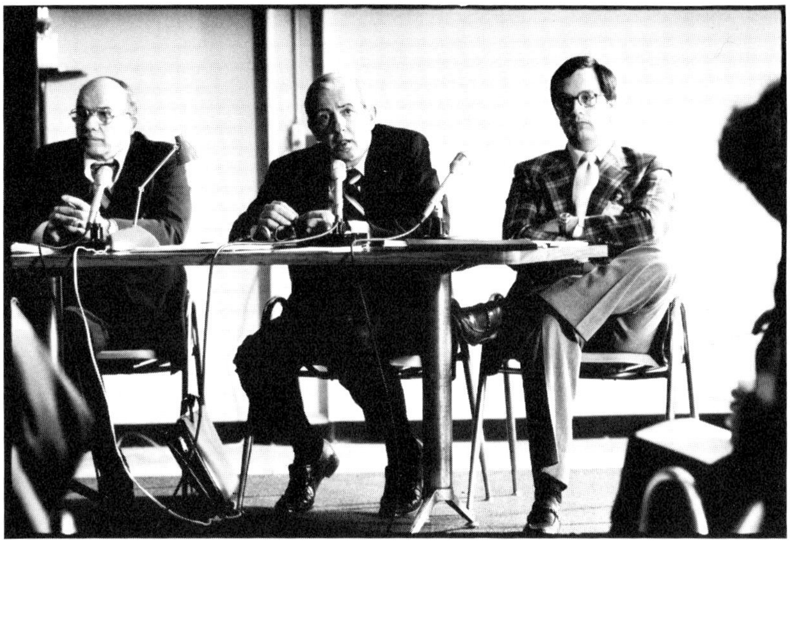

United Way meeting, U.S. Bancorp, Portland, Oregon

Karen Copenhaver, editor/
 photographer
U.S. Bancorp
Portland, Oregon

We do not always need intensely dramatic confrontations to make good meeting pictures. Even in routine exchanges of information, photographers can find responses, relationships, symbols, and details that reveal insights into the purpose of the meeting.

Once again, a speaker/listener pairing is used to convey a message, as Karen Copenhaver selectively records on film the varying responses of bank employees listening to a briefing at a United Way campaign planning meeting.

These women have been selected to lead fund raising efforts in various departments of the bank. They must have facts, examples, details—a grasp of the campaign's purpose and benefits. They listen to a spokeswoman for a home for children with severe emotional handicaps. They will see a film about the children, and through this combination of lecture and film they will come to understand the importance of a United Way service.

Copenhaver uses a telephoto lens to come in close, stressing some aspects of subject matter over others. In the shot of the four listeners, she focuses on the two women at center, contrasting their varying responses. The women at the ends appear in soft focus, adding still more variety in response. The picture implies that each is absorbing the information in her own way, yet all get the message.

The posters on the wall behind them can be read as symbols for various activities of the United Way, adding context to the message. Copenhaver shoots from a low position and waits until the women are absorbed in the proceedings. There were probably additional campaign coordinators at this meeting. But Copenhaver leaves them out. She realizes that the function of meeting photography is not to pay tribute to the participants or to take attendance. She must communicate the value and purpose of the meeting to her readers. She lets pictures of the few stand for the many others who may have also attended, creating an undiluted statement good enough to stand on its own.

She strengthens this picture by pairing it with a fine action shot of the speaker, caught at the moment she makes a point. Lips pursed, fingers pressed together, film at the ready, this woman is imparting important information. She believes in what she says, and her words are making an impact. The out-of-focus blackboard behind her carries verbal reinforcement. We can make out the name of the institution, its capacity, even some of its subdivisions.

The blackboard's dark surface links it effectively with the dark wall in the opposing picture, tieing both pictures together as a graphic entity. Copenhaver is not only linking responses and listener/speaker roles. She is using environmental similarities to bond the pair of pictures, making them work cohesively as a single editorial unit.

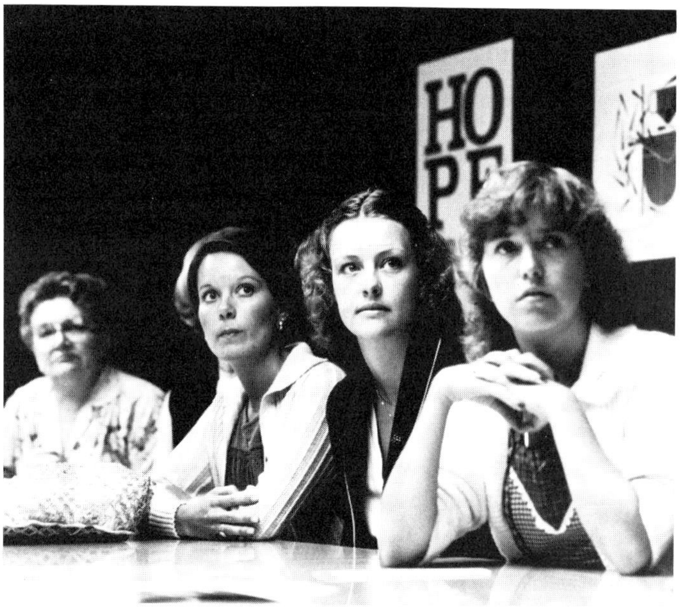

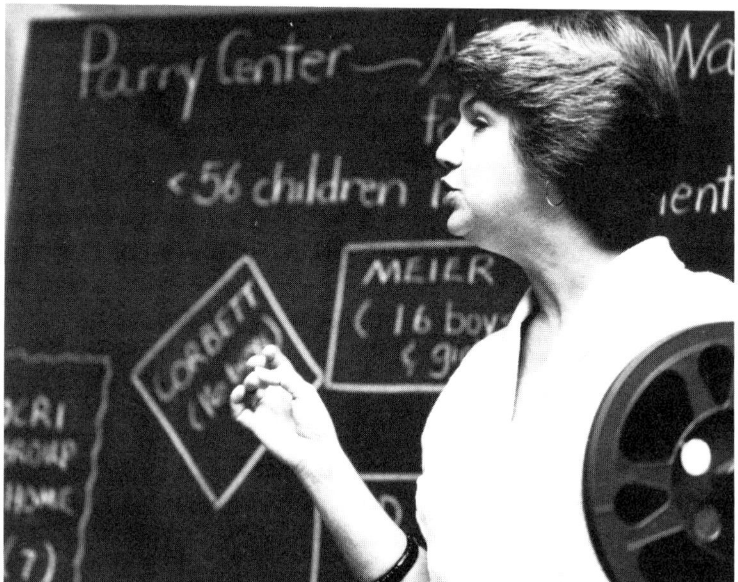
Parry Center
<56 children
MEIER

Don Ranly, IABC Conference Washington, D.C.

Jim Visser, freelance photographer
Client: International Association of Business Communicators
San Francisco, California

Many novice photographers complain about low lighting levels in meeting rooms and claim they need a flash to make good pictures in them. Such fears are groundless. To the contrary, most meeting rooms, particularly in hotels, offer lighting with more dramatic contrast than we find in most offices. The only photographers who still use flash to cover meetings are either fearful beginners, who are afraid "nothing will otherwise come out," or jaded hacks, who learned a handy lighting formula in 1958 and rigidly stick to it out of habit and fear.

Jim Visser, former staff photographer for Six Flags Over Mid-America recreation center and now a freelancer, proves that existing light in a hotel meeting room can add drama, emphasis, and meaning to a picture. Visser made this photo of speaker Don Ranly addressing a sea of heads at the 1981 conference of the International Association of Business Communicators in Washington, D.C.

The light is falling on Ranly from an overhead fixture. Since there is no light falling on the background, Visser can expose for the highlighted areas, making the background absolutely black. He eliminates distraction, concentrating our attention on Ranly's fervor.

Visser also selects a long telephoto lens, telescoping distance, blurring the audience into a soft mass that fills half the frame. He thereby puts the viewer of the picture into the audience, and through this vantage point, the viewer participates in the meeting as a spectator.

The softness is produced by the narrow focusing zone of the telephoto lens. Also, Visser probably "pushed" development of the film, rating his fast ASA 400 film at ASA 800 or 1600 and developing it accordingly. This produces some slight "grain," which in this case is not objectionable.

Note how the contrast between the sharp Ranly and the soft audience emphasizes the speaker. If the heads were as sharp as Ranly, he would be without emphasis, and a good portion of his strength as a speaker would be diluted. We are able to concentrate on Ranly's gesture, his facial response, the symbols of his authority—neck mike, badge with speaker's ribbon, silver hair and beard.

Through these symbols, gesture, light, and background, Ranly acquires a messianic quality. He urges his audience to join him in his thinking, to raise their standards to those he espouses. It is more than just a picture of a speaker at a meeting. It is a statement about persuasion, leadership, and inspiration.

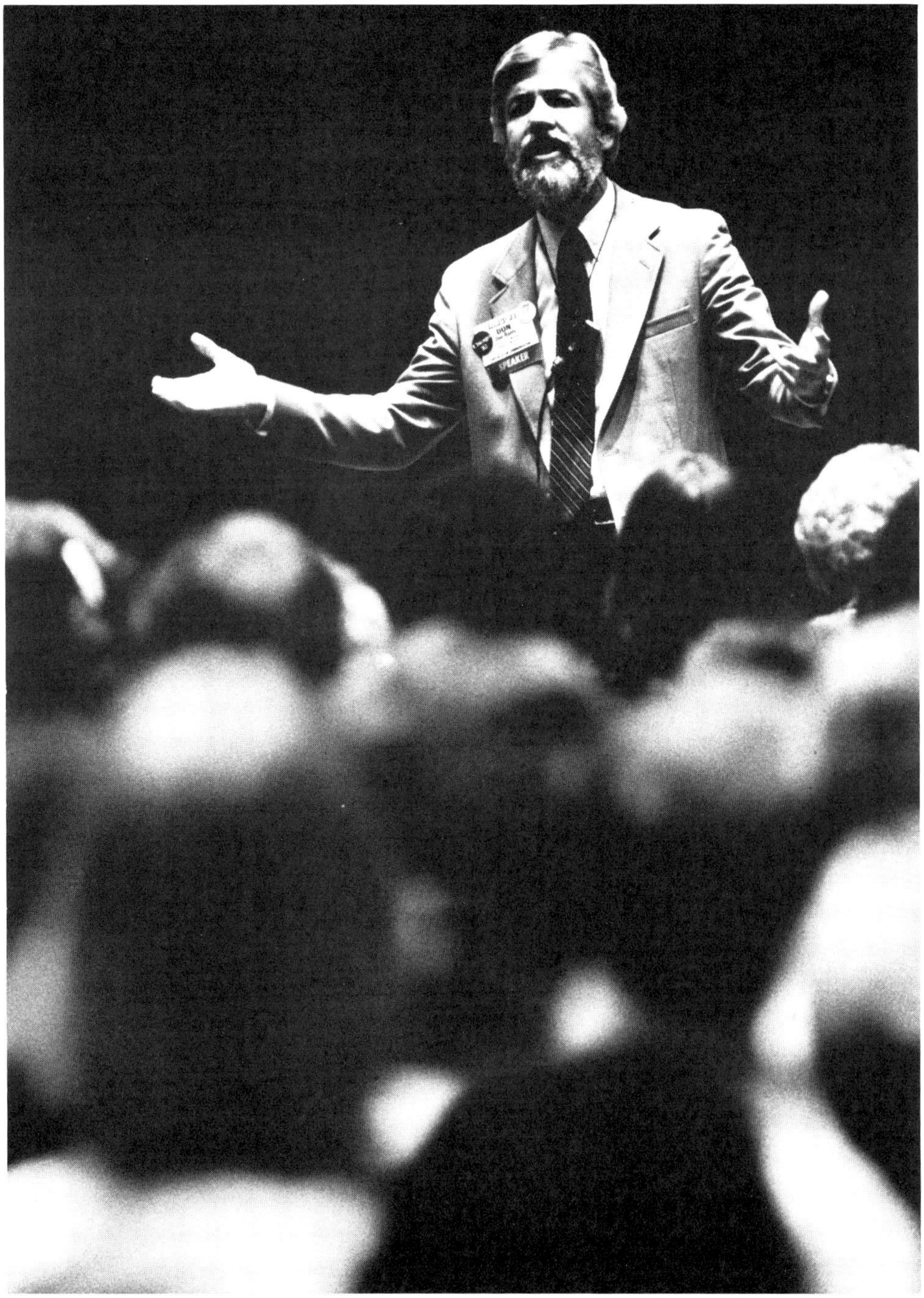
SPEAKER

Executive at back of meeting room

**Melissa Brown, manager of internal communications
Herman Miller, Inc.
Zeeland, Michigan**

"This is one of those situations everybody tells you can't shoot in," says Melissa Brown. "We were watching a slide show. All the lights in the meeting room were out, except the projector and a few low-level exit lights over the doors in the back of the room. I was halfway across the room, using the 100mm telephoto lens and shooting, hand-held, at 1/8th of a second." Brown does more than make the picture "come out." She makes a shot which expresses, through the appraising response of a company executive illuminated only by an exit sign over his head, the essence of the meeting.

This photograph shows us how far photography and its technical developments have come in just the last twenty years. There are still people in the business who tell us it can't be done. They remember only the photography they learned back in the days of slow film, slow lenses, bulky cameras, and obtrusive flash equipment. If they would only take advantage of technological progress, they too, could easily make images as memorable as Brown does here.

Years ago, there were no fast telephoto lenses. Today, telephotos with maximum openings of f/2 and f/2.8 are commonplace. Fast film used to be grainy. Today, the same film—Kodak's Tri-X—has been refined to the point where distracting grain structure is negligible. Tri-X can be routinely "pushed" to ASA 800. It even can be safely exposed up to ASA 1600 without serious loss of detail or clarity. Darkroom chemistry has changed, too. Developers are available to process at these "pushed" ASA ratings with clarity and contrast.

Of course, Brown must be very careful when releasing her shutter. At 1/8th of a second, there can be no camera movement or the picture will be blurred. Her finger can move only *before* she releases the shutter—a smooth, consistent pressure on the already depressed shutter button completes the release. She must hold the camera securely in the palm of her hand, with her fingers.

Brown sees the value of minimal light to emphasize the rhythm of the executive's lighted fingers holding the cigar. The softly focused aide provides context and contrast. The light on the collars and the cuff add to the message: We are seeing an executive appraisal, a calculated, watchful evaluation coming from a man standing under an exit sign at the back of a meeting room. We do not have to see the slide show. We do not see the audience at large. We only see one man, and he is only partially revealed. But that part says it all.

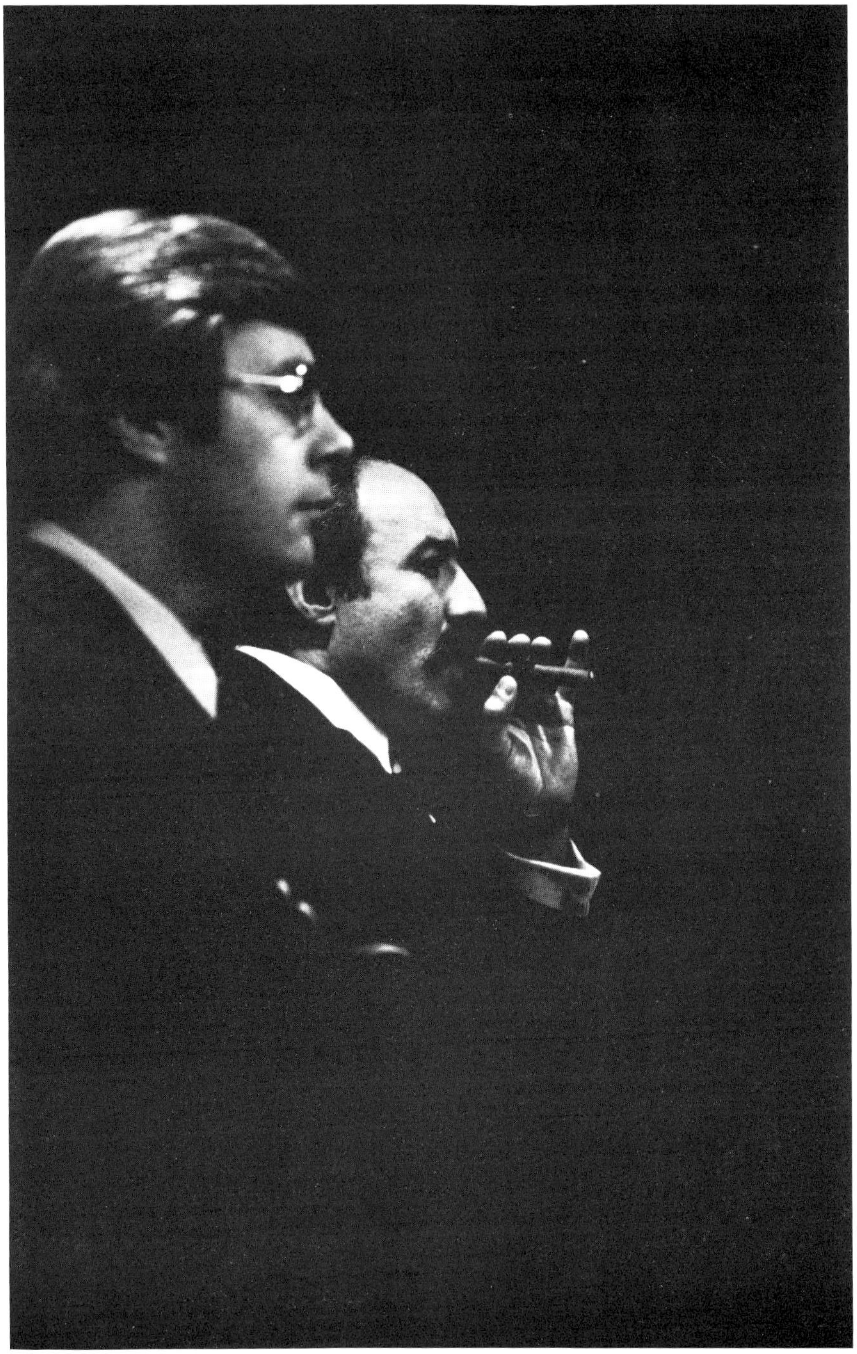

Environmental expert at meeting, Philadelphia National Bank

Ed Eckstein, freelance photographer
Client: Philadelphia National Bank
Philadelphia, Pennsylvania

When the Philadelphia National Bank wanted to feature the expertise of an environmental expert in its annual report, it turned to Ed Eckstein for help. Eckstein has long been among the country's finest corporate photojournalists. He calls his style "nonfiction photography." At a time when annual reports are becoming more and more devoted to slick abstraction and technical gloss, Eckstein's stress on human values provides a refreshing change of pace.

The environmentalist was addressing a meeting at the bank when Eckstein arrived to photograph him. He could have waited until the meeting was over and posed the man, arms folded, before a symbol of his profession. But Eckstein prefers to interpret the strength of the man's personality and, by extension, the depth of his knowledge. He can best do this by photographing the man as he actually *is* dispensing his expertise.

The strength of this meeting picture rests in the contrasts within it. While he leans on the lectern somewhat casually, his finger is jabbing towards us. And his face is split into contrasting light and dark halves.

Try this experiment. Place your hand over the light side of his face, and look at the shadowed side. We see a different person. There is a dark, brooding, almost surreal quality to the expression, with the light falling only around the open mouth.

Now cover the dark side and look at the light half. Open, free, and sure, the eye and mouth popping out at us. Now look at the entire face and view the interplay between the two sides. The sidelight stresses just one eye, and that eye is the focal point of the picture.

The blackboard behind him is softly focused but contains symbolic scribbling that tells of yield curves and interest rates. Perhaps these chalked notes are left by a previous speaker. The people in the room presumably know all about such things, yet they also come to hear from a man who brings them a view of the larger world and its potential impact on their business.

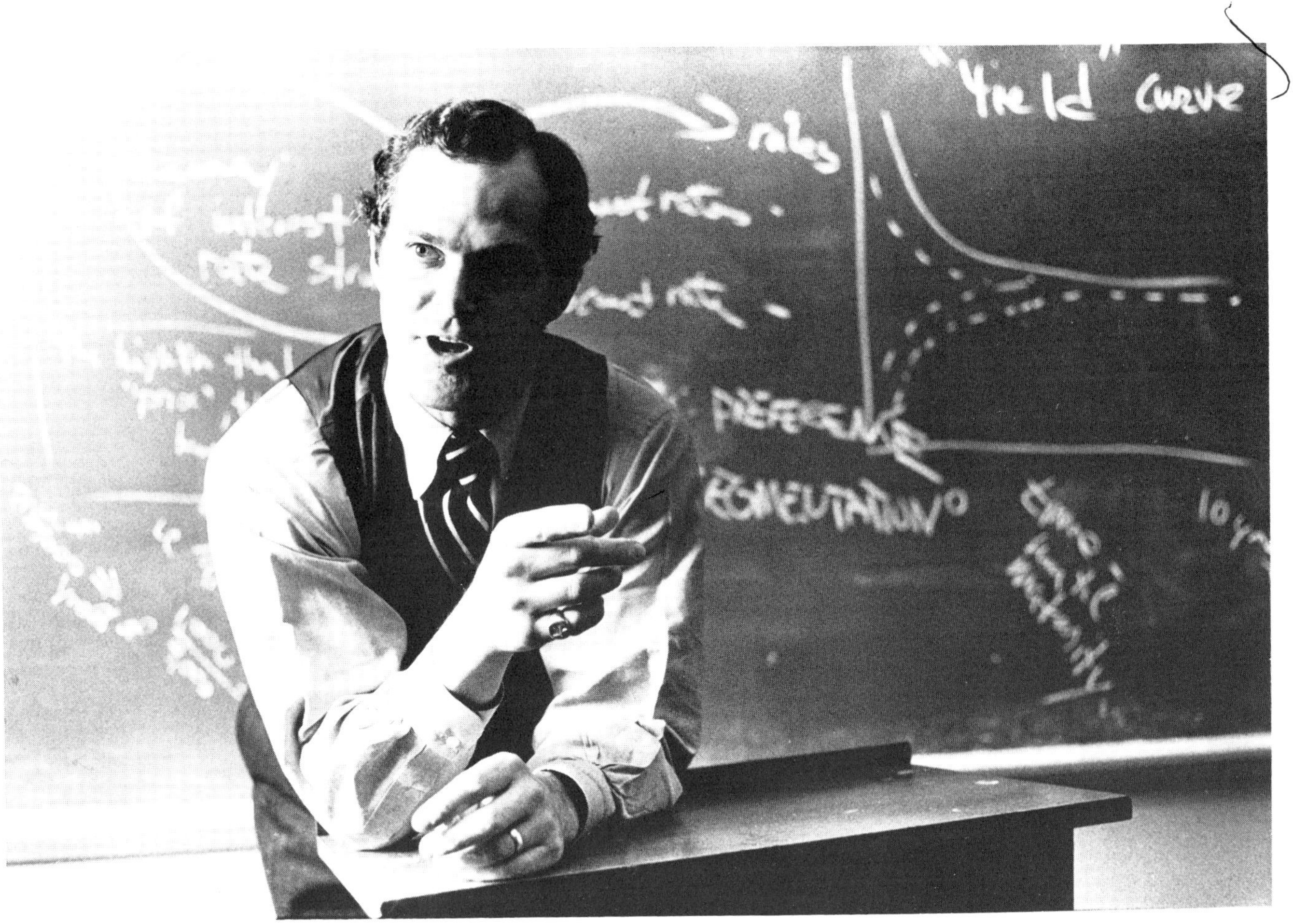
Yield Curve
rates

Management training program, Borg-Warner Corporation

Wm. Franklin McMahon, freelance photographer
Client: Borg-Warner Corporation
Chicago, Illinois

Meetings take place everywhere —in the formal setting of a classroom or ballroom, in offices, and even in hotel rooms. In an article called "Shirtsleeve schooldays," Borg-Warner's *Perspective* takes us into the heart of a management development program. It is 10:00 p.m., and while the day's official training schedule has long since ended, the discussions go on and on.

Photographer Frank McMahon enters the room and makes himself comfortable. He gets to know the participants, and they get to know him. He asks them about their work and comes to understand the problems they are dealing with. He opens the window shades to let in the night sky and the blazing city lights. And then he waits.

So engrossed in discussion are the trainees that McMahon is not even noticed as he climbs up on the bed. Using a wideangle lens turned vertically, he allows the reader to look over the shoulder of the softly focused man in the foreground, clipboard on his lap, pencil to his mouth.

Papers are strewn all over the bed. The man in the chair at middle distance is relaxed and appears to be almost asleep. Now our eyes reach the man next to the window. It is he who is doing the talking. His shirt is pulled out of his trousers, and his collar is open. He is barefoot.

This single detail is the key to this highly informal and unconventional picture. A barefoot executive at work in a hotel room late at night provides an incongruous, humane, telling image. He becomes an unforgettable symbol of dedication to a task. He does not care how he looks. He only cares about the job at hand. Learning.

The next day will find these men presenting a detailed Borg-Warner cash flow analysis and some ideas for changing it. Those ideas were developed here, in this hotel room meeting, late at night, in bare feet. The editors of *Perspective* run this picture as large as the tabloid page will allow. The bare feet come up in all their glory.

The power of key detail to provide incongruous, humane, symbolic touches is at the core of photojournalism. By becoming a part of the scene, McMahon is able to work unobtrusively, thereby making it possible to capture such detail as this.

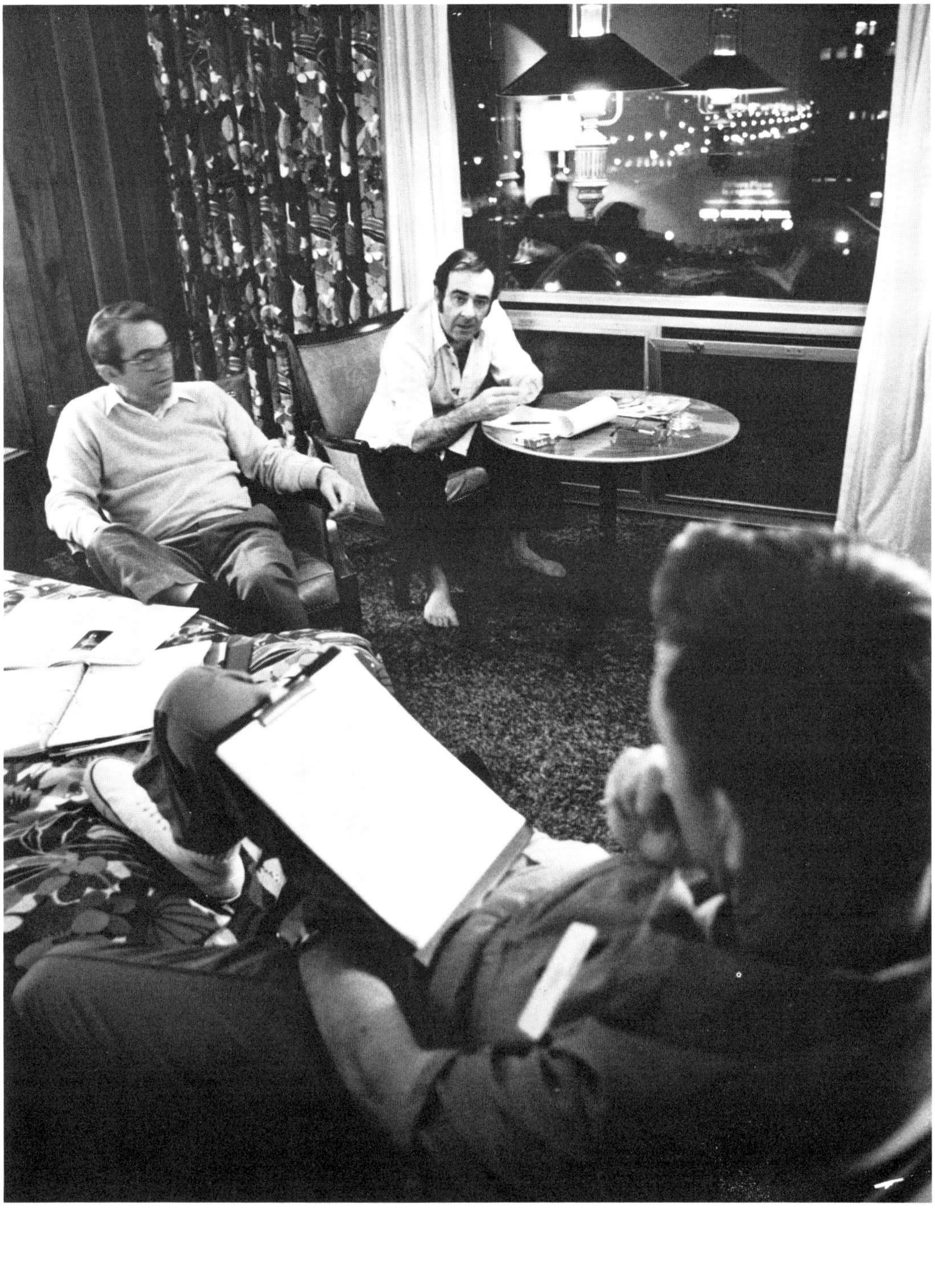

Chapter 9

The sporting life: people in action

Nearly all organizations offer recreational activities to their members for both social and health reasons. Sports, picnics, contests, and competitions offer the photojournalist spectacular opportunities to capture the excitement of people in action. At their best, such photos can offer insights into the skill, courage, and physical exertion of the competitors.

To go beyond literal, superficial descriptions of athletic activities takes a considerable degree of photographic expertise. The photographer must develop a sense of timing and an ability to anticipate what may happen. He or she must harness that skill to the mechanics of the camera: focus, shutter speed, vantage point. The sports photographer must also use optical tools such as long telephoto and super-wideangle lenses, getting the clutter out and the action in.

Sometimes, the finest sports shots occur when the action is over, and the competitors reflect on their victory or defeat. At their best, photographs of people at play can give us a measure of the human spirit, whether the subject is a child in the playground or a college athlete performing before millions.

Getting dusted

Kurt Foss, photojournalist
Hennepin County Public Affairs
Minneapolis, Minnesota

In order to make effective sports photographs, we must be able to anticipate what is going to happen. Foss, covering a county employee softball league game for his employee newspaper, noticed that a woman playing second base seemed particularly colorful and decided to concentrate on her play for a few innings. When a runner moved to first base, he knew there was potential action coming up at second base on the next play.

There is not enough time to focus a lens during fast action. So Foss uses a technique called "pre-focusing" to focus on second base *before* the action takes place. He uses a 300mm telephoto lens to reach across the field, soften the background, and fill the frame with players. Long lenses are hard to hold steady, and Foss does not want to burden his movements with a tripod. So he selects a fast shutter speed—1/250 second—eliminating "camera shake," and also stopping the action dead in its tracks.

When the next batter hits into a force play at second base, the ball and three players converge on the spot already in sharp focus. All Foss has to do is time his shutter release to coincide with the cloud of dust and the futile groping of the fielders. The result is a fine sports action shot, which ran across four columns on the front page of the employee paper. By capturing expressions, tension, frustration, and action simultaneously, Foss sums up the joys, and terrors, of the sport.

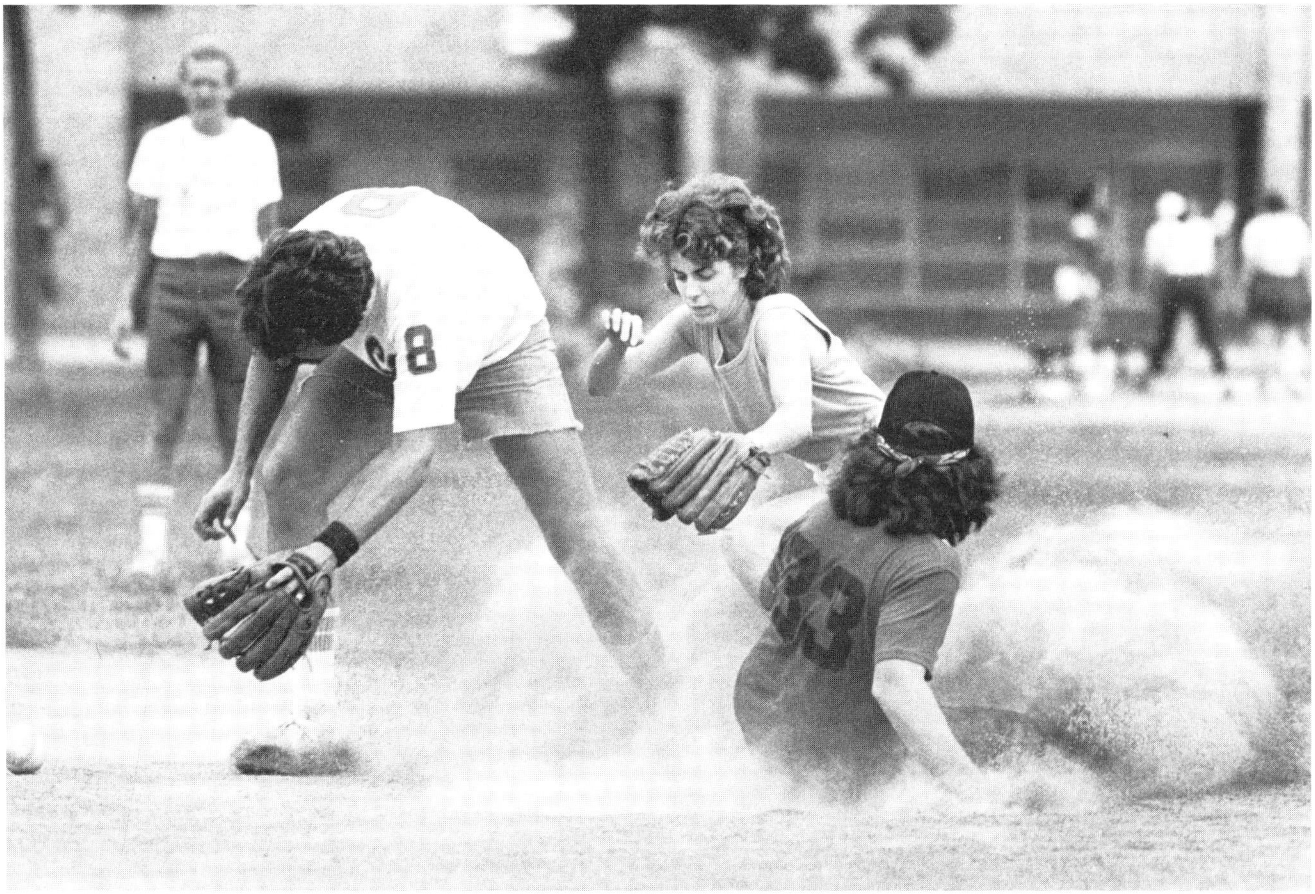

Young Eskimo boy, Kobuk, Alaska

Don Rutledge, photojournalist
Home Mission Board, Southern Baptist Convention
Atlanta, Georgia

Photographing people in action requires an exquisite sense of timing on the part of the photographer. French photojournalist Henri Cartier-Bresson calls it the "recognition of the decisive moment." There are, says Cartier-Bresson, no "maybes" in photography: "All the maybes should go in the trash."

In this photograph, Don Rutledge has eliminated the "maybes" by timing his shutter release at that precise moment when a moving ball approaches the hands of the reaching child. A fraction of a second earlier, and the ball would be merging into the school house beyond. An instant later, and the ball would be blocking the face of the child or already in his hands. There is only one instant that works, and Rutledge has seized it forever on film.

Rutledge has captured the spontaneity of childhood, the skill of a young athlete, the self-reliance of the frontier. It is more than just a sports shot. It is a statement about going it alone, something very close to the lives of anyone who lives in Kobuk, Alaska.

The photograph is timeless. Rutledge made it in 1967, but it could have been made yesterday. Photographs such as this, offering us the ability to suspend time, are, in the words of Cartier-Bresson, "once, and forever."

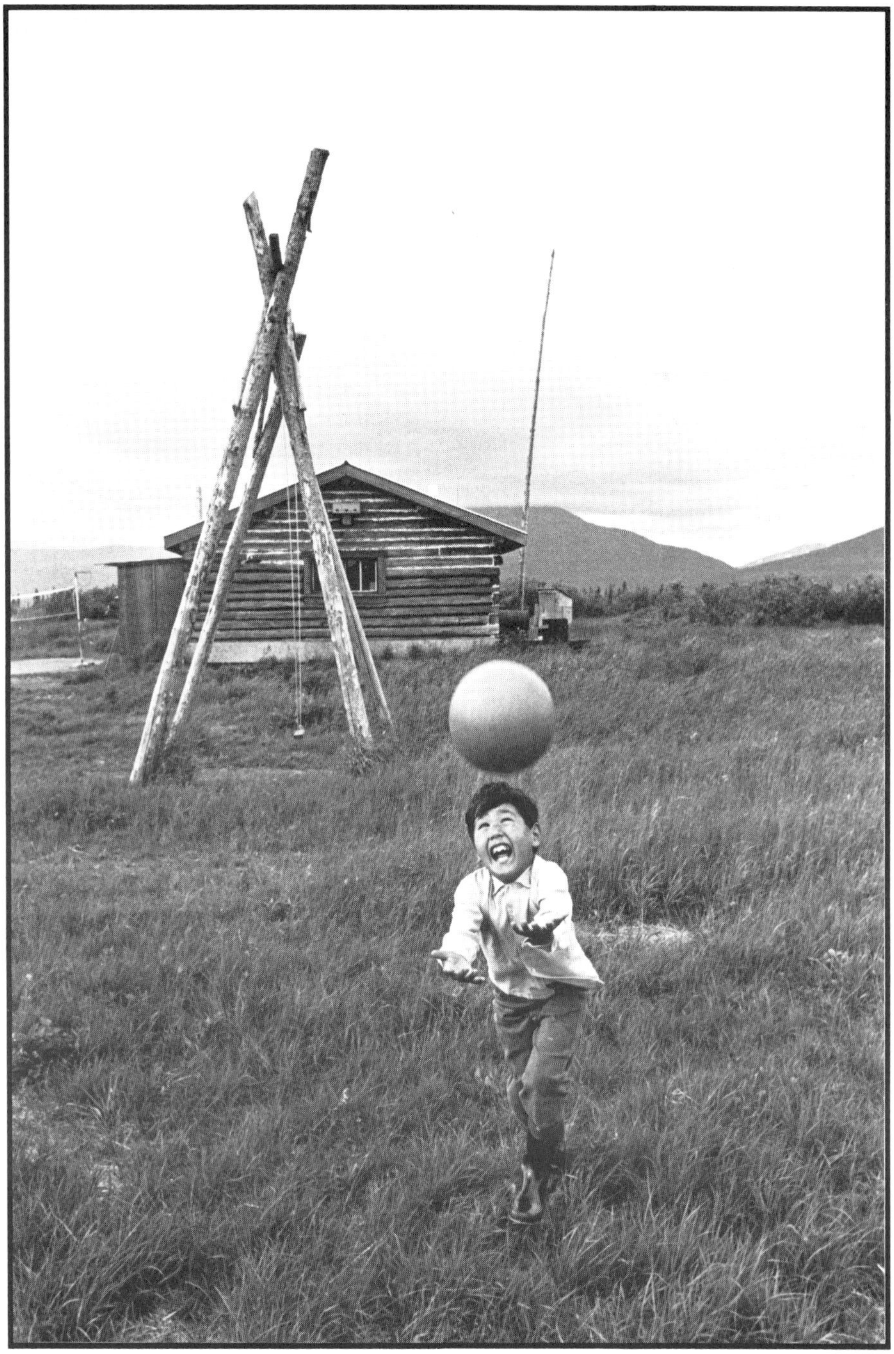

Moment of truth

Dale Geffs, staff photographer
Dresser Industries
Houston, Texas

Sports photos draw much of their impact from the emotions of the athlete. As in all areas of photography, the ability of the camera to depict human feelings in spontaneous moments offers great storytelling potential. In sports, "the thrill of victory, the agony of defeat" still rings true. For sports represent the world in microcosm —the struggle against the odds, the uncertainty of the outcome, the ability of people to challenge high standards and then go beyond them.

For Jim Hornung, a Dresser employee, the weight upon his shoulders at Houston's YMCA represents the limits of his strength. Can he lift it over his head? Dresser photographer Dale Geffs addresses this question with his camera, capturing the moment when Hornung begins his effort. Everything going on inside the man shows on his face. The crouching figure softly implied in the background seems to be urging Hornung on. The knee wrappings, the armadillo on the uniform, and those wonderfully incongruous shoes, add human touches to a supremely stressful moment.

If Hornung's lift gets beyond this point, all will go well. Unfortunately for Hornung, it didn't. Geffs's chronicle of the effort, though, honors not only this particular employee but everyone who defies the odds.

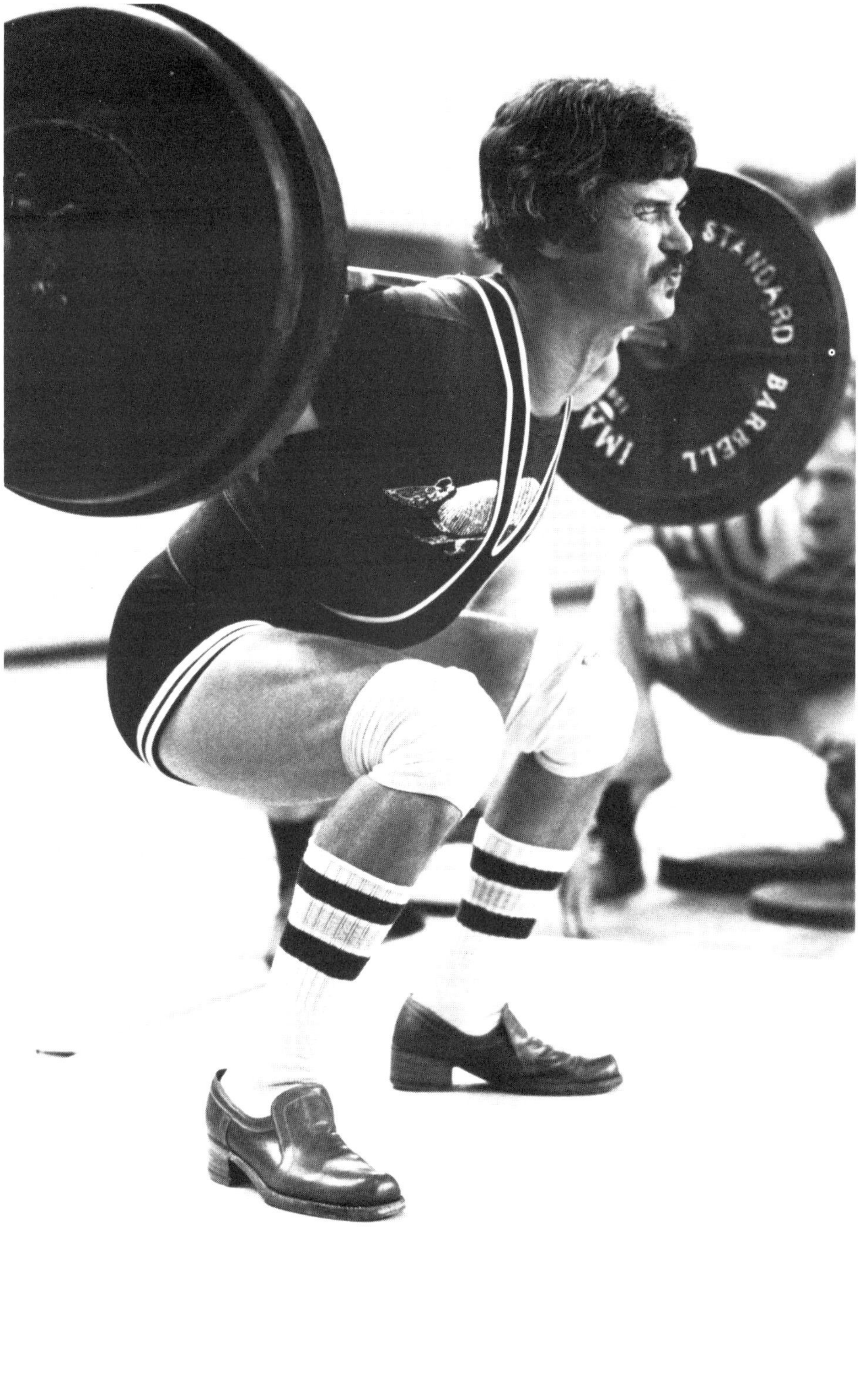
STANDARD
BARBELL

Slam-dunk

Mark Philbrick, university relations photographer
Brigham Young University
Provo, Utah

No matter how skilled sports photographers may become, they face the enormous challenge of making pictures of the same things over and over in fresh ways, with new meanings. Mark Philbrick meets and conquers this challenge with this spectacular image for the BYU basketball media guide. BYU's university relations department was also able to place this photo in two national sporting magazines featuring the school's basketball program.

Crouching directly under the opponent's basket, Philbrick uses a 16mm full frame "fish eye" wide-angle lens, which not only includes a vast amount of subject matter but also does not require precise focusing. It provides tremendous distortion. This distortion makes the photo unique.

The BYU player slamming the ball through the basket is only ten feet off the floor and is virtually on top of Philbrick. But the 16mm lens "pushes subject matter away," making the player seem to be much higher than he actually is. The backboard support is also forced up and away in a great curve. The opposing players seem to be lost in the distance, even though they are actually just a step or two behind.

But beware! Extreme wideangles can cause confusing background clutter. (Note how distant players merge into the crowd.) Philbrick's low vantage point, allowing him to shoot straight up against the dark ceiling, solves the problem effectively.

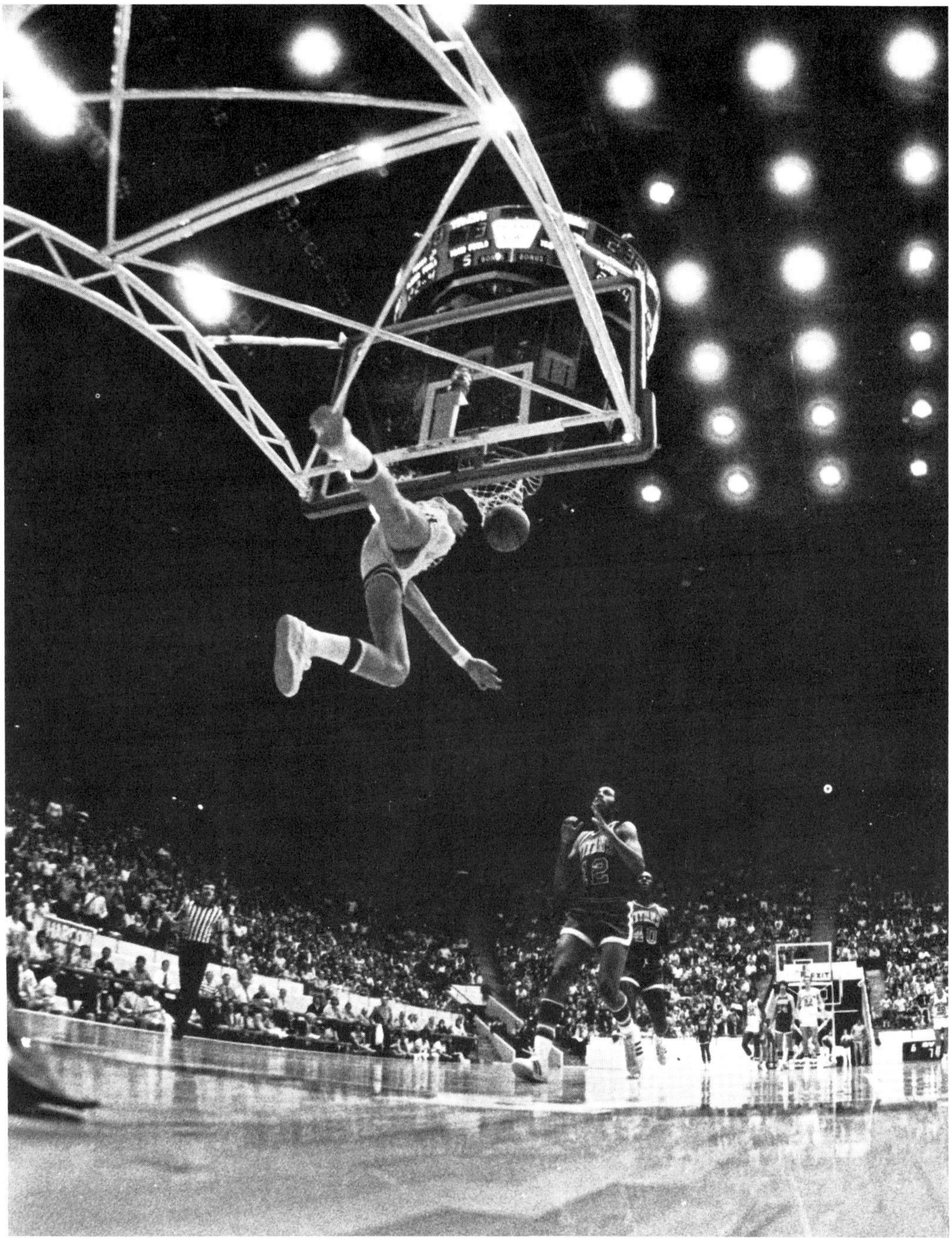

Olympic speed skater in training

Dave Denemark, publications coordinator
Medical College of Wisconsin
Milwaukee, Wisconsin

This photograph won an award of excellence for Denemark in the 1981 IABC Gold Quill news photo category. It demonstrates that sometimes the best sports photo opportunities come not in actual competition but, instead, during practice sessions. Here, Dr. Mike Woods, who took a year off from his residency at Medical College of Wisconsin, works out with his trainer for the Lake Placid Olympics. (Woods would finish fifth in his event, well behind teammate Eric Heiden.)

Denemark uses deliberate blur to intensify the feeling of speed, which is, of course, the purpose of the sport. Instead of completely stopping the action, Denemark extends it. He uses a slower than usual shutter speed and pans the camera—moving it horizontally at the moment of exposure—thereby turning the background into an undefined flowing mass.

The trainer, scrutinizing every move of his colleague, is also blurred, leaving only Woods and his determined expression in clear definition. The two skaters create a rhythmic pattern, typifying the movement of the sport.

The picture is free of distracting background clutter, one of the biggest problems in sports photography. Denemark is using selective focus, a long lens, and deliberate blur to simplify the image, as well as to express the flow of the sport.

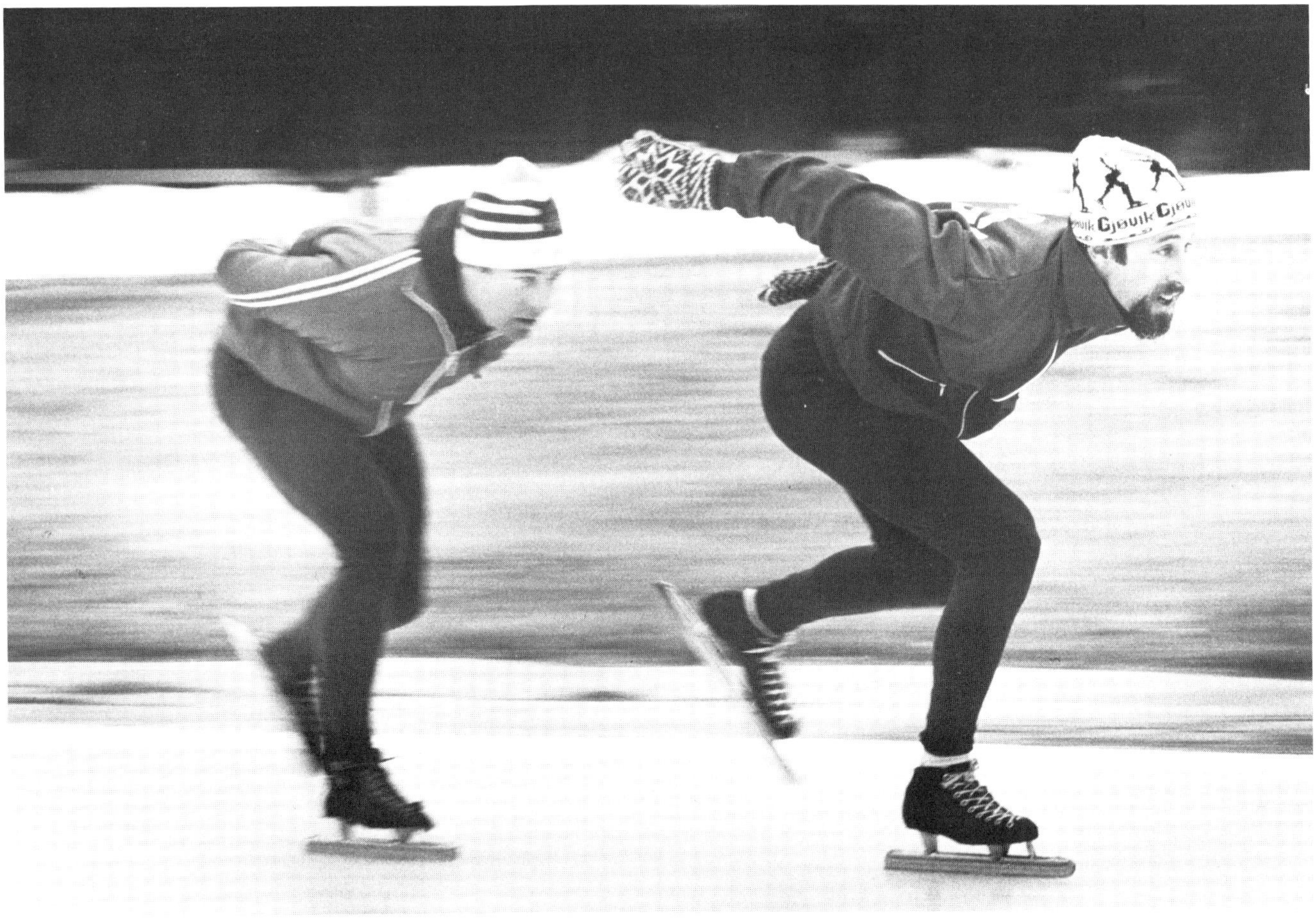
Gjøvik

Missouri State frisbee champions, 1978

Jim Visser, photographer
Six Flags over Mid-America
St. Louis, Missouri

Sometimes photographers can't be present at a sports event and are asked to "get a picture of the winners" after the fact. Such photos are almost always cliches, stiffly posed trophy-bearers displaying inane grins. But Jim Visser, then a staff photographer for the Six Flags over Mid-America recreation center, goes beyond the cliche with this photo of an event sponsored by his employer.

Visser posed the *situation*, not the picture. He asks the three winners to demonstrate their form. Using a wideangle lens from a close vantage point and a fast shutter speed to freeze action and expressions, Visser creates a surrealistic recap of the event.

A picture of just one frisbee winner in action would not have been enough. It is the interrelationship of all three participants that gives this picture its bizarre quality. Each person displays a totally different expression, style, and body language. They are off in their own worlds, seemingly unaware of each other. The frisbees defy gravity, hanging in space in a triangle around the center participant.

The picture does not only tell the story of the event by showing off the skills of the participants. It offers viewers a flight into fancy, allowing them to use their imaginations and become part of the action themselves. The picture was not only used by Visser's employee publication; it was picked up and distributed by UPI as well.

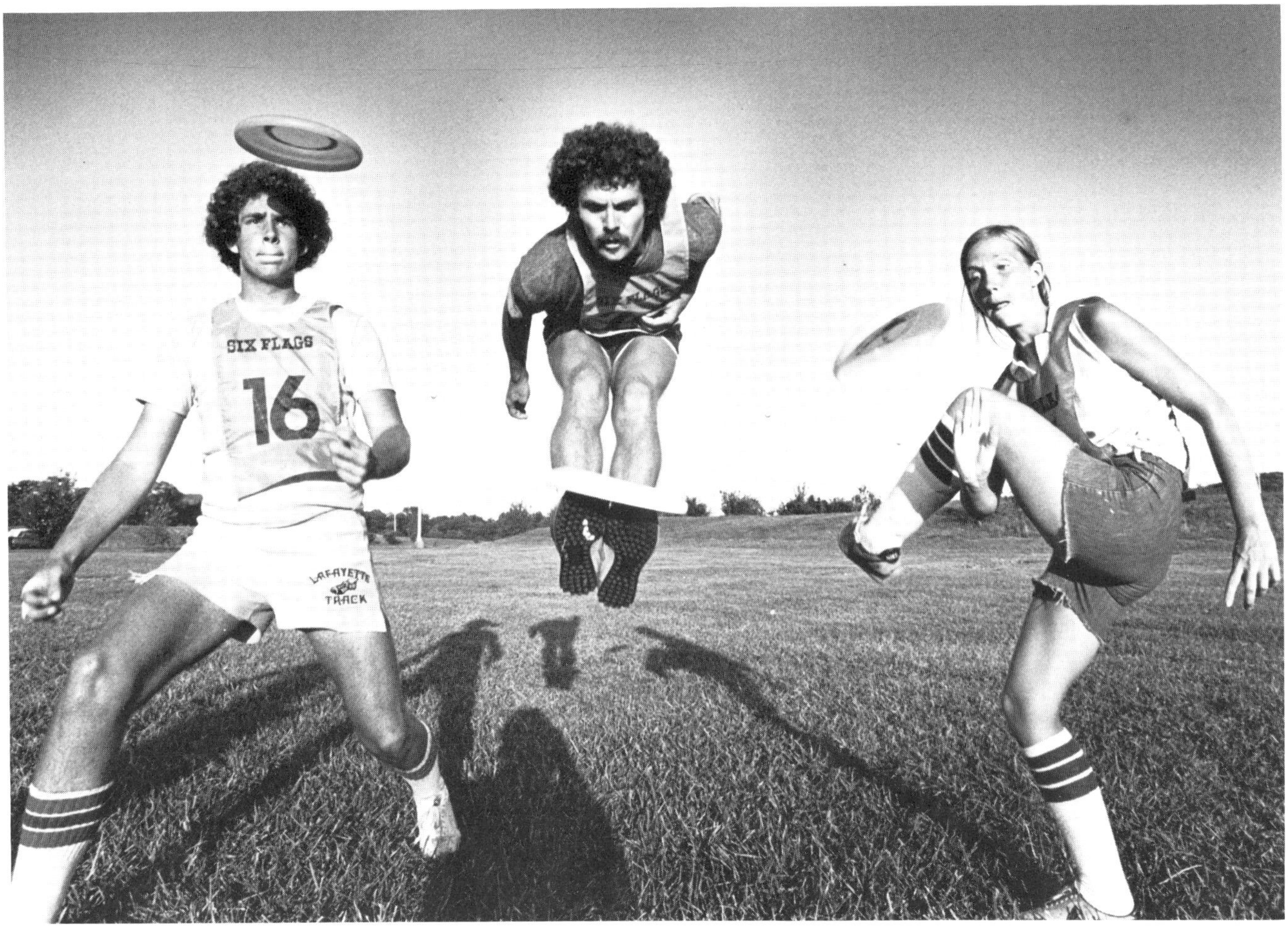
SIX FLAGS
16
LAFAYETTE
TRACK

The playground

Bruce Stromberg, freelance photographer
Client: Episcopal Community Services
Philadelphia, Pennsylvania

Symbolism offers a visual shortcut, a way of saying something in photographs without complex, comprehensive description. Visual description for its own sake is usually boring. Imagine illustrating a day care program by making a picture of a day care center. Yet that's just what unthinking photographers and editors do every day.

Bruce Stromberg moves far beyond that level of literal description with this image made for the 1979 annual report of Episcopal Community Services of Philadelphia. To Stromberg, this little girl at play *represents* day care. In trying out her skills on the playground equipment, she is acquiring a degree of independence. While her parents work, she is learning and growing.

Stromberg does not even show us her face. Her appearance is not important. The message is in her body language, the precarious sense of balance she has obviously achieved. To show her expression would negate the power of the symbol, which is far stronger in abstraction than in description. Instead he shoots from behind, isolating her against a softly blurred background. The long telephoto lens, with its ability to create a shallow zone of focus, is an essential tool. Any background detail would add a distracting element, destroying the utter simplicity of Stromberg's symbolism.

The rear vantage point helps us identify with this playground athlete. Although she can't see us, we are there to help her if she takes a tumble. Perhaps this, too, is part of the message Stromberg is communicating.

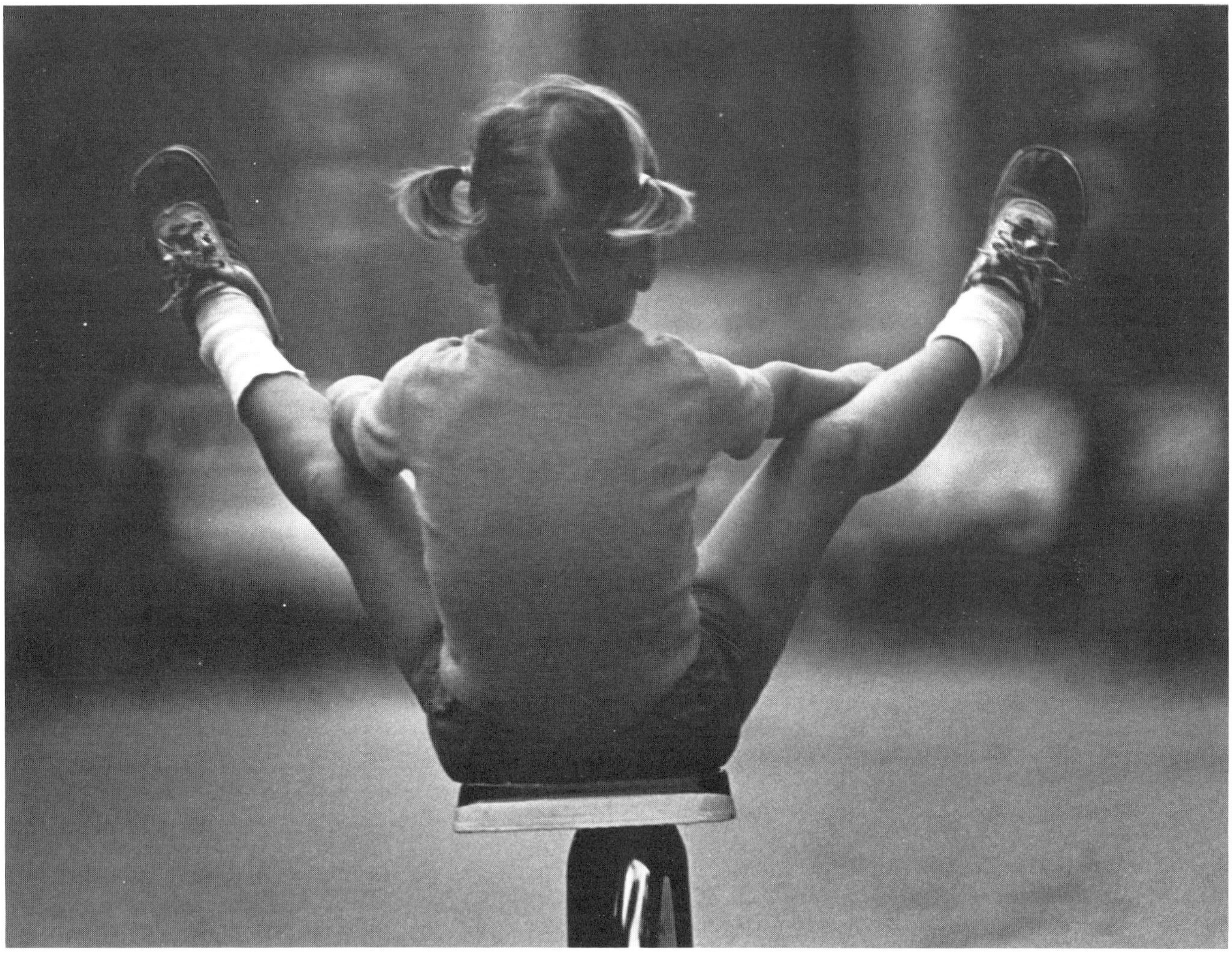

Chapter 10

Ceremonies and rituals: turning lemons into lemonade

The bane of organizational publications is, of course, the ancient ceremonial cliche—those handshaking, ribbon-cutting, check-passing embarrassments that have for so long stigmatized the "company house organ" as a repository for pompous, vainglorious ego-boosting. If even a single photograph is devoted to puffery, all else in the publication becomes suspect.

Organizational publications still print them because editors and managers often don't know any better. But institutional ritual can be photographically conveyed in intelligent, substantive ways. Such pictures can still "recognize" the subjects, making them feel "important." Yet they can go far beyond that level to engage the reader's emotions and intellect.

A publication must be more than an organization's scrapbook if it is to become a valid communications medium. Ritualistic photo cliches must be replaced by humane interpretations offering insight into the award or honor in question. This involves more than cosmetic solutions. Getting a "more interesting angle" of a ceremonial cliche is still portraying what remains, in essence, a phony situation. Organizational photographers must instead be able to record on film the genuine feelings of those involved in order to convey the meaning of the occasion to their readers.

To remove cliches and replace them with substantive coverage of ceremony and ritual requires editorial control over the planning and execution of the publication itself. And this, in turn, sometimes calls for courage on the part of both editor and photographer, as well as the trust of the organization's management.

Service award—a picture that never ran

Karen Copenhaver, editor/
photographer
U.S. Bancorp
Portland, Oregon

Everyone would agree that this is the way a service award picture should look. It has everything going for it: spontaneity, warmth, enthusiasm, caring, credibility. It captures the essence of the moment far better than the dreary mugshots that have come to represent the anniversarians of most organizations.

All we need do now is print it, and we can say something to all readers about the nature of the award and the people concerned. Unfortunately, this picture was not printed. In its place, Copenhaver says, readers of her publication saw instead "a picture showing each of the members of the 25 year club, all seated in rows, so as not to leave anyone out."

This decision, obviously taken out of Copenhaver's hands, was made for political, not journalistic, reasons. She lost editorial control in this particular case. We can also be sure that every member of the club will probably prefer the all-inclusive shot to this one. The desire to see one's self in print runs strong. That must have been considered by those who made the decision to run the all-inclusive picture and kill this one.

In their zeal to make award winners feel good and recognize employee accomplishments, corporate decision-makers without professional communications backgrounds usually cannot appreciate the value of pictures as journalism. They prefer to make people feel good by "recognizing" them en masse. But recognition for its own sake is not communication. It is something else—ego-boosting, perhaps. And sometimes, political nest-feathering. These intentions cater only to the individuals concerned. Nobody else cares.

The professional communicator, on the other hand, usually serves a larger interest, that of the organization as a whole. Why not publish a separate booklet for service anniversarians? Fill *that* with recognition pictures. Set up special, nonjournalistic media for rewards and recognition: bulletin boards, flyers, posters, inserts, pamphlets. This will free media designed for *editorial* communication—magazines, newspapers, and newsletters—to function as organizational journalism. For journalistic use of photographs is intended to activate the minds and emotions of *all* readers—not just those who appear in the pictures.

The photograph that Copenhaver makes does this quite well. It says more about the depth of feeling people have towards each other in her organization than pictures of dreary rows of bodies could possibly say. It is only a shame that the readers of her company's magazine are unable to enjoy it with us.

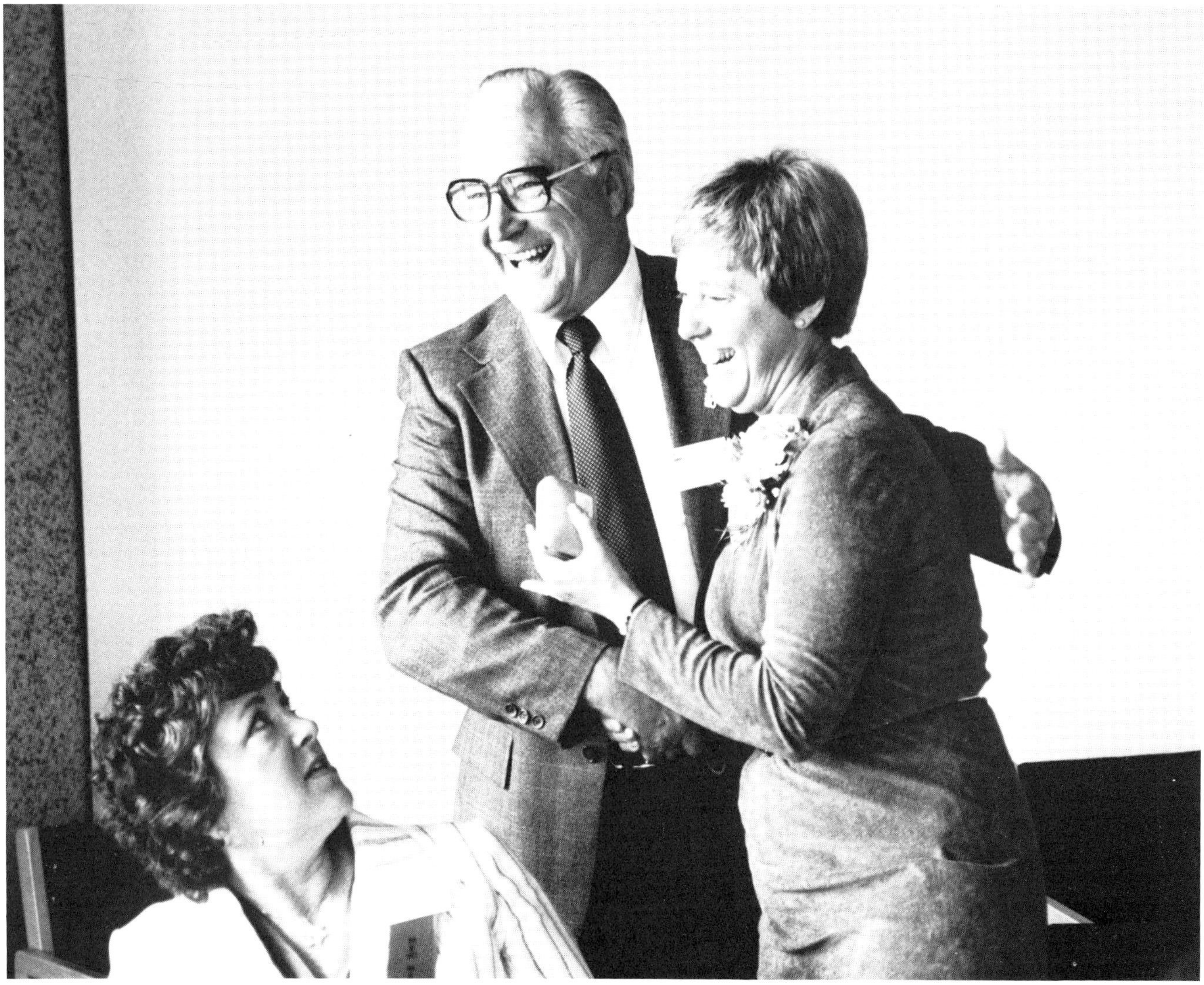

Aviation hangar opening

Beverly Freeman, senior editor
Transco Companies, Inc.
Houston, Texas

Making effective ceremonial photographs depends largely on the amount of control editors and photographers have over their own jobs. Some photographers are told exactly what to do by the person in charge of the ceremony. No deviation is allowed. Then the editor is told by an assortment of authorities to print the picture as it was made. The entire situation has been taken out of the hands of the communicator. No communication can take place under such circumstances. The so-called "communicator" has become little more than an information processor.

Editors and photographers gain control by taking responsibility for as much of their jobs as possible: taking risks, offering alternatives. Here is a good example of that process.

Beverly Freeman is told by a department manager to make a picture of a ribbon cutting ceremony opening a new Transco aviation hangar. A vice president is equally insistent that the picture be used in the magazine. Freeman is not pleased with these orders, but she is not in a position to refuse them. Her apprehension grows when she arrives at the hangar to find that the officials have decided to use a narrow stairway for the ceremony instead of the hangar itself, which at least would have offered a more symbolic environment.

Faced with few alternatives, Freeman decides that the only chance the picture has of saying anything to the general readers of her publication rests in the responses of the people themselves. The chairman of the board arrives to cut the ribbon. Department executives gather around him. Freeman decides to take a spur of the moment risk. "I grabbed a bunch of employees at random from the audience and made them get up on the stairs to watch."

The employees are amused at becoming stars. They laugh as the chairman cuts the ribbon. The laughter is infectious. Even the chairman and his executive colleagues chuckle as the ribbon is snipped. The ceremony becomes an informal, humorous performance for Freeman's camera, with everybody getting into the act.

Freeman's shot will win few awards as photography. But it does convey the fact that Transco people are willing to bend a little, relax, have fun, even at a formal ceremony commemorating the opening of a structure costing a lot of money. While it does not tell a story or have much to do with the structure's function, Freeman's effort at least turns what would have been a boring cliche into a display of spontaneous responses that may help humanize the institution.

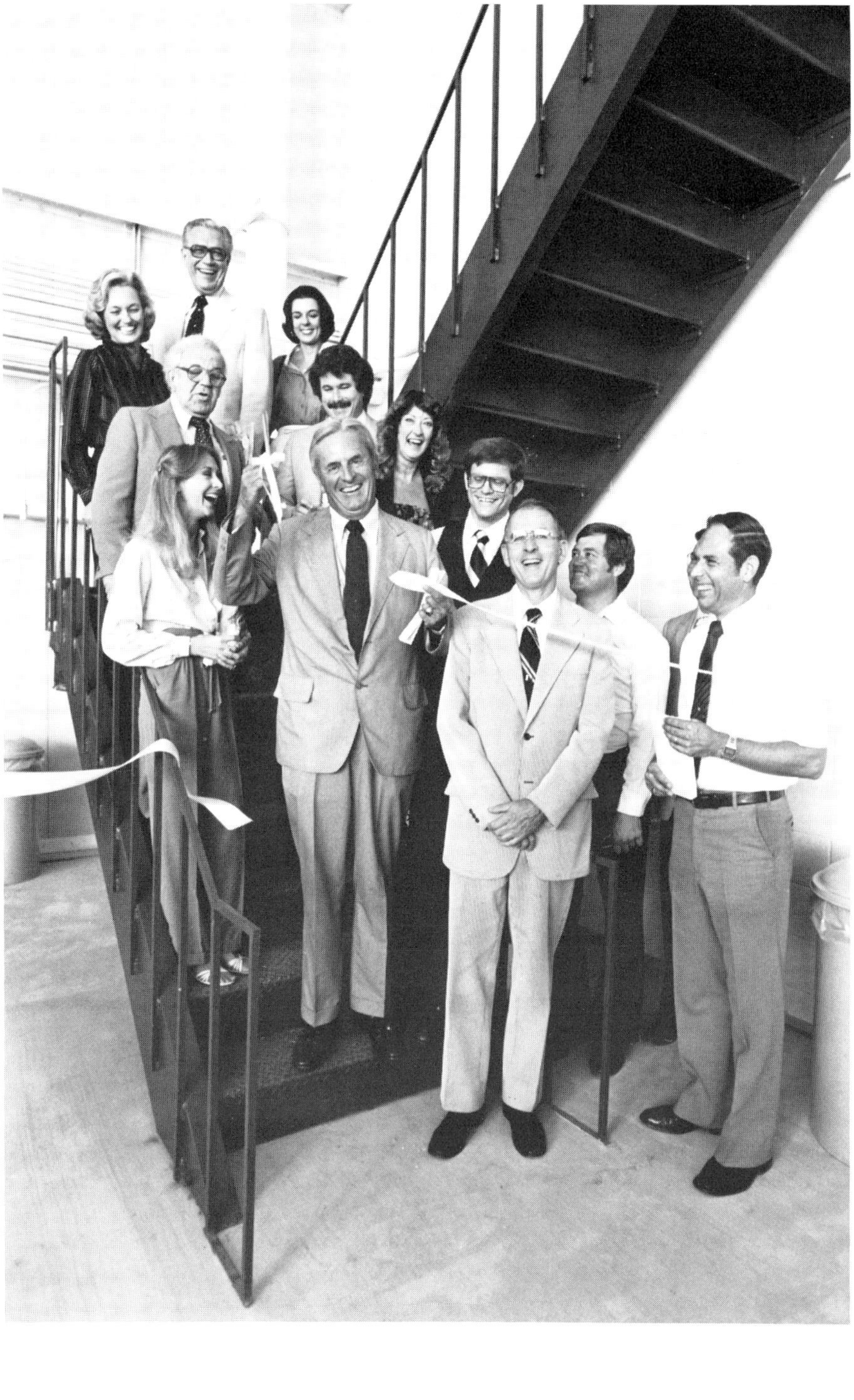

In honor of Robyn Fulton

Dale Geffs, staff photographer
Dresser Industries
Houston, Texas

This trio of photographs is as fine a set of solutions to the age-old problem of "what-to-do-about-the-grip-and-grin-cliche," as we have seen. Dale Geffs is asked to cover the "40-year-luncheon" of Robyn Fulton, president of Dresser Industries Magcobar Division. Like all anniversary luncheons, it features speeches and gifts and handshakes all around. But Dale Geffs has a larger mission ahead of him. He is determined to make pictures that convey Fulton's feelings about the event, as well as those of the people who came to honor him.

From the range of vantage points and the variety of situations Geffs is covering here, we can see that he moves with the flow of the action, not standing rigidly in one place. He does not limit his shooting to the brief pump of the hand at the lectern. Geffs says that "photos like these are not made by photographers who sit around with their lens cap on while eating dessert. One must pay extremely close attention to the subject at all times."

The picture of the men embracing at the lectern is effective because of the incongruous tennis racket and public hugging. Neither tennis rackets nor such intense hugs are normally seen at business functions. To see them here is to enjoy them, and Fulton is viewed as a person beloved by his colleagues.

When Fulton turns to leave the rostrum, Geffs stands before him, and through his camera, we see what Fulton cannot see. The range of response to Fulton's remarks is tremendous. He is cheered by some, silently watched by others. For Fulton himself, the moment brings satisfaction. It is written all over his face as he walks towards us, racket in hand.

Later Fulton stops to reflect on his long career with some colleagues. Geffs is still shooting. He finds a vantage point peering past the shoulders of onlookers, creating a peephole effect that barely allows the viewer to squeeze into the conversation. The quality of the light in this third photo is rich and warm, providing a place in the sun for the man of the hour.

Tallying the sum of the three shots, we come to know and like Robyn Fulton. Although few of us have ever heard of him before, we have all gained insights into the kind of person he is from the images Geffs has given us.

This is the ultimate value of ceremonial photographs. The ceremony itself is incidental. It is the quality of the human values expressed *within* the ceremony that is important. It is this quality that determines, to a large extent, our impressions of the institution itself.

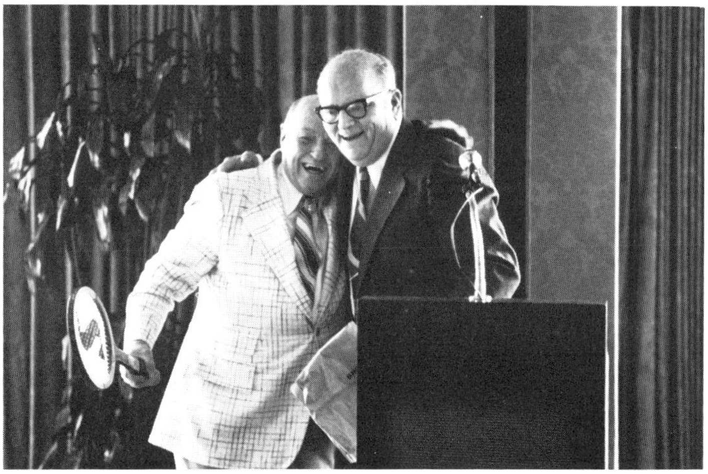

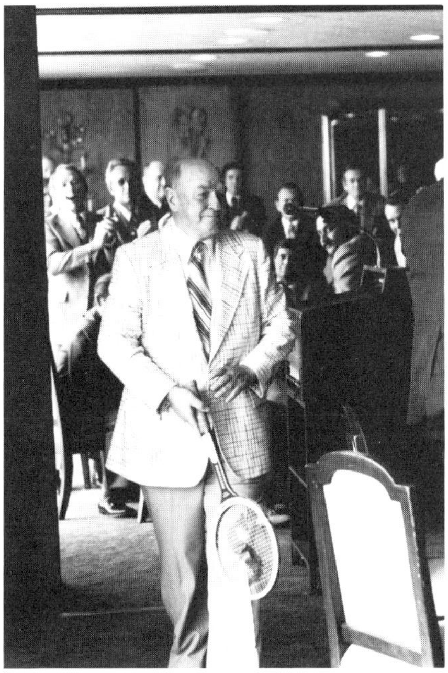

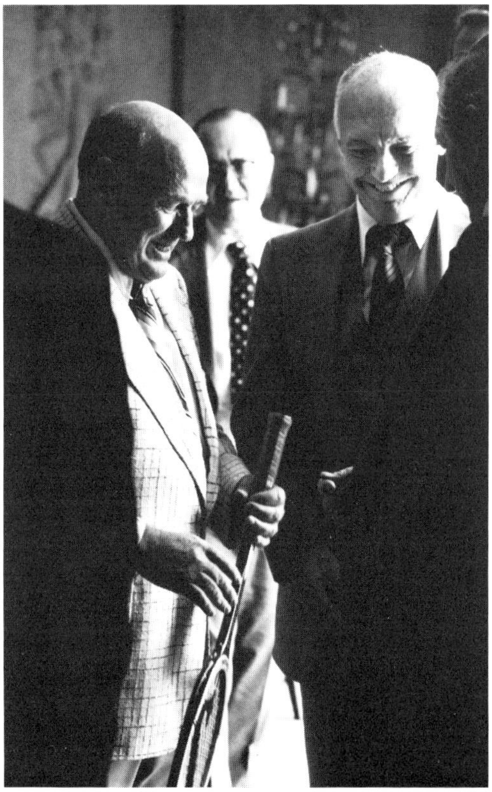

The goodbye party

Chris Craft, freelance photographer
Client: Albany General Hospital
Albany, Oregon

If we are to get humane responses into the stiff formality of organizational ceremonies, we must use certain techniques to loosen people up. Chris Craft uses some of them to make this effective interpretation of a goodbye tea party for a manager who has accepted a job in another state.

Craft shoots a lot of film, probably several rolls—a small investment providing huge dividends. The very fact that a photographer keeps on shooting, eventually helps the subjects forget that pictures are being made. The photographer no longer stands at the center of the event. The clicking camera soon becomes as much a part of the scene as the hum of the air conditioner. Some photographers have even been known to enter a room with an empty film cannister in the camera. They will shoot without film in the camera for fifteen or twenty minutes just to get the stiffness out of people. Then they load up with the real thing. By that time, people are going about their activities without even thinking of the photographer.

Craft starts out by shooting the obligatory posed pictures—happy souls holding teacups and grinning at the camera. These will make nice gifts which Craft later sends to the people who appear in them. This is good public relations, and it also helps meet people's expectations. They want their pictures taken in certain ways, and they deserve to have them as souvenirs of the event. But such pictures should never be printed in a communication medium, because they are not communication. Craft will shoot communicative pictures of the event later, after all the ceremonial photo-duties have been accomplished.

At the end of Craft's preliminary souvenir-shot session, a husband and wife volunteer team approach the departing manager (who had been Albany General Hospital's director of volunteers) and ask Craft to take one more souvenir picture. She takes it for them. But after she shoots it, the husband spontaneously decides to give the departing manager a kiss. Craft is ready—and not only gets the kiss, but records the contrasting responses of both the manager and the man's wife to the gesture.

Craft prints *this* picture. For it represents the heart of the event. As the editor of the hospital's publication, she plays it across a spread, under the headline "Enjoyed this job? Oh, yes!"

In the hands of many other photographers, this event would have been covered with a dismal tea party cliche. But Craft turns the depiction of the event into a human document, rich in spontaneity, incongruity, and human values. The picture underscores the feeling these people have for the departing manager, and, by extension, characterizes the human qualities of the entire institution.

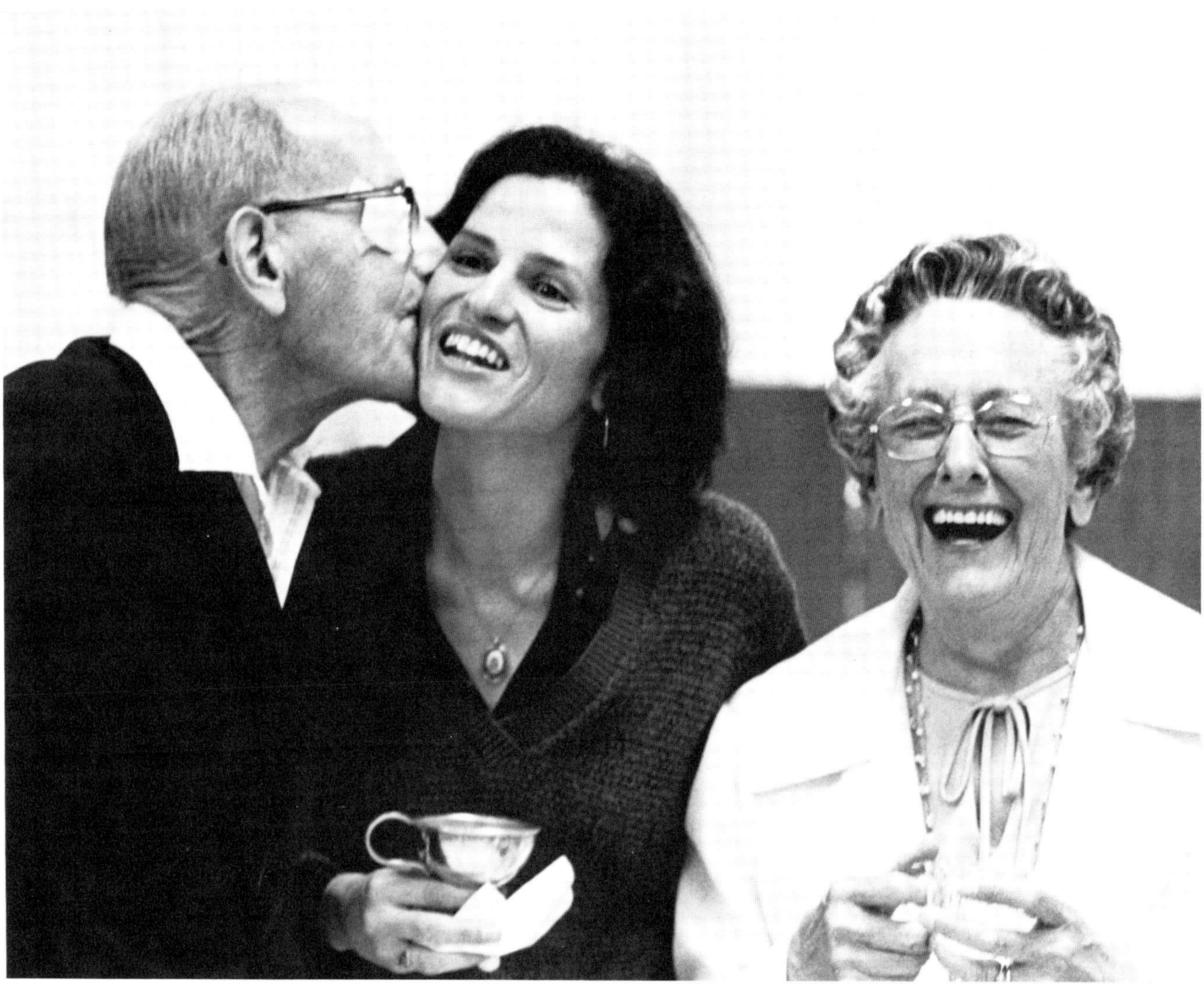

Law and orderliness

Kurt Foss, photojournalist
Hennepin County Public Affairs
Minneapolis, Minnesota

Once each year, the Hennepin County Sheriff's department requires its 320 deputies to assemble for a full-scale inspection where the sheriff examines uniforms, weapons, and equipment right down to the shine of the badges. Photo-coverage of this annual ritual for external publicity and in-house publications could easily have been conceived in typically stilted fashion: a line-up of hundreds of deputies gathered behind the sheriff and his staff. But it is not. Hennepin County does not believe in cliche photographs, at least not as long as Kurt Foss is the resident photojournalist.

Foss already knows the sheriff and is on good terms with him. They chat before the ceremony, and Foss suggests to the sheriff that he go on with the inspection instead of posing for a group picture. Foss gives the assemblage time to get used to his camera, as he shoots the unfolding ceremony.

Foss is using an important principle in covering this ritual: He is shooting the event itself instead of making a picture of people having their pictures taken.

Using a 180mm telephoto lens, with a large f/2.8 opening which allows him to get very shallow focusing depth, Foss greatly simplifies the event. He does not shoot all 320 deputies. He narrows it down, stressing just two people —one deputy and the sheriff himself. He is letting the few stand for the many. Seven or eight other deputies are also in the picture but they are out of focus, part of the environment. They offer context to the face-off between the two people we see in sharp focus.

There is a contrast in responses. The deputy is smiling. The sheriff, wearing his badge of authority on his jacket, is not. But Foss catches him with a grin just waiting to surface.

Foss not only goes beyond the cliche. He softens our general impression of law enforcement officers — who often seem distant, authoritarian, and humorless. This may be a spit and polish inspection. But it is also a chance to imply that beneath the formality and the fuss, human hearts still beat.

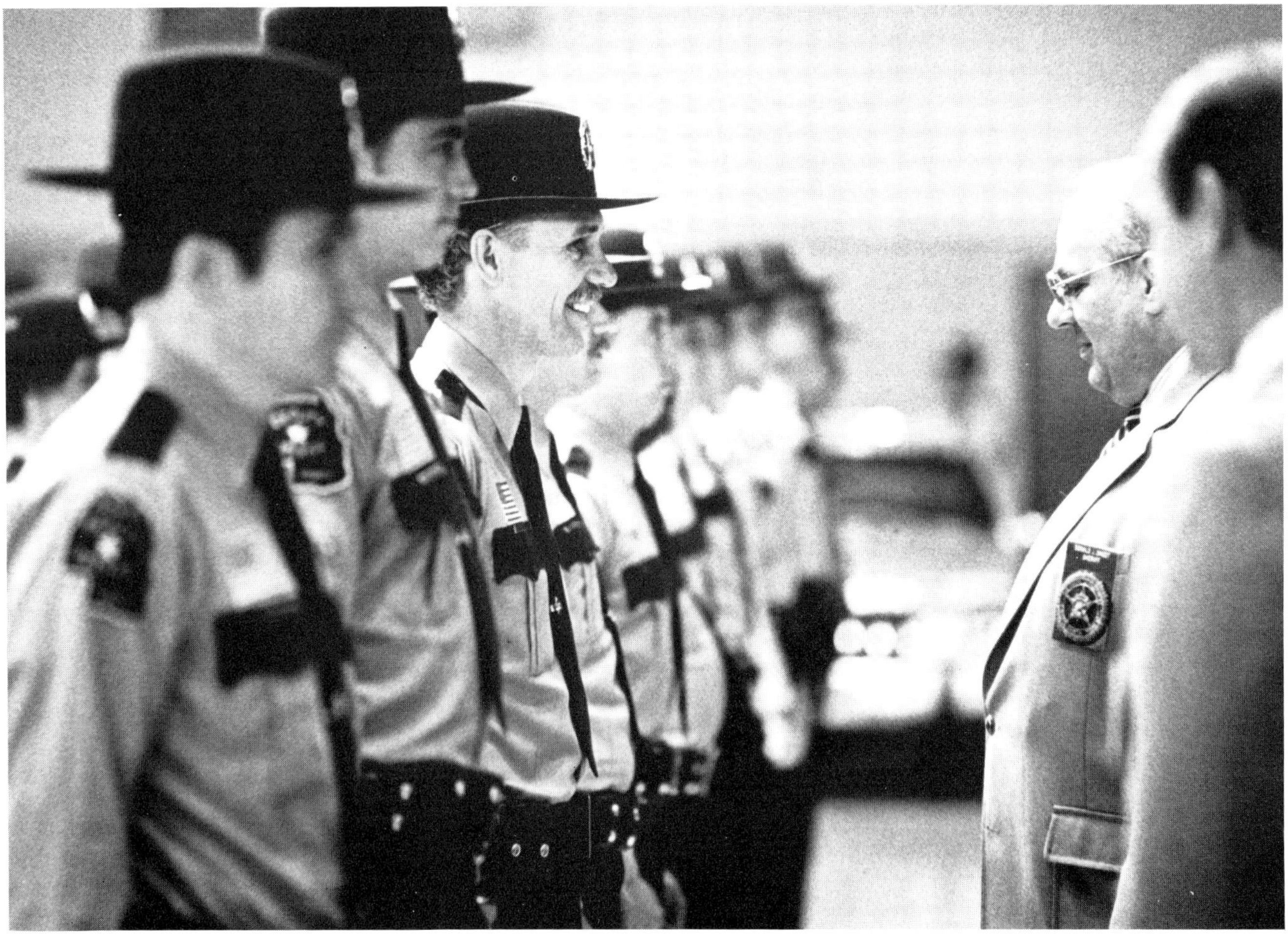

Presidential speech

Mark Philbrick, university relations photographer
Brigham Young University
Provo, Utah

The speech picture is another organizational chestnut. When we have viewed one talking head, we have viewed them all. Some photographers even specialize in stopping talking heads in action (for example, the mentality of the White House Press Corps as it makes motor-drive studies of presidential lips in action at four frames a second). A picture of a talking head never does much for a reader.

One way to break the talking head syndrome in speech pictures is to relate the body language of the speaker to the environment of the meeting hall. Mark Philbrick does this, giving us an insight into the personality of the incoming president of Brigham Young University as he addresses the student body.

The key to Philbrick's approach is his vantage point and lens choice. He decides to get in just enough background and foreground information to add important context to the picture. He also chooses a telephoto lens that will throw the students in the background out of focus. If they were sharp, the president would merge into the background.

Philbrick adds ceremonial detail to strengthen the idea that the speaker and the event are both important. Two flags, potted plants, a multi-leveled rostrum, and the softly defined mass of people add pomp and circumstance to the ceremony. Without these symbols, the picture would portray just another man making a speech.

Philbrick chooses a moment when the president-elect folds his hands before him. It is an unusual gesture for a public speaker addressing thousands in a huge arena. Platform speakers are trained to use their hands in forceful, dramatic ways, not in quiet contemplation. Folded hands are for intimate conversation, a symbol of relaxation, thought, calm. We can assume that this man is unconventional. He, who publicly addresses thousands in the same way he would talk to a person across his desk, has to be unique.

The picture was used with a news release featuring the speaker's upcoming inauguration as president of BYU.

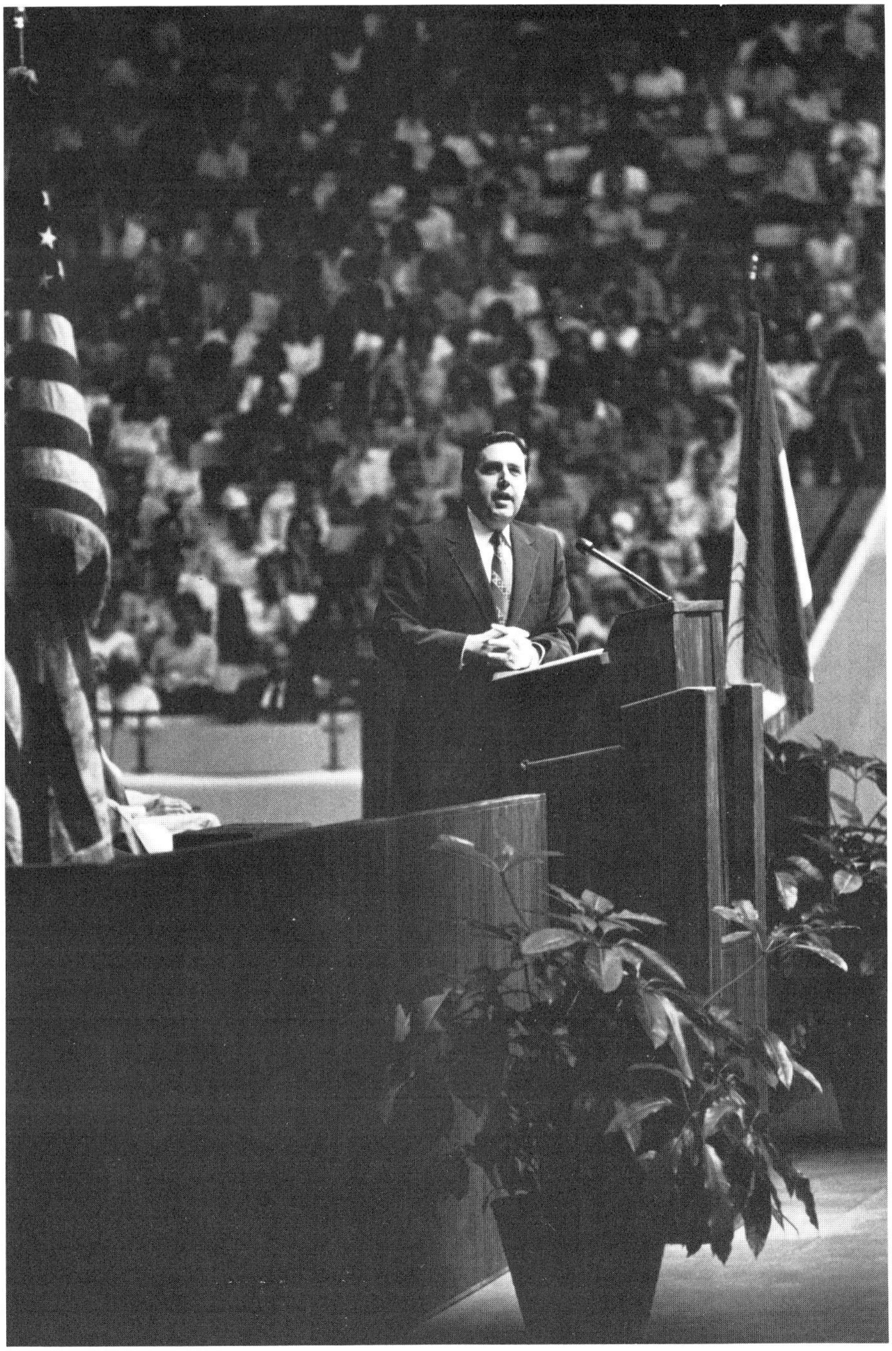

Chapter 11

Photographing hobbies and arts: using one art to define another

An endless stream of feature stories on outside interests of employees and other organizational members parades across the pages of institutional publications. Hobbyists, artists, and performers—ranging from guitarists to quiltmakers, ballerinas to beer can collectors—are duly enshrined in print and photos, most of them in a depressingly superficial manner.

Such photos generally show us only what the person "looks like." Sometimes we may see them actually "doing" whatever it is they do. But that's where the message ends.

We must go beyond literal description and somehow tell the reader something about *both* the person and the activity, perhaps something never realized before. Opportunities for photographic interpretation exist both in the nature of the art or hobby itself and in the energies, personalities, and skills of the person involved in it.

There is an opportunity here for the photographer to practice one art—photography—while interpreting another. It will be the viewer who ultimately gains the most from this dual experience.

Ceramic artists

Dave Denemark, publications coordinator
Medical College of Wisconsin
Milwaukee, Wisconsin

The environmental portrait is among the most useful methods to use when photographing hobbyists and artists for feature stories in organizational publications. Such portraits are particularly effective because they can relate artists to their craft with directness, simultaneously exploring both the character of the artists and the nature of their skills.

Denemark uses a high vantage point and a wideangle lens to make this portrait of two ceramic artists. The photo was shot to be used in a brochure promoting a local "whole earthworks" organization. This portrait would function just as well as an illustration for a feature story on the artists. While portraiture such as this is not in-depth photojournalism, it does give the viewer a sense of personality and avocation.

The artists look up at us, seeking our appraisal. Their body language is relaxed. Each differs from the other. One crosses his hands, the other folds them. One wears mustache and hair at moderate length, the other is more hirsute. One wears paint-spattered trousers, the other doesn't. Yet both use the same studio, create similar artifacts, and seem confident in their abilities.

The light is mellow, adding a sense of peace to the scene. Denemark does more than show us what these men and their work look like. He has given us some hints as to who they are and where their art comes from.

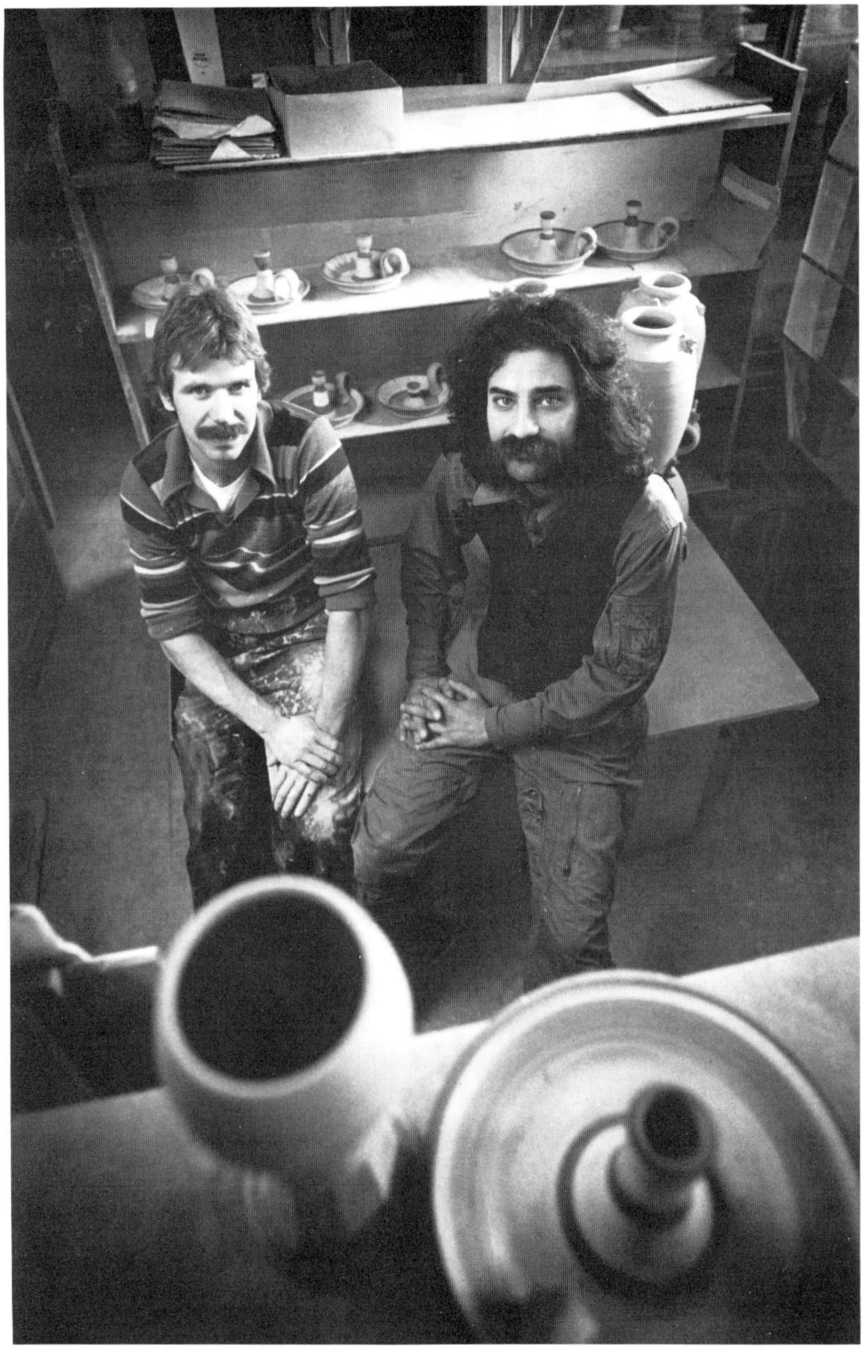

The professor

Bruce Stromberg, freelance photographer
Client: Haverford College
Bryn Mawr, Pennsylvania

In this environmental portrait of a Haverford College professor of music, created by Stromberg for the school's alumni magazine, we see how geometry works to organize visual information.

The boundaries of a photograph form a geometric shape—a rectangle. This becomes Stromberg's starting point. He works in from the limits of his frame, drawing our eyes to the subject through a progression of lines and rhythms.

Stromberg finds highlights to stress the vertical lines within the open piano. A horizontal bar bisects the picture, echoing the horizontal rhythms in the background. The musical score rests on that horizontal bar. The open pages reflect light onto the face of the professor. Behind him, the blackboard, filled with horizontal lines, is partially truncated by the angle of the piano lid. Within this triangular shape floats an eerie reflected image of the subject.

The professor sits just to the right of center, the target of the flowing verticals coming at him from below. Stromberg organizes the picture coherently, bringing us to the focal point: the relaxed, informal pose of the professor. The symbols of his art surrounding him, the man becomes a study in authority, expertise. He is at home with his art, master of his craft, an appropriate person to teach it to others.

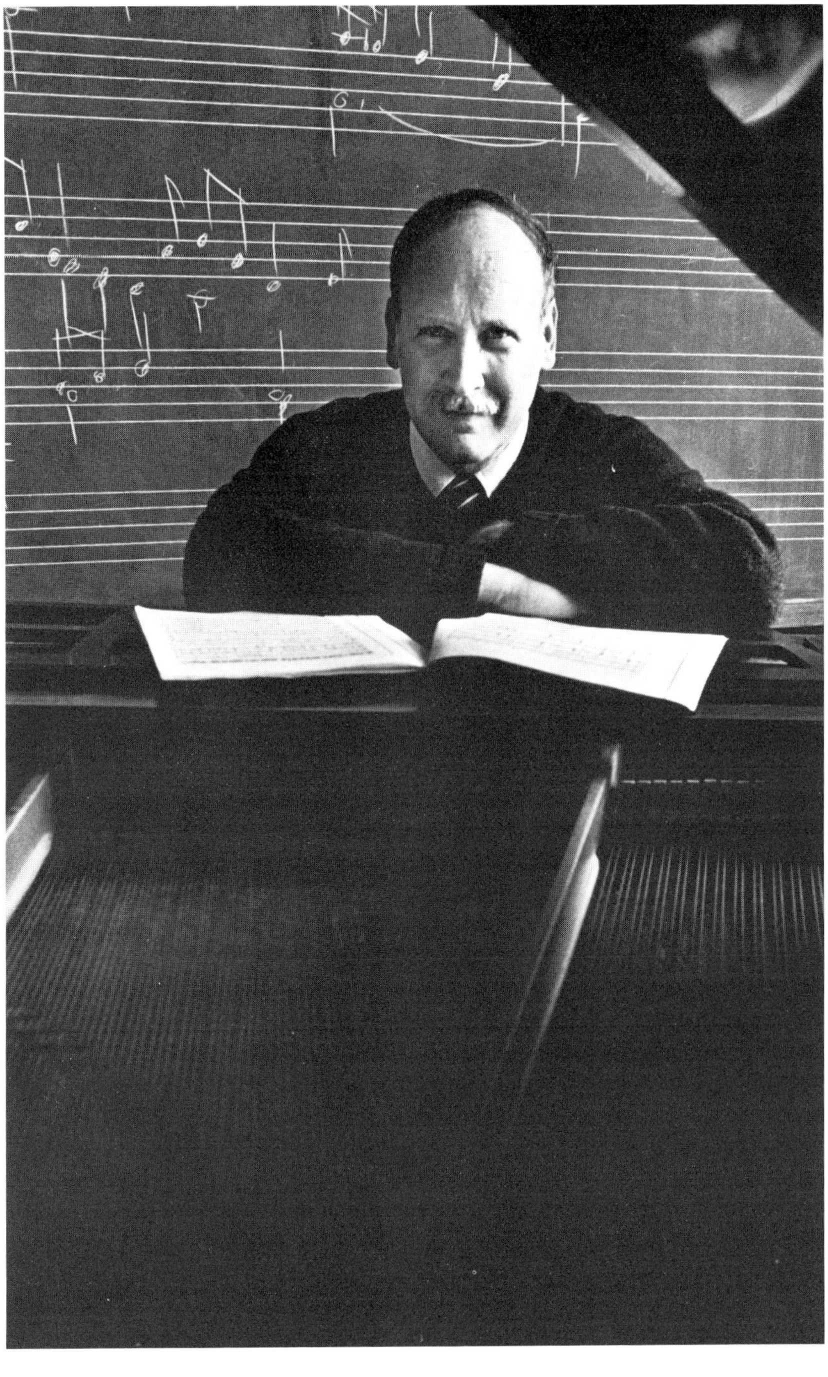

Music all around

Kurt Foss, photojournalist
Hennepin County Public Affairs
Minneapolis, Minnesota

Sometimes it is just one detail or juxtaposition that lifts a photograph out of the ordinary and makes it unique. Such an incongruity presented itself to Kurt Foss while photographing a Shriners' band performing outside the Hennepin County Government Center.

As he shifts his vantage point, Foss notices a large tuba in the back row of the band. It can be used to give any performer in the foreground a "halo" effect. By putting the tuba out of focus, the halo will become abstract enough to suggest a rising moon, thereby reinforcing the moon and star symbol on the caps of the performers.

Foss selects a clarinetist bearing a particularly intent expression as the focal point of the picture. Carefully placing the tuba directly behind the clarinetist's head, Foss uses a large lens opening to narrow the focusing zone, making the man sharp and the tuba soft. The musicians in the background are also put into soft focus so as not to compete with the expression of the clarinetist.

The effect is sublime. The picture becomes highly musical, a fitting interpretation of an afternoon's entertainment. The photo was used in the county's 1979 annual report as part of a center spread featuring the use of the Government Center as a public space.

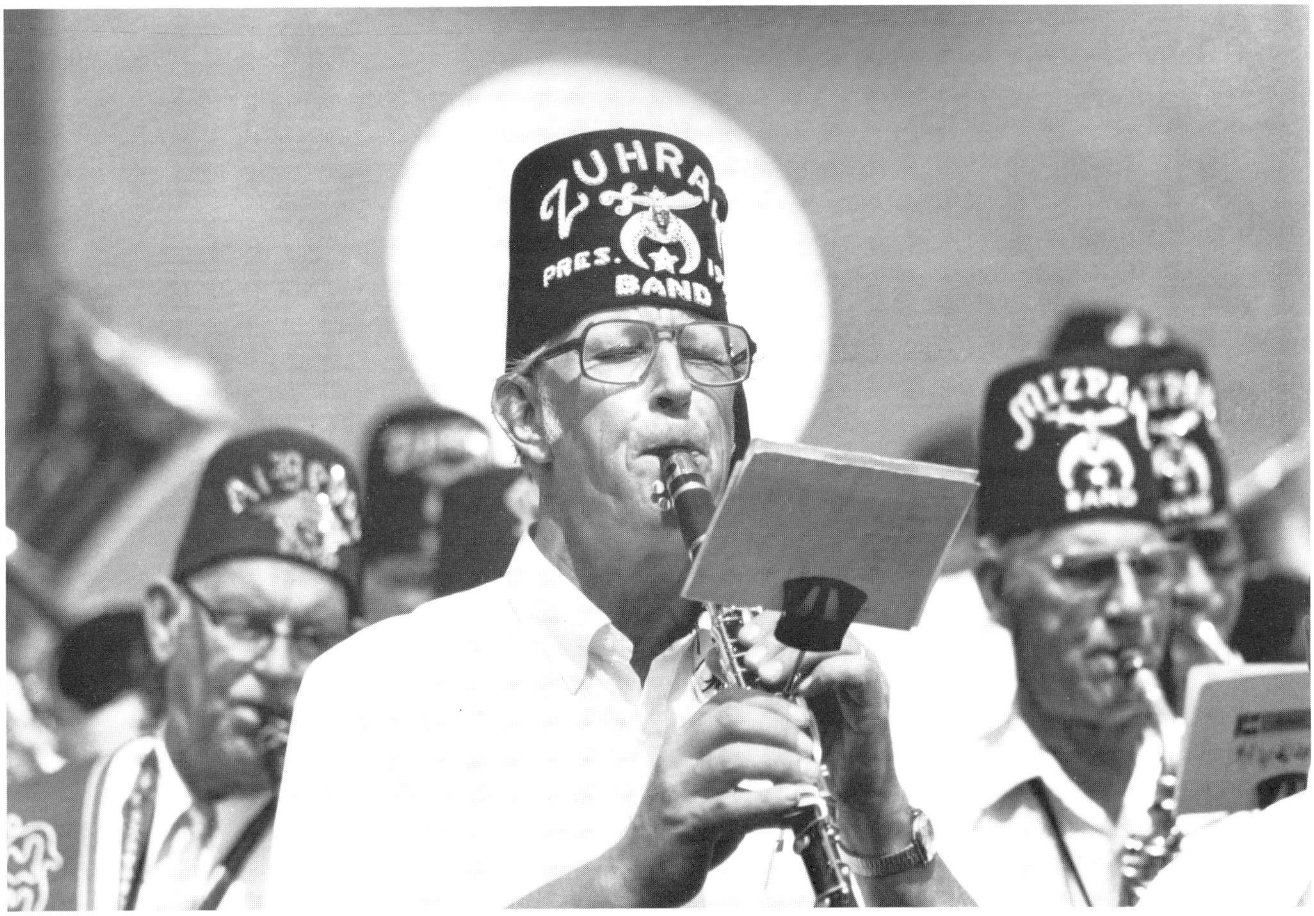
ZUHRA
PRES.
BAND

Dancer at rest

Bruce Stromberg, freelance photographer
Client: Ile Ife Black Humanitarian Center
Philadelphia, Pennsylvania

One of the most memorable brochures ever published by an organization was a 1973 fund raising effort on behalf of the Ile Ife Black Humanitarian Center of Philadelphia. The organization invited freelancer Bruce Stromberg to create a stunning portfolio of 10" by 10" unbound photos printed on one side only. The Center later packaged a dozen of them in a handsome folder along with one sheet of text material. The recipient could view the pictures in any sequence. The printing was fine enough to give the pictures the quality of original prints, suitable for framing.

The twelve images—among them this study of a dancer at rest—spoke eloquently of the center's activities. Stromberg uses light to sculpt the dancer's form, revealing musculature. The highlighted areas define body language.

The purpose of the Center is to nourish the human spirit through the arts. This photograph presents an aspect of that spirit, using abstraction, response, costume, and light.

It is obvious that Stromberg cares about his subject. We feel that care in this photograph. It comes as no surprise to learn that Stromberg donated his services to the Center in order to create such personal statements, which evoke both the nature and spirit of the organization.

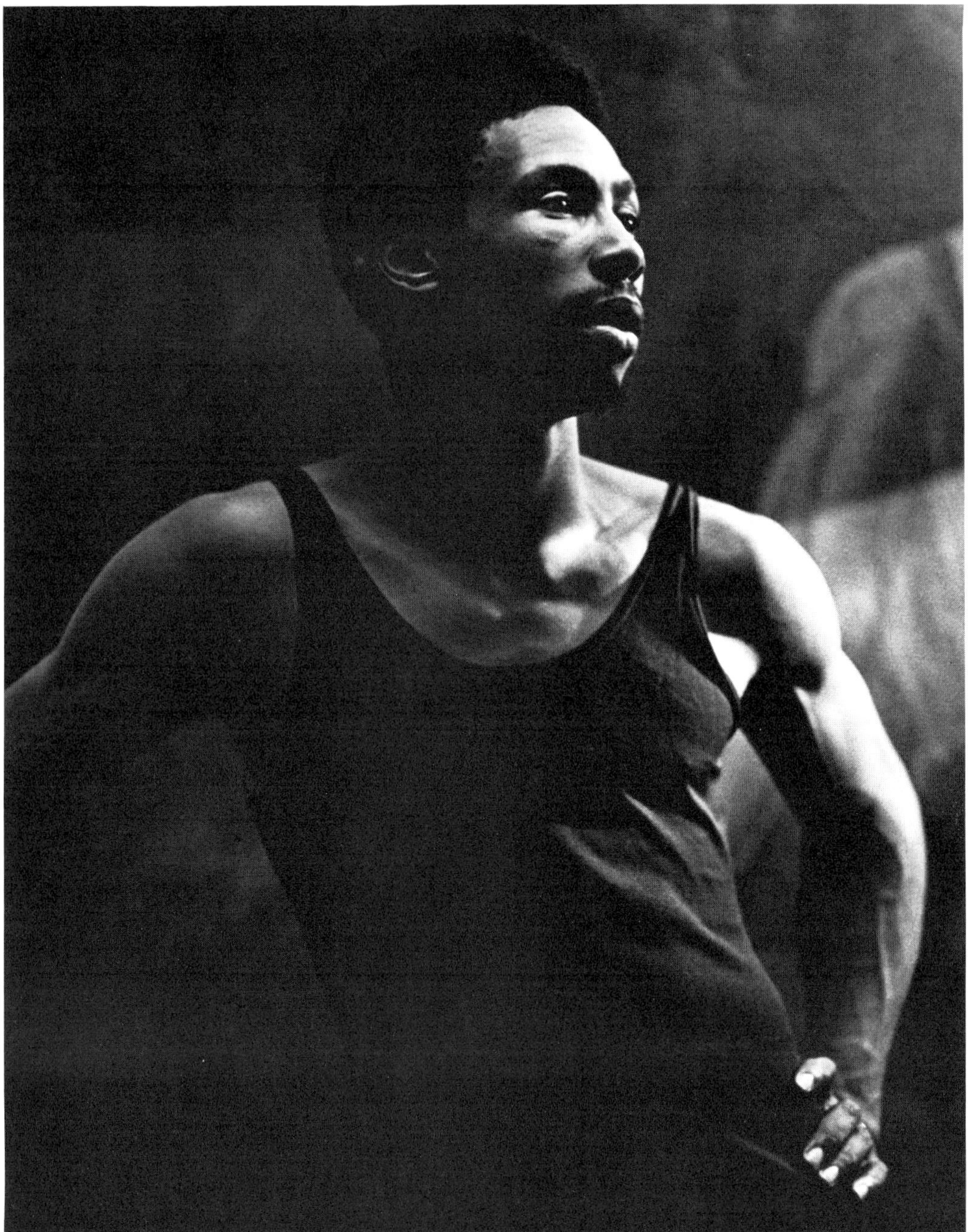

The flute

Bruce Stromberg, freelance photographer
Client: Ile Ife Black Humanitarian Center
Philadelphia, Pennsylvania

Less is more. This aphorism, attributed to architect Ludwig Mies van der Rohe, is at the heart of interpretive photography. Nowhere do we see a better example than in this study of a flute player created for Philadelphia's Ile Ife Black Humanitarian Center by Bruce Stromberg.

Only a fragment of the face can be seen. The highlights play over the musician's cheek and nose, bringing us down to the lips pressed to the flute. Stromberg places the subject to the far right of the frame, leaving a large black area filling the left and center of the picture. Within this area we can imagine the sound of the flute itself.

Through such abstraction, the photograph invites the participation of the viewer. Our imaginations are activated; we become part of the event ourselves. Stromberg exposes his film for the highlights only, allowing the balance of the picture to fade into darkness. If any background information came through on the negative, we can be sure that Stromberg eliminated it through further underexposure of the print in the darkroom.

The essence of visual literacy is respect for the intelligence of the viewer. We are not obligated to reveal *everything* within a scene. We can suggest, imply, and tantalize through abstraction. We can allow viewers the latitude to enter the photograph and make of it what they will.

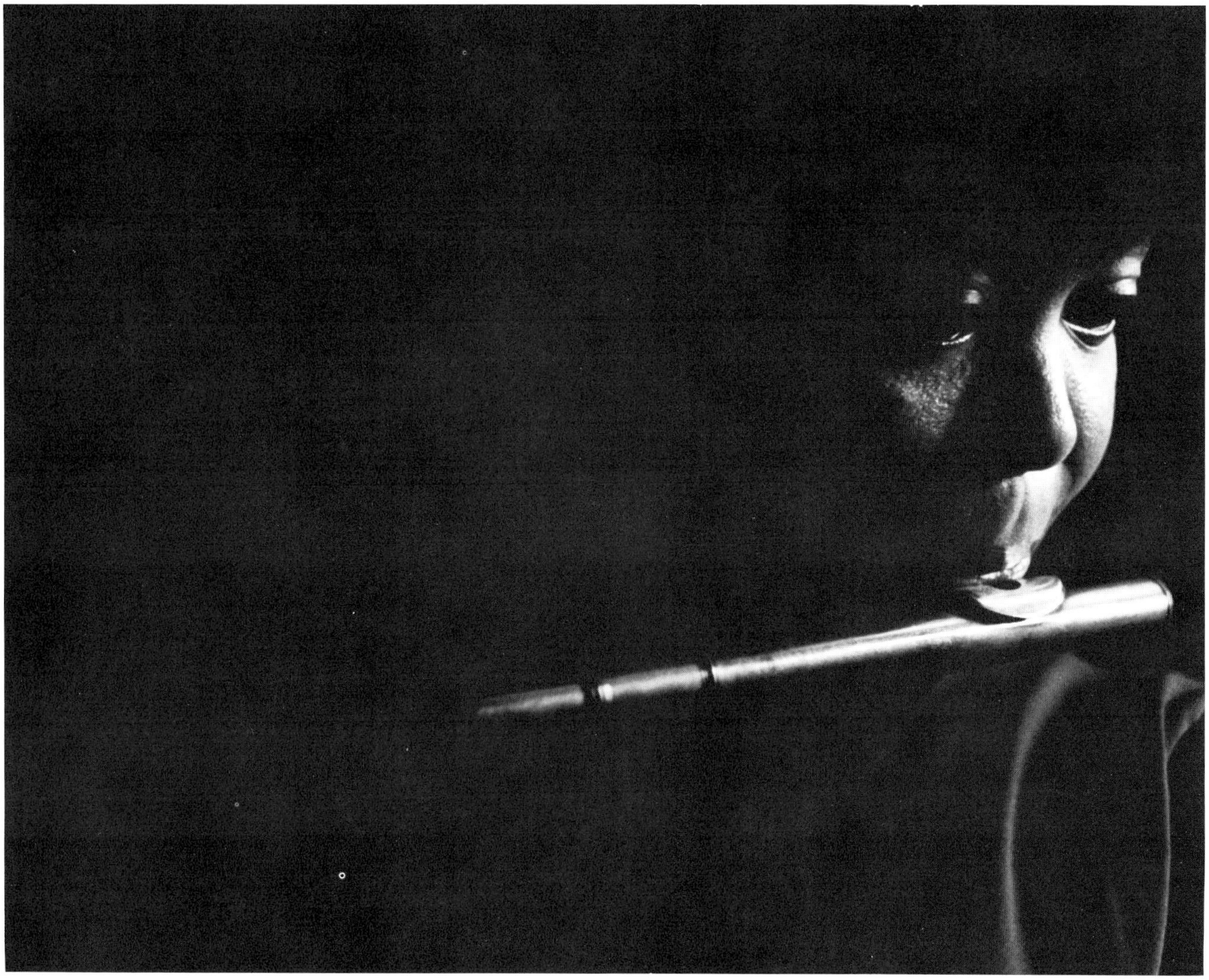

Sculptor

Bruce Stromberg, freelance photographer
Client: Philadelphia Corporation for Aging
Philadelphia, Pennsylvania

When photographers attempt to show us artists at work, they must do more than just record the scene randomly. They must hone it down to convey the essence of the skills artists bring to their craft. This often requires patience, waiting for that moment when every element combines to express the feelings and talents of the artist.

In this photograph of a sculptor at work, Stromberg is also making what he feels is a positive statement on aging. Age brings wisdom, and this is a woman most assuredly experienced in her art. She holds her arm to her body, expressing absolute confidence in her own abilities. She places the tiny tool in just the right place, ever so skillfully. Stromberg stresses this by shifting his vantage point to silhouette the bust and the sculpting tool in the window behind her. A tiny shift to his left, and there would have been no silhouette, no emphasis on detail, no clear delineation of key action.

The window provides "rim lighting," outlining the profile to stress the skill of the artist. There are quivering tensions running through the spaces between artist, table, bust, and the edges of the picture, another by-product of Stromberg's vantage point. Yet those tensions are countered by a solid base—the legs of both table and woman, firmly planted upon the floor.

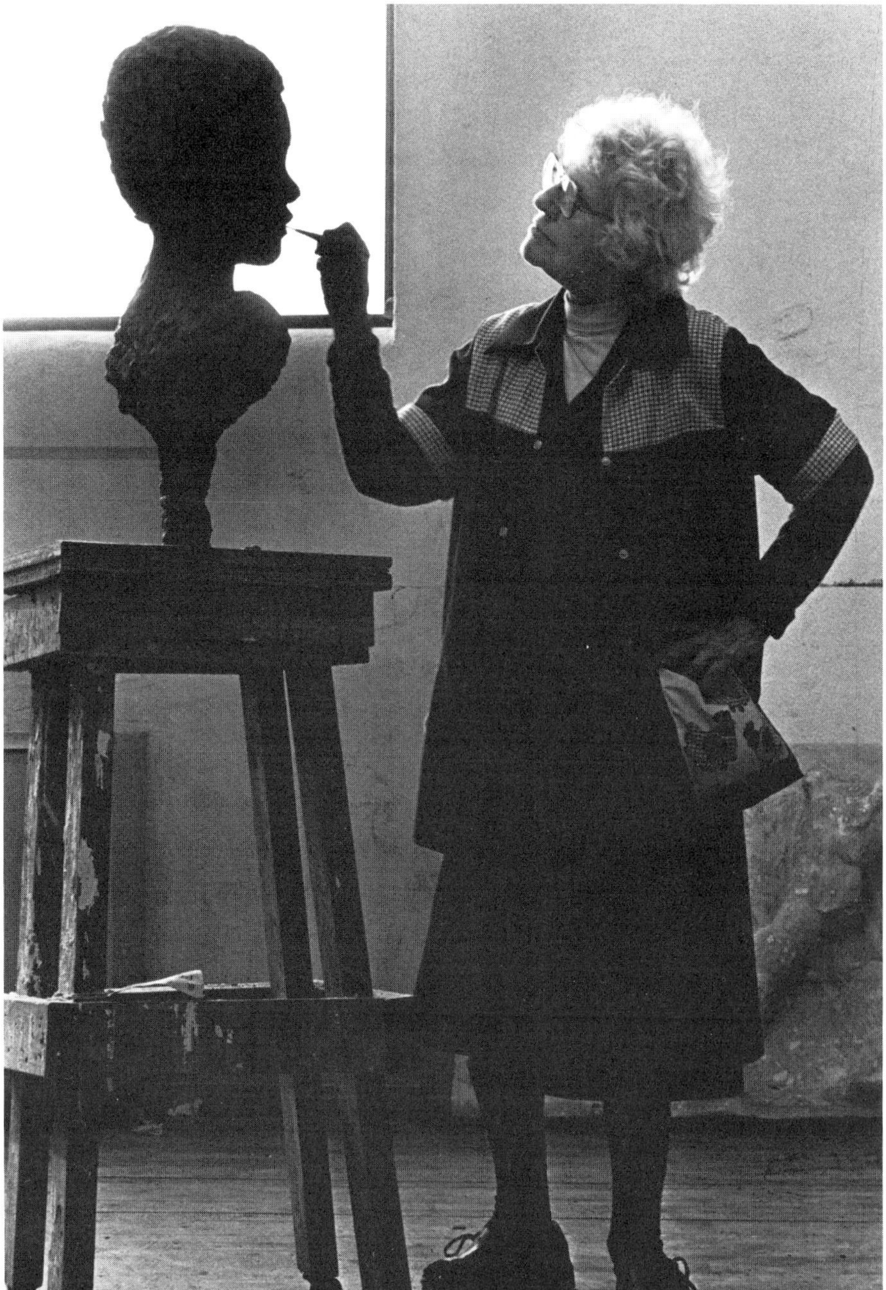

Chapter 12

Photojournalism and religion: interpreting issues of our times

The organizational press embraces not only vast numbers of publications from businesses, hospitals, government, educational institutions, and associations. It also includes the publications of hundreds of religious denominations. Only a few, however, make serious use of photojournalism to communicate to parishioners, staff, employees, missionaries, and the general public.

By far the most consistent and effective use of visual communication in print for religious purposes is the work of the Southern Baptist Home Mission Board, based in Atlanta, Georgia. Close behind is its sister organization, the Southern Baptist Foreign Mission Board, based in Richmond, Virginia.

On the following pages (and scattered throughout other chapters, as well) are examples of how the Southern Baptists use pictures to interpret the issues of our times to thousands of missionaries. It is unique work—probably the most consistent use of in-depth photojournalism practiced by *any* organization, anywhere.

We can learn much from their gifted photographers—and from the far-seeing editors and managers who employ and direct them.

Early morning for Bailey and Luvenia King, Quentin, Mississippi, 1979

Don Rutledge, photojournalist
Home Mission Board, Southern Baptist Convention
Atlanta, Georgia

This pivotal photograph in Don Rutledge's monumental photo-essay on the poverty of Bailey King and his family, appeared in *Missions USA* in late 1979. (See the chapter on incongruity for background on this assignment). In it, Rutledge does what few organizational photographers have ever done. He strikes to the core of this complex issue with one powerful image.

King is wasted by physical ailments. He rests frequently, gathering his strength just to walk. Bailey and Luvenia King share whatever is possible to share. But some things each must do alone. This is one of those moments when their paths diverge. Mrs. King works to feed a large family, while her husband stretches exhausted on the bed before us. This is a very private picture, yet only through such a moment can the truth be adequately conveyed. While it works in concert with the other photographs in the essay, this photo brings more to them than they bring to it.

The very fact that it even could be made is a measure of the mutual respect between Rutledge and the Kings. If effective photojournalism is to take place within any organization, it must be preceded by understanding and trust shared by both subject and photographer. Rutledge is a courtly, gentle man. He walks and talks softly, yet makes images that will communicate as long as there are people around to appreciate them. Shortly after this essay was completed, he left the Home Mission Board to join its sister organization, SBC's Foreign Mission Board in Richmond, Virginia. He now roams the globe, interpreting significant issues for SBC's missionaries around the world.

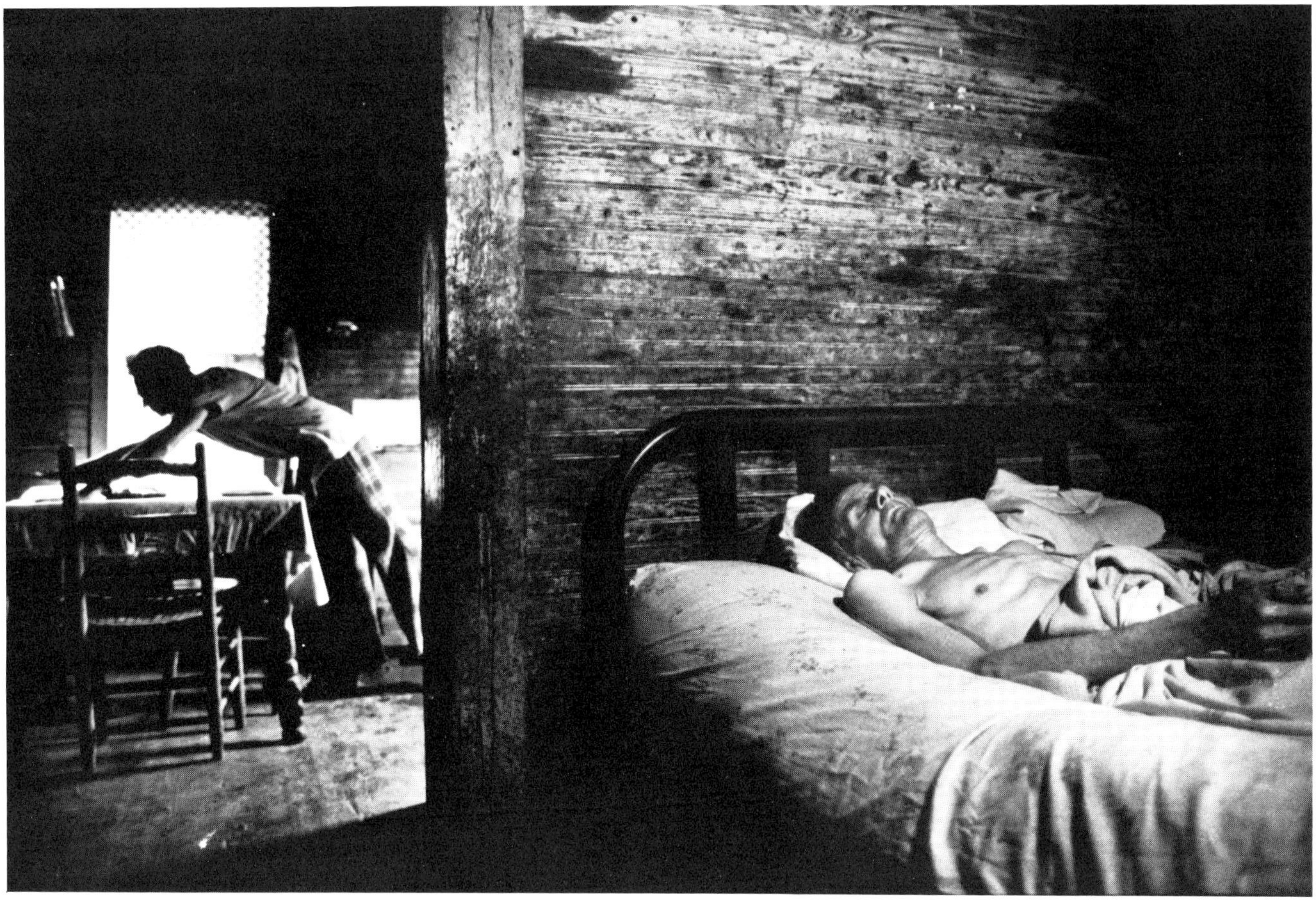

Ritual

**Don Rutledge, photojournalist
Home Mission Board, Southern Baptist Convention
Atlanta, Georgia**

Missions USA and its sister publications often examine the issues faced by people in the early years of their lives: education, religious training, peer pressures, the differences between right and wrong. Don Rutledge records the moment when Rochelle Davis, pastor of the Temple of Faith Baptist Church in Detroit, grasps the shoulders of young Anthony Owens. Before a sanctuary filled with adults, the child experiences the ritual of his religion.

There are no smiles. The solemnity of the ritual stands in counterpoint to the more typically carefree scenes of childhood we expect to encounter. Young Anthony, however, is invited to join an adult world.

Rutledge neatly divides the photograph in half. On one side are the pastor, the child, the audience. On the other side, a woman, perhaps Anthony's mother. She stands a few feet away, yet remains a generation apart.

The vertical thrust of the pastor's arms and gaze moves our eyes up from Anthony to the unseen, yet obviously implied, presence of a higher authority. Pictures like this one hardly need captions. Rutledge has said it all.

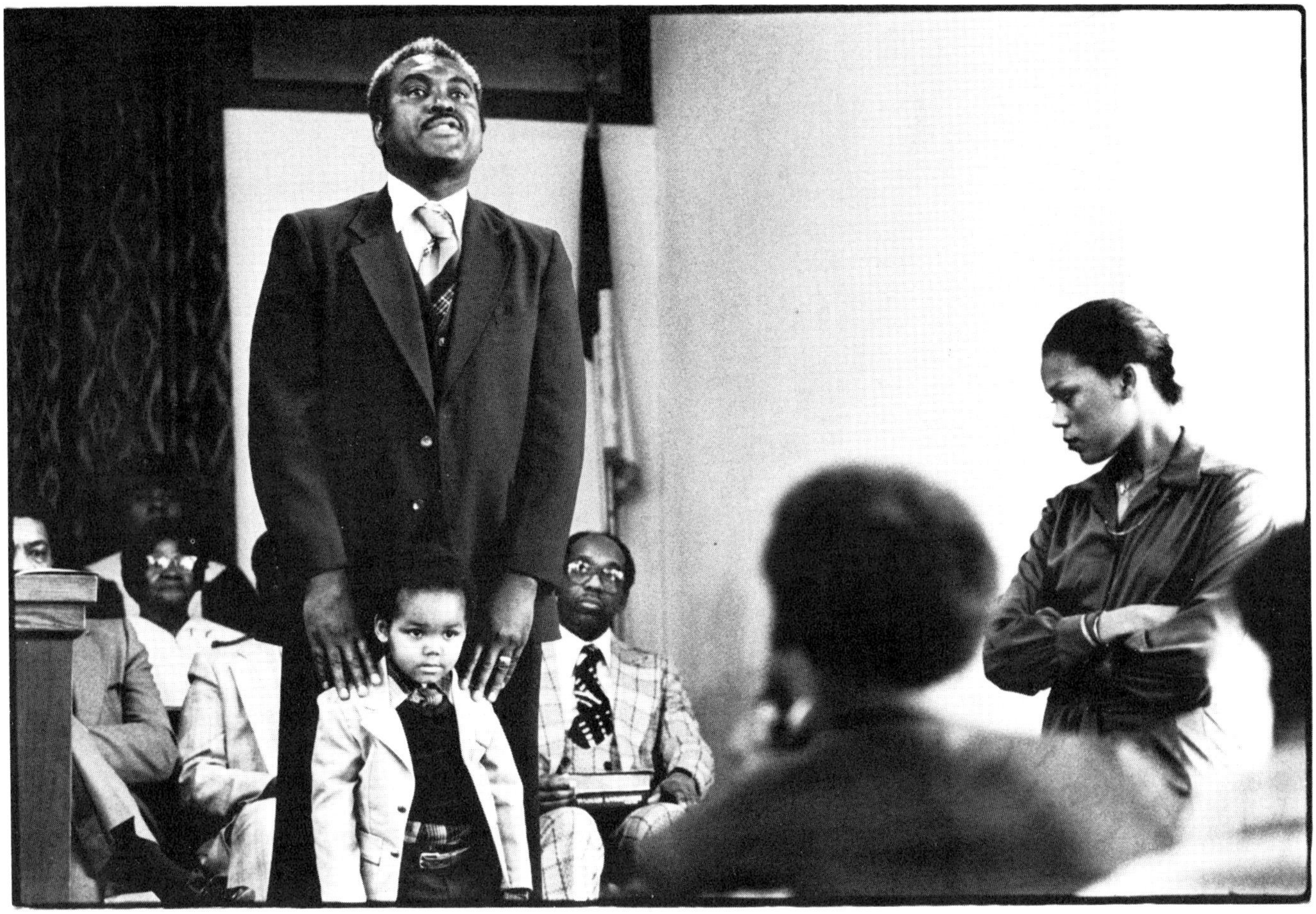

Missionary at work: Pascua Village, Arizona

Mark Sandlin, manager,
  photographic services
Home Mission Board, Southern
  Baptist Convention
Atlanta, Georgia

Once again, a *Missions USA* photojournalist makes two pictures in one, this time to comment upon a missionary's experiences in a remote Arizona village. The contrast between the left and right halves of the picture is fascinating and the interplay between them gives the overall image its meaning.

Mark Sandlin remains outside the open door, focusing on the scene within the next room as missionary Ross Hanna visits an 84-year-old woman. The quality of the light on the woman is striking, bathing her gesture in an ethereal glow. It is she who seems to be instructing the missionary, instead of the other way around. It would be fair to assume that she may well know something that the missionary doesn't.

The left half of the picture is a complete statement in itself, but it acquires added context from the plaque on the outside wall, offering us a symbol of her faith, as well as reminders of her past. Over the religious homily, we see an ancient photograph of four soldiers bearing rifles before an American flag. A tiny snapshot is placed, in turn, upon that. We are viewing a picture within a picture within a picture.

It provides an unintentional comment on the role photography plays in everyday life. For only photographs can overcome the limits of our memory. Photographs offer us substitutes for reality. For this 84-year-old-woman, the memories in her life no doubt provide much of what is left to her.

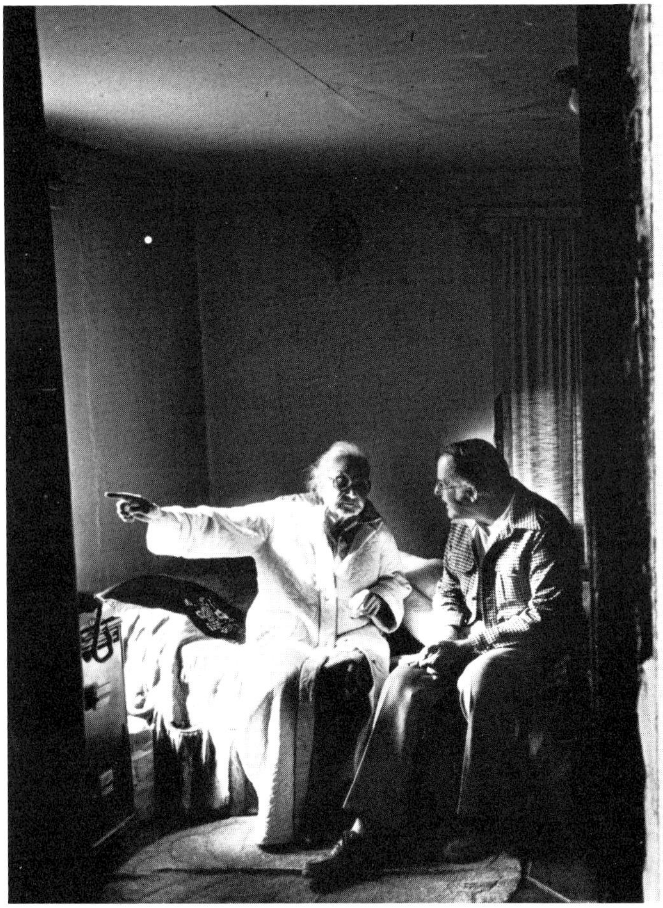

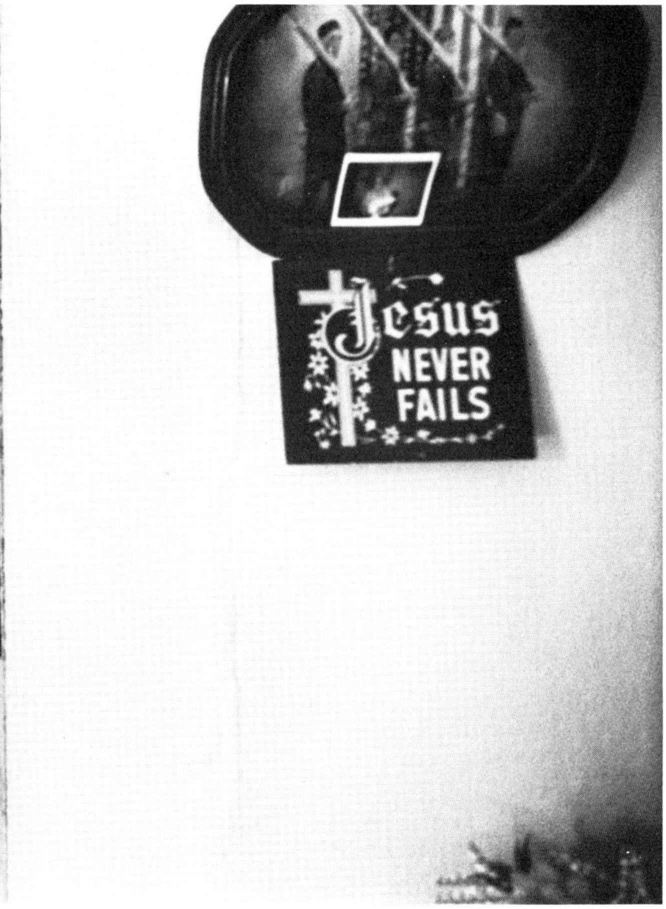
Jesus
NEVER
FAILS

Sikh temple, Los Angeles

Paul Obregon, senior photographer
Home Mission Board, Southern
   Baptist Convention
Atlanta, Georgia

Still another task for photojournalists shooting for the SBC Home Mission Board publications is to make their readers familiar with the customs and activities of other faiths. Here Paul Obregon humanizes what might seem to some to be an obscure and unfathomable set of rites—those of the Sikhs.

A large religious portrait divides the brightly lit room in half. Except for the painting, it seems to be just another room. But it's not. It is a Sikh temple. Strange, then, that the space to the left of the painting is alive with dancing children. Obregon tells us that he made the photo minutes before worship began. Somehow, the spontaneous rituals of childhood are more universal than any formal ceremony, and Obregon shoots the frivolity to tell his fellow Baptists that the Sikhs are, in some ways at least, no different than any of us.

The photo, which appeared in the SBC book *Your God, My God*, also comments on a fact Obregon feels is worth remembering: "The future of any religion," he says, "rests upon the children."

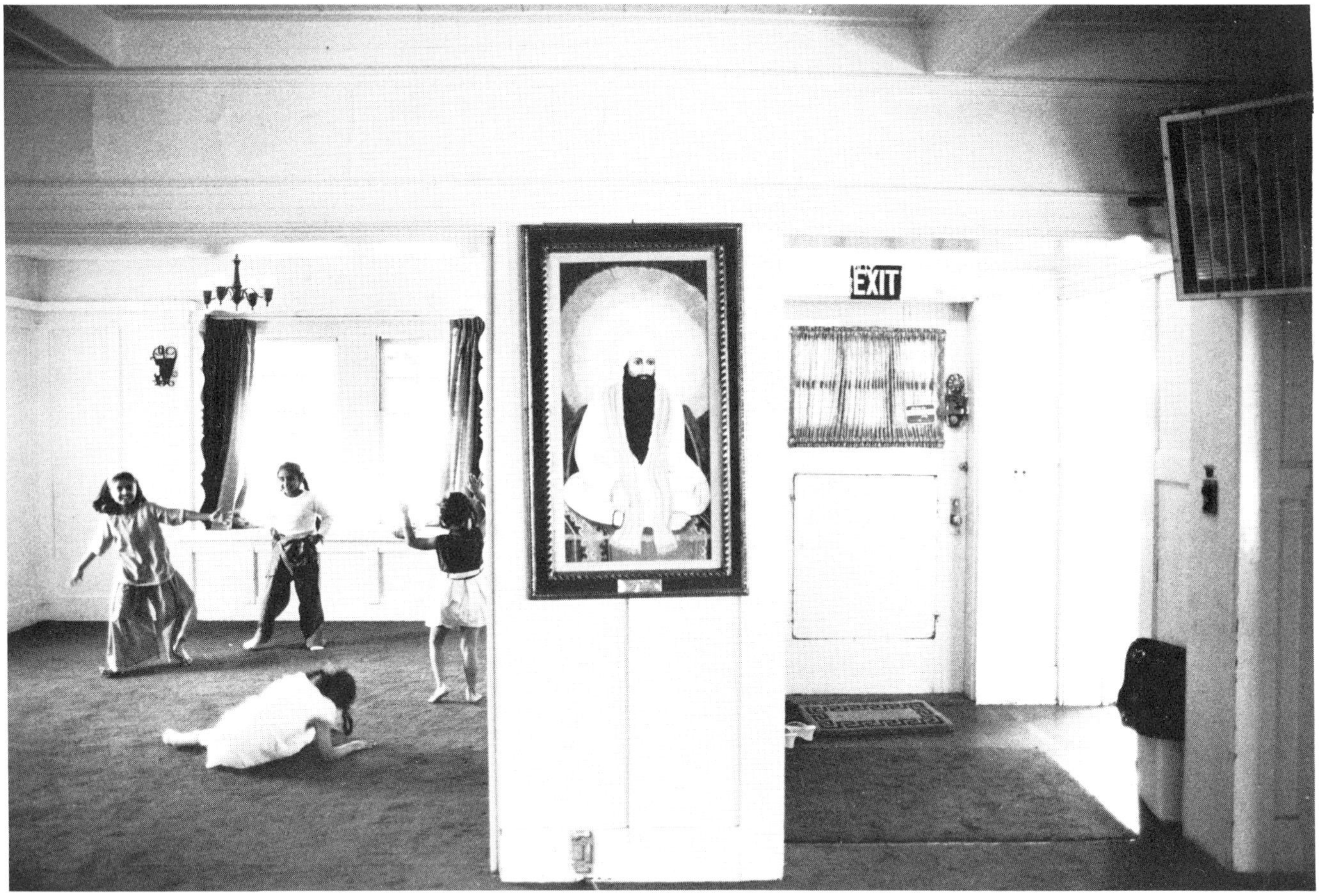
EXIT

The Hispanics

Paul Obregon, senior photographer
Home Mission Board, Southern Baptist Convention
Atlanta, Georgia

Hispanics are among the most rapidly growing ethnic groups in the country, and Obregon attempts to symbolize with this group shot (or "multiple portrait," as he calls it) the personality of that culture. The photograph was used as the opening spread for a major story on the SBC's missionary work among the Hispanics. Obregon does a fine job in conveying some of those qualities that he feels typify the group.

It is, however, dangerous business to try to typify any group, for we run the risk of stereotyping. But Obregon speaks the language of these people. He was born in the town of Laredo, Texas, where he made this picture. He says "When I took their photo, it was very natural. I took them just as they were."

There is no self-consciousness here. The three people confront us directly without hostility, fear, or embarrassment. They share certain mannerisms; the two older men hold their hands in similar fashion. All of them squint in the bright Texas sun. The two at the left are members of the same family, and the young man's body language bears this out.

Obregon did not pose them. He found them on a wooden bench before a plain cracked wall. His multiple portrait has defined a cultural and physical bond they all share. In a larger sense, this group represents a heritage shared by an entire ethnic group.

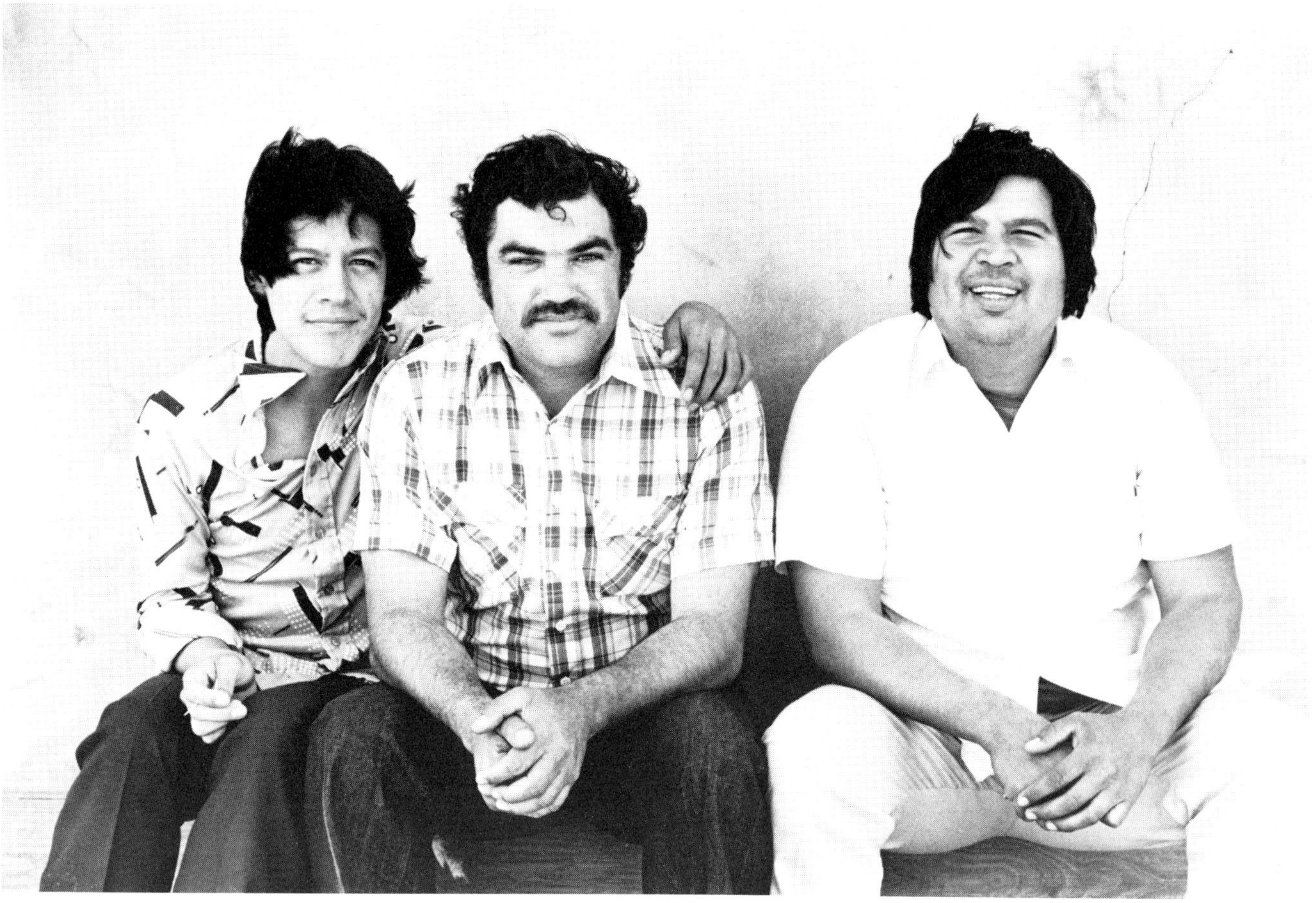

The visit

Paul Obregon, senior photographer
Home Mission Board, Southern Baptist Convention
Atlanta, Georgia

The power of Home Mission Board photography does not depend on spectacular subject matter but on how subjects are handled. Most of these subjects are ordinary people, living ordinary lives. Yet somehow Rutledge, Sandlin, and Obregon manage to find the extraordinary within ordinary, daily life, and they have the ability to record it indelibly on film.

The 1978 annual report of the Southern Baptist Convention featured a photo essay called "A day in the life of a Southern Baptist." To cover comprehensively one of the largest religious groups in the United States, the scope of the essay had to be as broad as the everyday lives of the population at large.

This is one of the finest photographs in that essay. Paul Obregon was covering the Sunday routine of a woman who started the day by visiting her neighbor across the street, a woman who could not talk because of a stroke. They communicated with their eyes, says Obregon, with the younger woman asking questions and also answering them after looking into the eyes of the ailing woman. The kiss came unexpectedly. Obregon fortunately had the scene already focused and framed and was able to record this beautiful moment. It speaks for itself. If ever there was a visual "thank you," it can be found in the face of this elderly woman.

People need the care and support of other people. This photograph makes that point in an unforgettable way.

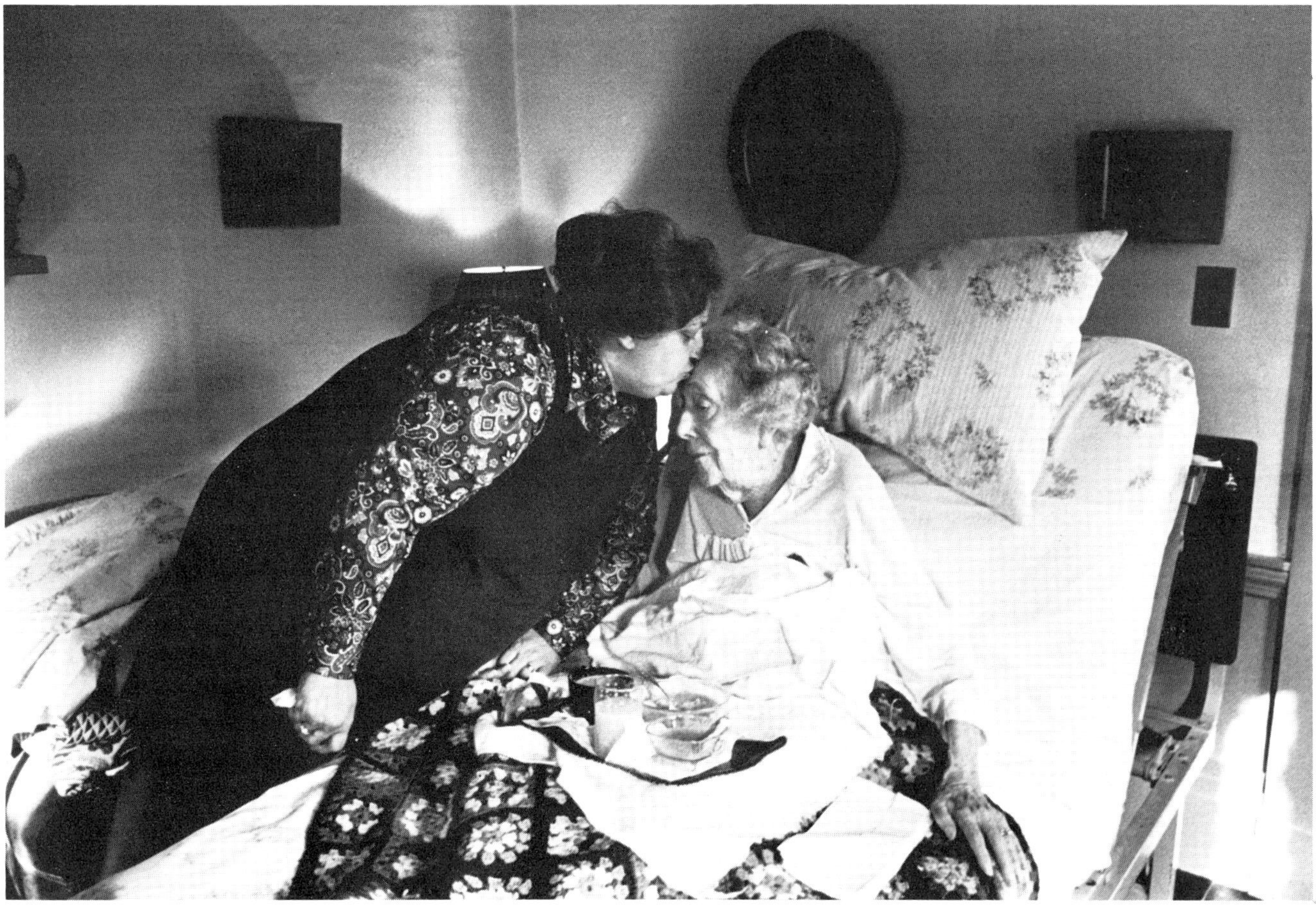

Chapter 13

Portraits: revealing the person inside

Portraits comprise the largest single category of organizational photographs. Most appear in print to "recognize" the *subject*. Little thought is given to the value of such photographs to the *viewer*. Hence depressing rows of embalmed-looking mugshots blight the typical organizational publication.

It is possible to both honor the subject and still say something about that person to the reader. This requires the photographer to leave the artificiality of the studio and shoot people where they actually perform their organizational tasks.

There are three basic approaches to the portrait. We can seek responses that say something about how people feel about what they are doing, capturing moments on film as candid insights. We can pose people straightforwardly in an environment that symbolizes their function. Usually such pictures relate the subject directly to the viewer, avoiding faked, self-conscious responses. We call these environmental portraits. Finally, we can blend both the candid approach and the environmental portrait, by posing the subject in the right environment and drawing the subject into a conversation, releasing the shutter when the spontaneity of the moment reveals the inner person.

Ultimately, portraits must do more than just show what someone looks like. That is acceptable only for use on badges and in personnel folders. Effective portraits for journalistic purposes must instead reveal who that person really is.

Portrait of Herb Denenberg, consumer advocate

Ed Eckstein, freelance photographer
Client: Saturday Review
Philadelphia, Pennsylvania

Photojournalist Robert Capa once said, "If your pictures aren't any good, you're not close enough."

In portraiture, close vantage points are usually essential. Here are three tight views of consumer affairs advocate Herb Denenberg, shot on assignment for *Saturday Review* by freelancer Ed Eckstein. The first is close; the second, closer; the third, closest.

How does Eckstein get so close without intruding? He uses a telephoto lens, probably 100mm, considered the prime portrait lens because it doubles the size of the image, bringing us twice as close as we would otherwise be. Yet it is a lens with a large enough maximum opening to allow us to shoot under low lighting conditions with available light. It also lets us focus selectively, stressing key aspects by contrasting sharply focused against softly focused areas.

Eckstein also makes sure the subject is otherwise occupied. He shoots his pictures while Denenberg is being interviewed. Eckstein can work unnoticed in the background while the subject responds to the interviewer's questions.

This technique not only allows the photographer to work unobtrusively but also allows the subject to respond naturally, unselfconsciously. If editor and photographer are one and the same person, he or she should get the interview first and return later to make photographs when the subject is occupied in normal working activities.

This trio of portraits offers us choices. We would not want to use all three in a sequence because they do not vary that much. But there are some differences. The longest view suggests the presence of somebody else and offers good body language in the arms. The desk suggests a busy man. The medium view is a more aggressive, less worried head-and-shoulders shot. The third portrait is by far the most unique—a very thoughtful profile, fingers to lips. The softly focused face complements the sharp fingers.

The three choices are a testimony to Eckstein's ability to work quietly, shifting vantage points during the portrait session. He gives the editor the luxury of choice, a chance to pick a picture that best captures the man depicted in the story. That's what a portrait has to do if it is to work as communication.

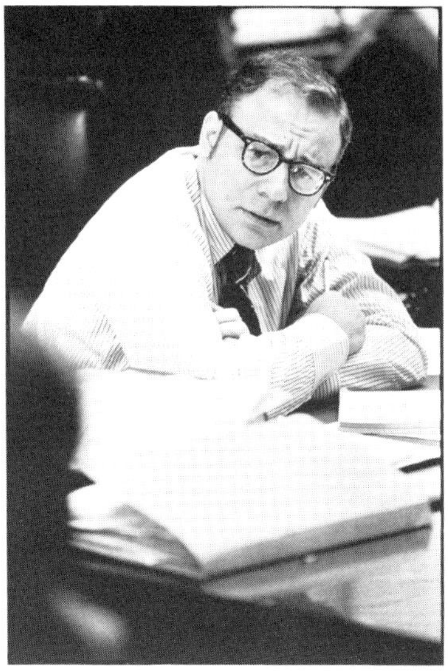
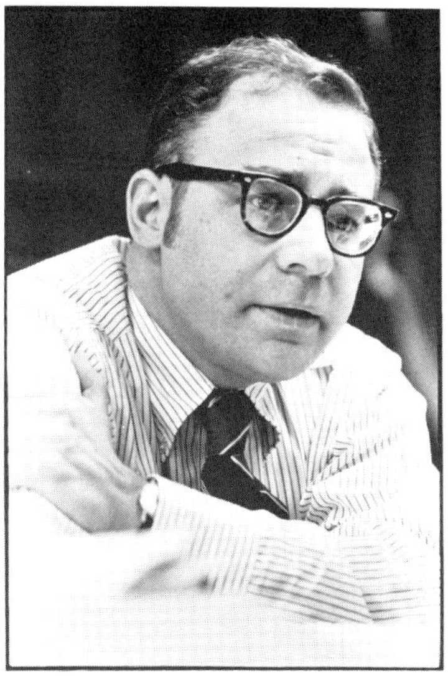
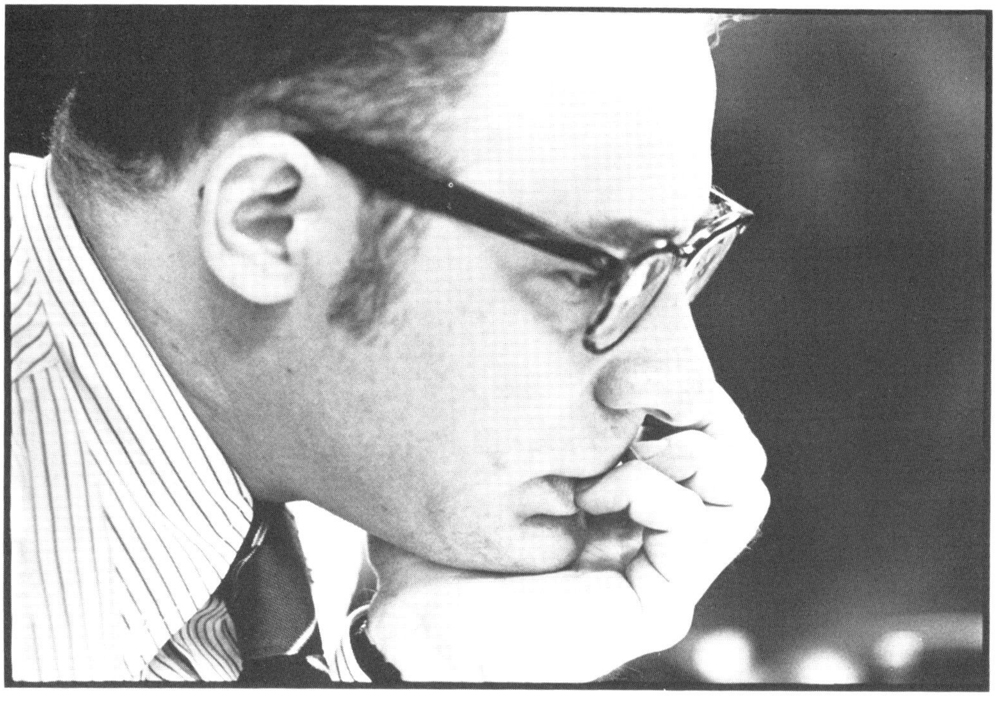

Margaret Page, RN

Stormy Fitzgerald,
   chief photographer
Methodist Hospitals of Memphis
Memphis, Tennessee

Many institutions would not publish a portrait as true to life as this one. The subject is not happy. She appears somewhat tired, and certainly concerned. Such insightful portraits must be published if the institution and its employees are to be perceived as credible.

Margaret Page is a consultant to nurses. She helps them to help their patients deal with psychological needs and problems. She is seen here during a consultation, sidelight illuminating her profile, stressing her strength as well as her vulnerability. Stormy Fitzgerald had less than a year of experience as a photojournalist when she made this portrait of Page. Yet she was able to master what is perhaps the most difficult challenge facing a photojournalist—getting to know the subject as a person, in order to effectively reveal that person, inside and out.

Sometimes this knowledge works against this goal. Fitzgerald says that a close friendship with the subject creates problems. "They're too aware of you, knowing that you know their weaknesses as well as their strengths." But Page and Fitzgerald together transcend that problem. Page is so deeply involved in her counseling that she has long forgotten Fitzgerald is even there. Fitzgerald draws on her knowledge of Page to help her find the right position and the right moment for this portrait.

The mutual bond of trust between photographer and subject as well as the strength of Margaret Page's character help to see this picture into print. Page did not object to being portrayed as she actually appears when she works. She does not see the role of a portrait in the employee publication as flattery. She sees it as communication.

Other subjects caught as candidly as this might well object. To them, communication may not be the goal of a portrait. Yet it is important to remember that the *subject is not the editor* of the publication. The picture is being published for the benefit of the *reader*, not the subject. Candid portraits often can only be employed when subject, photographer, editor, and manager trust each other and agree that the goal of the publication is communication. If there is no trust or no commitment to communication, such fine portraits as this may wind up on the cutting room floor.

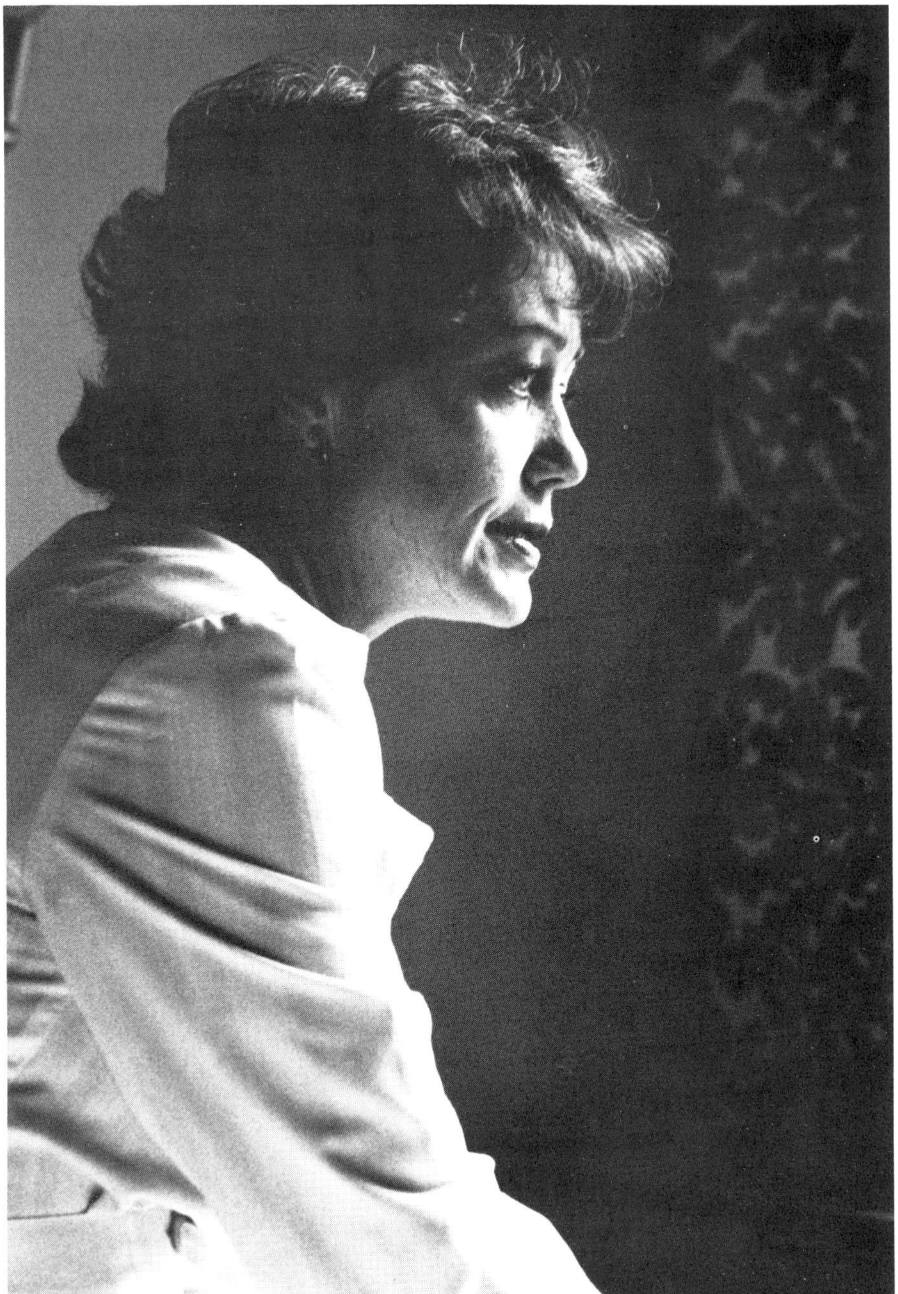

Retiring executive, Herman Miller Inc.

Melissa Brown, internal communications manager
Herman Miller, Inc.
Zeeland, Michigan

We see this fine informal portrait in two versions—before and after it was retouched with an airbrush. Retouching is a dangerous business, for it merges fantasy and artifice with reality, producing at times a misleading hybrid. But in this case airbrushing is essential for coherence.

Melissa Brown appears in Hugh DePree's office to interview and photograph him. Before the interview begins, DePree asks Brown to wait while he finishes some reading. As he becomes absorbed in the letter, Brown begins to shoot. She and DePree had worked together before, and there is no need to ask permission to photograph. Brown sees the glasses come off, the open tie, the open collar, the wonderful response, and gets it on film.

But a big problem went unnoticed at the time. In her eagerness to get DePree's response, Brown fails to notice that the shelf behind him merges into his jaw. Although she gets it out of focus, it is still a terrible distraction.

After Brown saw the print, she probably wished she had swung the camera a bit to her left, putting DePree in front of the blank wall instead of the shelf. But it was too late. A great portrait had suffered a serious flaw. In such situations, there are no retakes.

The skill of the airbrusher saves the portrait for Brown and her audience. Now that we know it is airbrushed, the cosmetology is obvious. But to those who have never seen the original, the grey background looks like a wall. DePree comes through without background static. Airbrushing is legitimate in photographic communication only when it does not alter the situation or personality concerned. Is the picture still true to life? If so, we can get away with cosmetic surgery such as this. Retouching should never be used, however, to change the appearance of a face or to remove a person from a scene. That approach changes the subject itself and presents a lie to the world.

The portrait says a lot to us about Hugh DePree. We can assume he is open, relaxed, kind, and humorous. He is not vain. He is secure enough in his position to "risk" being seen at ease. His warmth comes through. This picture was used later as a retirement tribute honoring him and his long career. Brown says the response to the portrait was enthusiastic. This was the man the employees knew, cared about, and wanted to remember. The airbrushing was never even noticed.

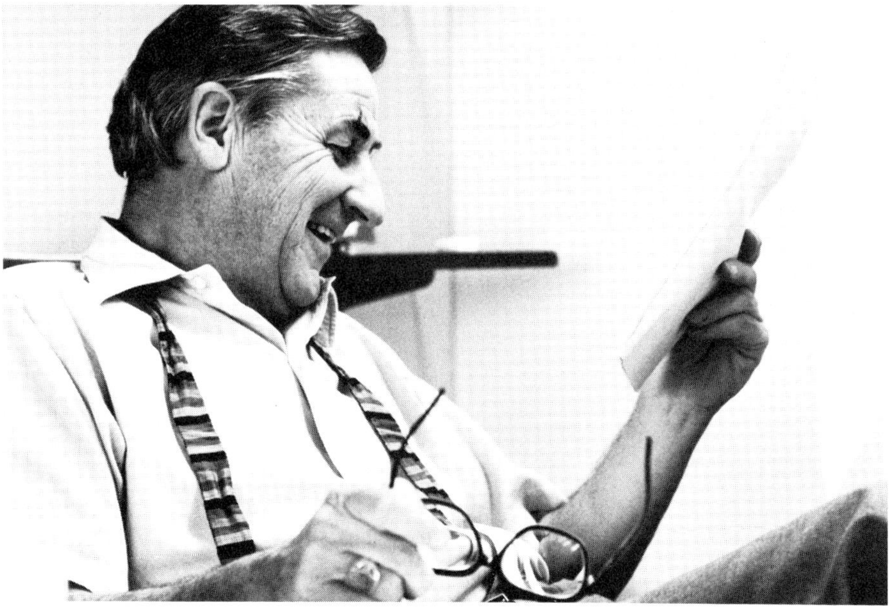

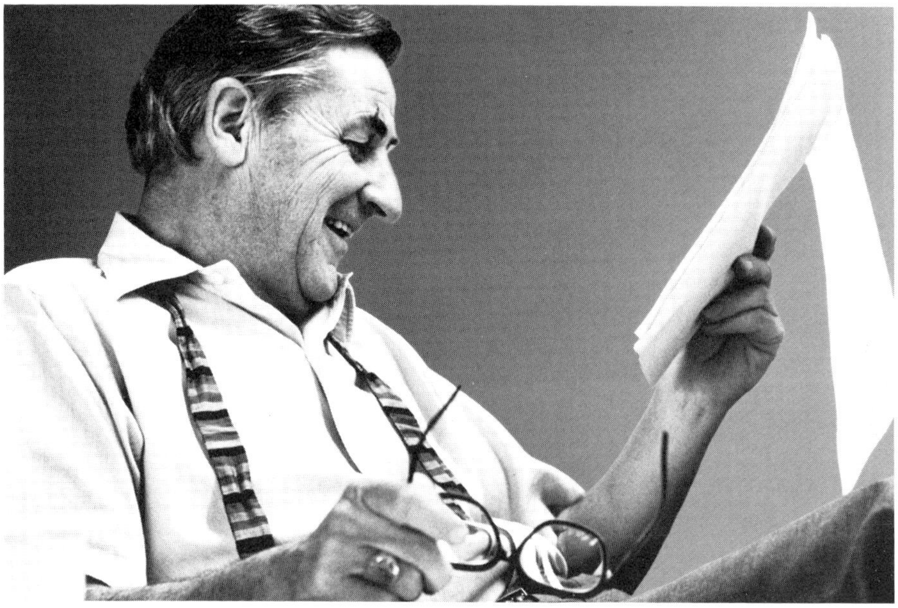

Architect Otto Riechart

Bruce Stromberg, freelance photographer
Client: Otto Riechart Associates
Philadelphia, Pennsylvania

Sometimes candid portraiture is impossible. When architect Otto Riechart hired Bruce Stromberg to produce a publicity portrait, he knew exactly what he wanted to tell the world about himself. Dignity, strength, professionalism, experience—all must be conveyed in Stromberg's interpretation of Riechart if the assignment is to be successful.

To do this, Stromberg chooses to control carefully every aspect of the portrait. Nothing can be left to chance. This approach is called an "environmental portrait." Such pictures are the result of a partnership between sitter and photographer. The setting, the costume, the props, the expression are all mutually acceptable.

Environmental portraits can tell us as much about a subject as a candid portrait. And they can tell us much more than those standard mugshots that fill so many organizational publications. They are generally straightforwardly posed, but the nuances of expression must usually be spontaneously drawn out by the photographer.

Reichart chooses to view the lens seriously. An architect's plan emerges from behind his shoulder, mirroring the slight tilt to his head. The only touch of informality in this portrait is the cigar in the hand. It is an important detail, providing a touch of human values, a contrast to the serious expression.

The environmental portrait makes an excellent safety valve. There are situations when some people simply will not accept a candid shot as a way to represent themselves to the world. Such subjects want to be in control of their emotions and leave nothing to chance. In these cases, organizational photographers usually avoid the candid approach, going to environmental, posed portraits. Yet this method can still say a great deal to readers about what these subjects do and what kind of people they are.

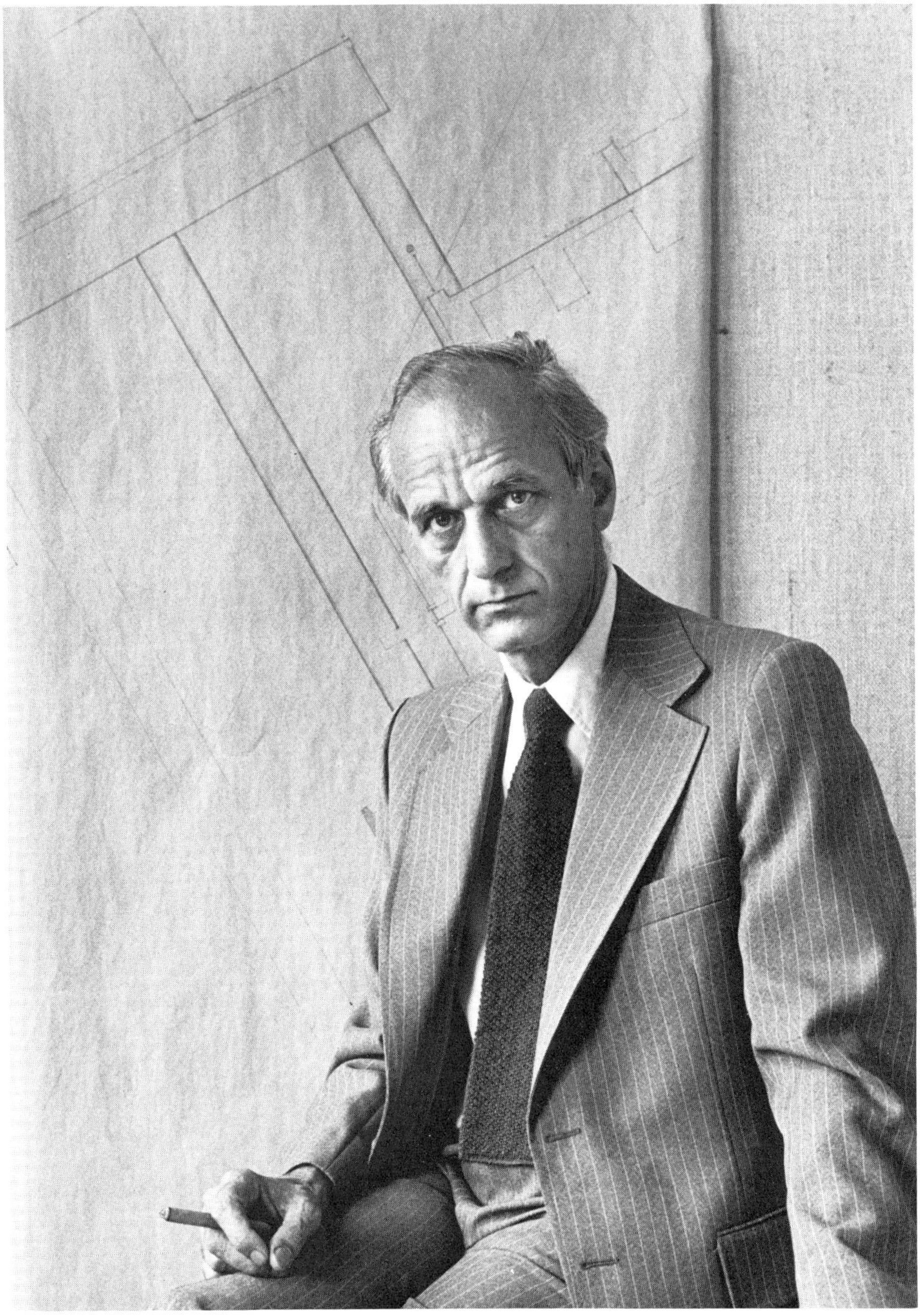

Kenneth Vaughn, MD, chief of staff

Chris Craft, freelance editor/photographer
Client: Albany General Hospital
Albany, Oregon

Environmental portraits can often communicate subtle points that illuminate the character, occupation, and position of the sitter. They can also make points that are unable, for one reason or another, to be discussed in the story.

Chris Craft not only describes the appearance of this important doctor, but she goes on to tell us something about the doctor's position in his profession and society, the influence of his hobby in his life, and the way he views himself as a person. She could have posed him in a medical environment, but that would be the expected solution. Instead, she finds in his office visual symbols that are far more revealing assets in a portrait.

Kenneth Vaughn is also a big game hunter; the painting over his desk features the king of beasts. Craft is able to tie that painting into the portrait by using a wide-angle lens. This lens also emphasizes the hands, and the hands of a doctor most effectively embody the skill and strength of the profession.

Craft drops to her knees to bring Vaughn and the painting together, catching the window light on the symbolic white coat and the oversized hand. The hunter, the physician—the power inherent in both—are vividly interwoven.

Vaughn sits in the huge chair, but he does not rest. His self-assured body language contrasts with the potential comfort of that chair. Craft says she shot an entire roll to bring it all together. She knows that film is the cheapest part of a photographic assignment and is not afraid to use it.

The photo was used for publicity on Vaughn's appointment as chief of staff. It was also used in the hospital's magazine. Nowhere in the article is there mention of such things as authority, skill, or self-assuredness. It is left to the portrait to make those points to the reader.

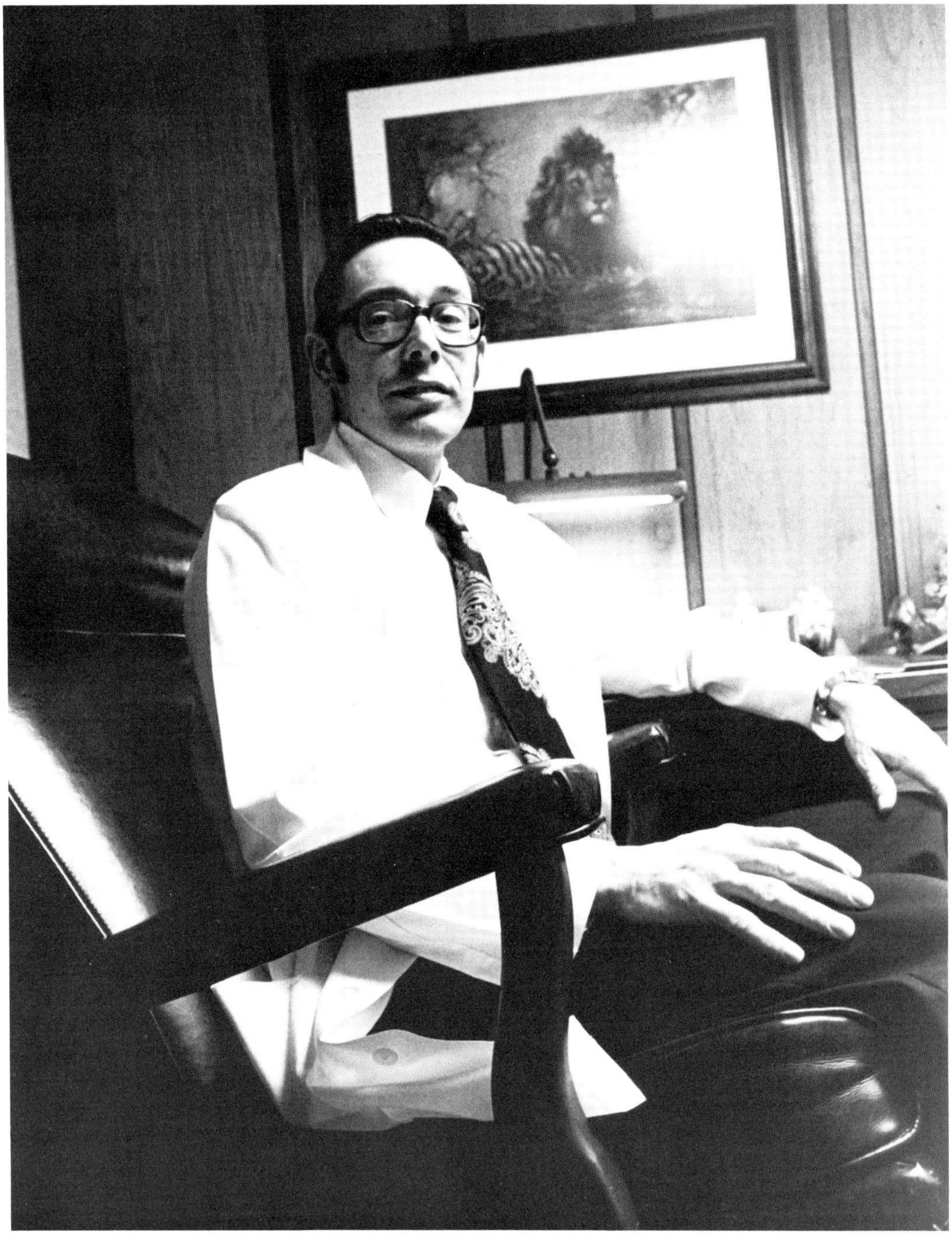

Delfina Soto, Pascua Village, Arizona

**Mark Sandlin, manager, photographic services
Home Mission Board, Southern Baptist Convention
Atlanta, Georgia**

Details are critical to photographic meaning, and this portrait of a Yaqui Indian woman relies on detail to underscore the poverty in which she lives. Mark Sandlin wants the photo to tell us exactly what it is like to live in a shack made of plywood, scrap metal, and cardboard.

For this task he chooses a razor-sharp wideangle lens. Because of their design, these lenses offer photographers tremendous depth of field, allowing crisp detail in both foreground and background. If Sandlin wanted to stress just the woman and merely imply her living conditions, he would have used a telephoto lens, which has a narrow depth of field, and would have placed the background into soft focus.

Editorial photographers must be equipped with both wideangle and telephoto lenses in order to provide the emphasis needed for a particular message. Very few professionals use the normal 50mm lens. It is not as effective in offering them the power to emphasize subject matter selectively.

Study the detail closely in this picture. The electrical outlet is skewed at an angle. The bottom of the window is broken and sealed. The ceiling has obviously leaked and is patched with plywood. A painting of a child with huge eyes hangs crookedly on the wall. The child seems as resigned to her life as Delfina Soto is to hers.

Sandlin places Soto off center, under the crooked painting. He does this not by moving Soto but by moving himself so that the woman shifts in the frame. By using such placement, Sandlin creates tensions throughout the picture.

The wideangle lens turned vertically includes a sweep from the hem of Soto's dress all the way up and onto the ceiling. Sandlin is able to virtually wrap the room around Soto to make the point: This is how she lives.

The picture appeared in *Missions USA* with a story on an SBC missionary at work in Arizona.

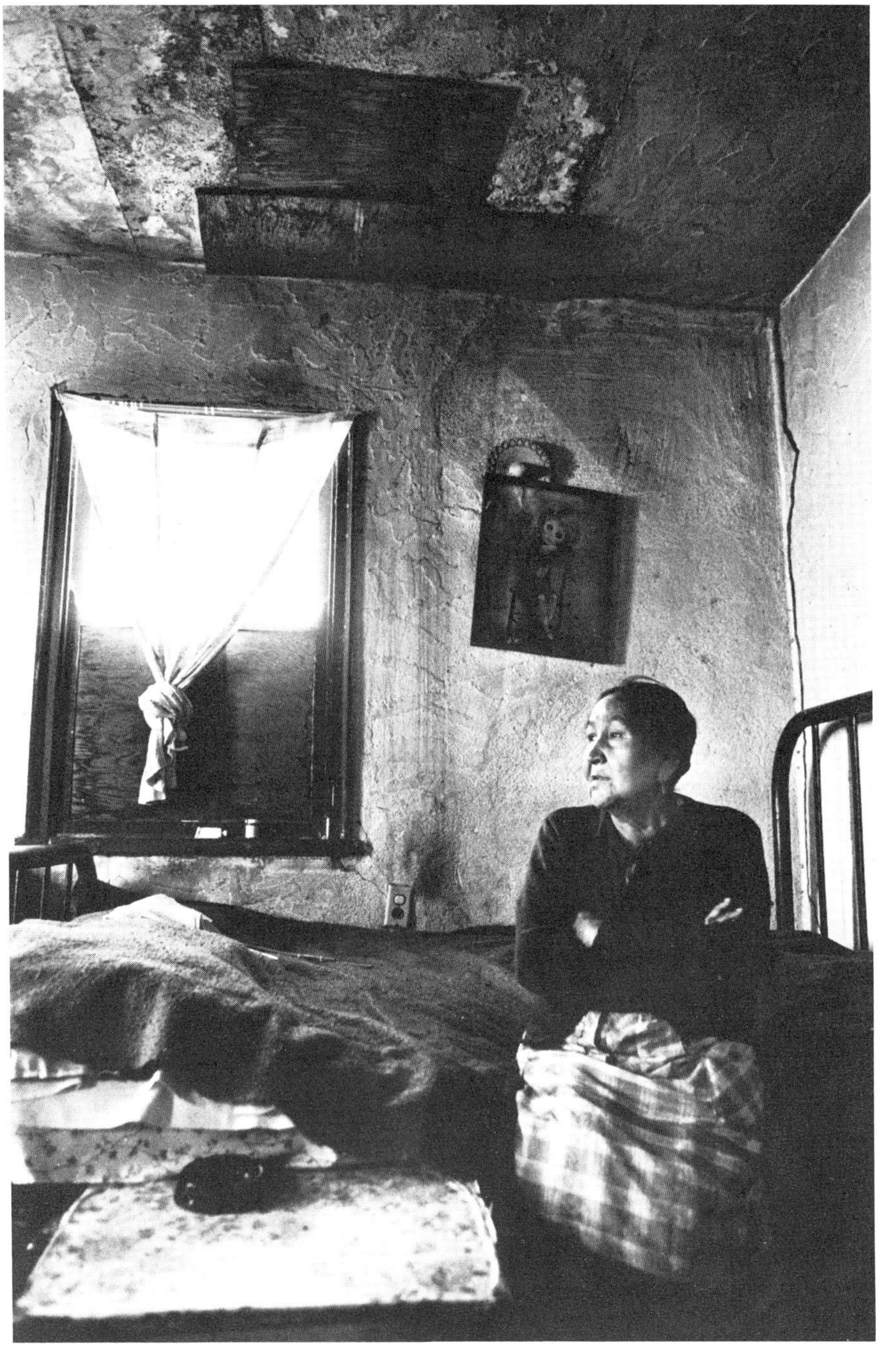

Dick Morville, maintenance supervisor, York Automotive division of Borg-Warner

Michael Mauney, freelance photographer
Client: Borg-Warner Corporation
Chicago, Illinois

Photographers can't make effective environmental portraits simply by placing the subject in front of a symbolic background and shooting. They must use environments that naturally embrace the character and occupation of the subject. People must not look awkward or out of place. They must fit the environment like a hand in a glove.

This portrait of Dick Morville graced the front page of *Perspective*, the quarterly management tabloid of the Borg-Warner Corporation. Morville is not posing for his own sake. He is acting as a symbol of a larger idea. He and his fellow supervisors are trying out new ways of supervising workers, solving problems, and learning from those solutions. The portrait symbolizes all foremen involved in "quality of work" programs in the division.

The programs are moving along with mixed results. The article is balanced, informing Borg-Warner managers of both success and problems. Mike Mauney is asked to produce a photographic synthesis of the story through a portrait of a foreman.

The lighting suggests two sides to Morville, underscoring his mixed experience with the program. His face is severely divided down the middle into darkness and light, symbolizing the good and bad, the known and unknown. The materials he and his team work with surround him. His mood is serious. His body language seems to be asking us, "Well, what now?" The caption tells us that all has not gone smoothly. Morville says that when the program started, a lot of foremen were mad: "Some of them felt they were gonna get their toes stepped on—or worse."

The portrait does not come by this strength accidentally. Pictures are not an afterthought at Borg-Warner. The company's internal communications people plan the approach to every picture, communicating the goals of a story to photographers well in advance. Photographers are given a set of objectives for each assignment. Mauney did not find this man, this mood, this setting, by chance. It represents a team approach to photojournalism. Borg-Warner's internal communications director Barry Nelson likens his role to an orchestra conductor. To play great music, it must be interpreted according to the goals of the man on the podium. But nothing will happen unless the musicians are gifted interpreters as well, working together to breathe new life into the work.

In this case, Mauney is the man with the instrument—the camera. He is not told *what to take*. No competent photographer should ever have to be told that. He is not told *how to take* the picture either. But he is told what his editors are trying to *accomplish*. He uses his talents brilliantly to define, through a portrait of one man, the nature of the story.

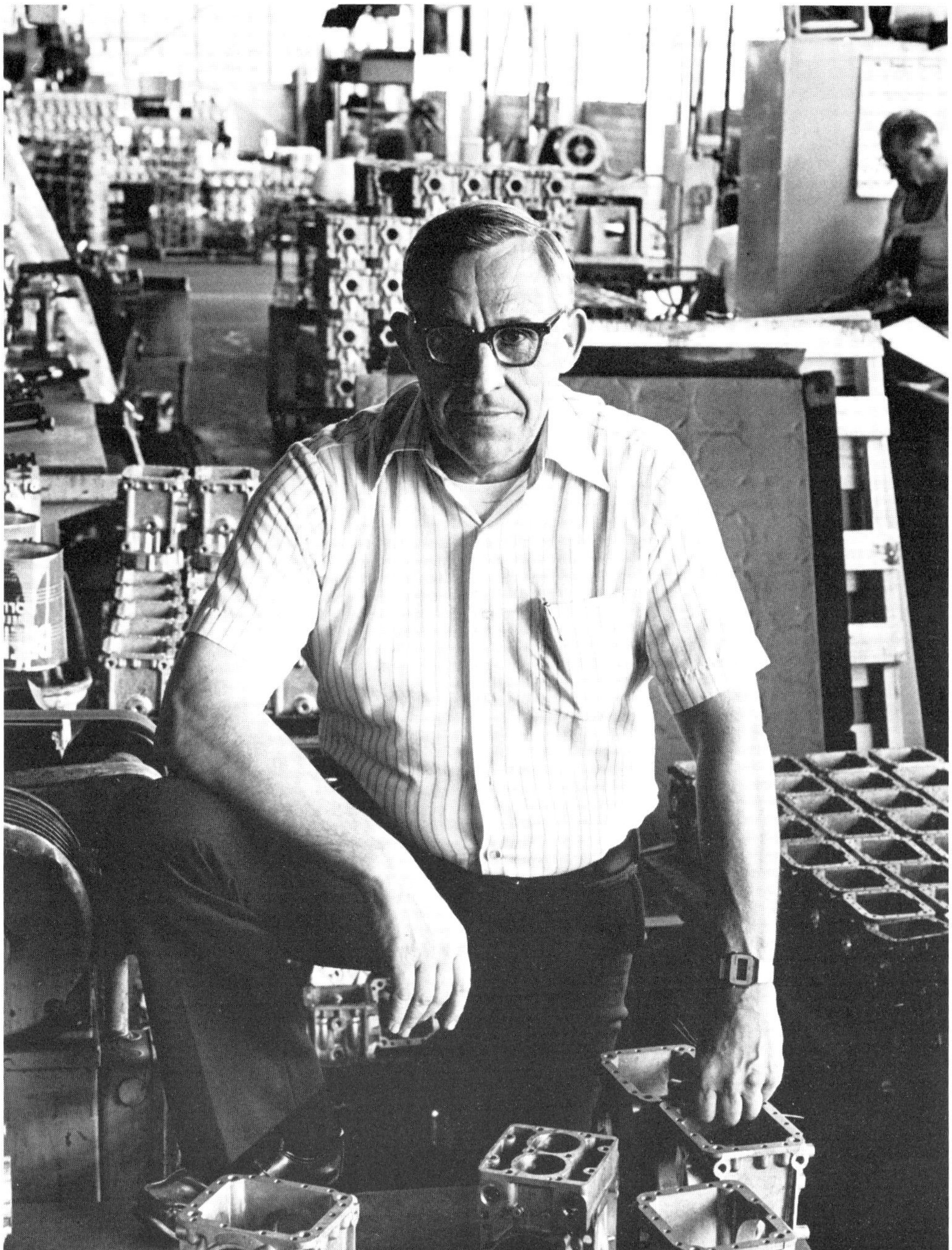

Chapter 14

The group portrait: the bonds we share

As with the individual portrait, the group shot must transcend physical description in order to work as effective editorial communication on behalf of an organization. Instead of defining the nature of an individual, the group shot must express a *collective* insight into the nature of the group and its activities.

The key principle governing the interpretive group shot is the ability of the photographer to depict the nature of the *bond* that ties the group together as a group. The portrait must be more than a picket-fence lineup. It must relate body language, appearance, and environment into a cohesive visual statement.

Group shots can be formal or informal. The subjects can pose directly for the camera, or they can interact among themselves. We must be able to link the people to their setting as a symbol of their existence as a group.

The dress or costume of the subjects becomes important in the group portrait. So does the nature of their expressions, body language, and the details which surround them.

In the end, a reader must come away from a group shot with an understanding of what makes that group into a group. It is a challenging assignment, one of the most difficult in photography. It is hard enough to concentrate on the emotional nuances of one person, let alone the many simultaneous responses within a group. But it must be done if the group portrait is to function as journalism on the printed page.

Eskimo family inside the Arctic Circle

Don Rutledge, photojournalist
Home Mission Board, Southern Baptist Convention
Atlanta, Georgia

The most effective group portraits are also environmental portraits. Instead of relating just one person to the environment, however, such portraits link a group to a particular setting and thus relate each of the members of the group to the others.

Body language, the way people occupy space, and facial expressions also add meaning to the environmental group portrait. Sometimes, photographers will carefully place subjects in position. But often the photographer just chooses the general setting, and the people arrange themselves naturally within it.

Don Rutledge chooses the latter course to express the relationships within an Eskimo family. We learn where the family lives and also see how its members feel about that life and about each other. In spite of the primitive building and the lonely landscape beyond it, we sense spontaneity, joy, and a touch of whimsy emanating from the group.

The focal point is the mother and child on the front step. The other children fan out behind and around her. One even peers at us through the window at left. The girl at center bends her body, the youngster behind her hangs from the doorway, the child at rear stays in the background, nibbling on her hand. All are expressing respective roles within the family.

Rutledge watches as they assume these positions. Only then does he release the shutter, telling us not only where this family lives, but also how it lives.

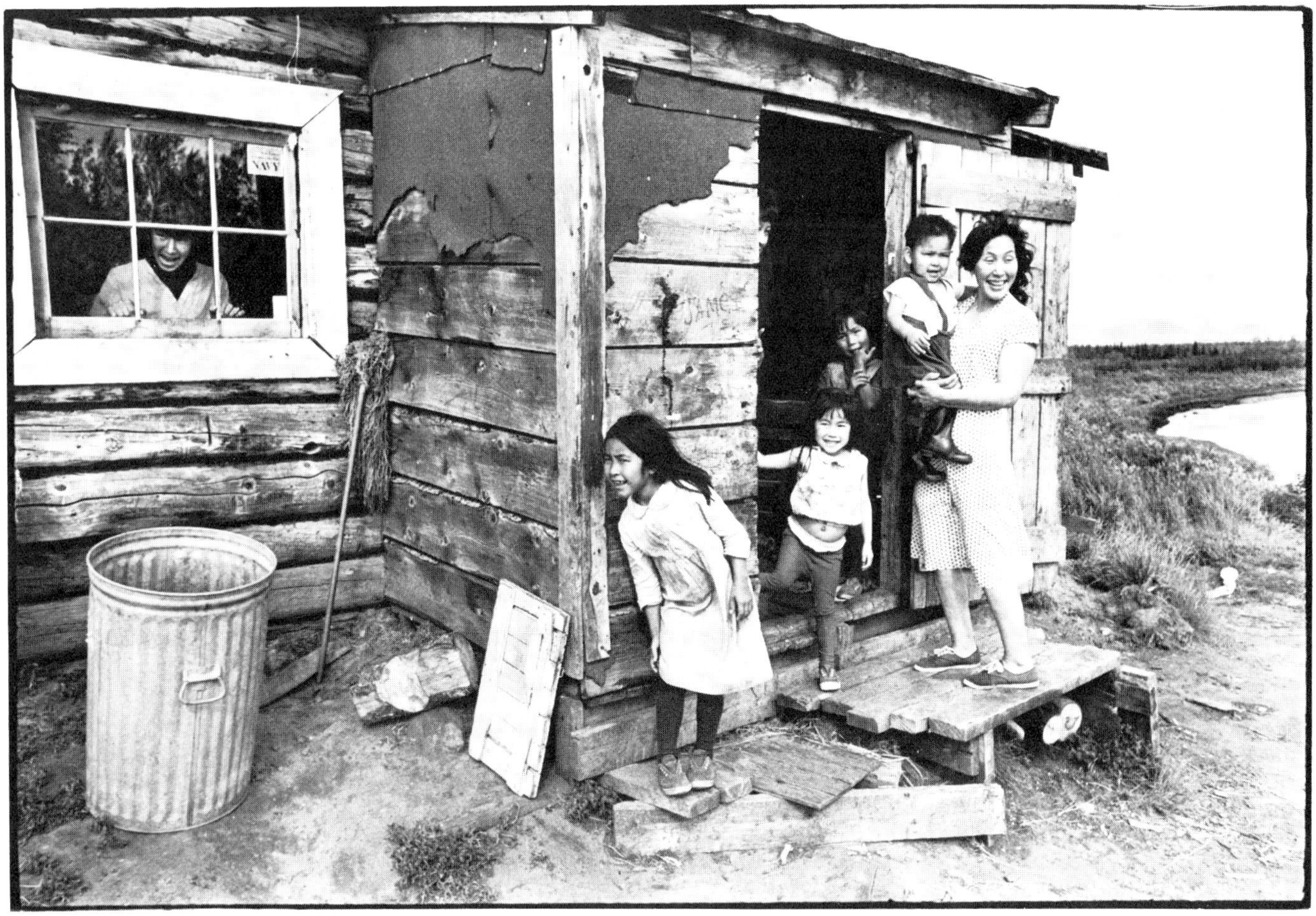
NAVY

Portrait within a portrait

Melissa Brown, internal
   communications manager
Herman Miller, Inc.
Zeeland, Michigan

Some group shots just happen. Herman Miller corporate executives and some famous industrial designers, including the late Charles Eames and his wife (far right), are being posed by a professional photographer to commemorate the opening of an industrial design exhibition at a museum. As the photographer adjusts the lighting between shots, the group relaxes. People make a few jokes, assuming natural instead of posed expressions. At this point, Melissa Brown, editor/photographer of Herman Miller's employee magazine, moves in to photograph those who are being photographed.

The group reacts to the incongruity of the situation. They also laugh at Brown's technique. Although she wears a lady-like dress, she kicks off her shoes, scrambling over a sofa to get the shot. The group responds spontaneously, offering subject matter the other photographer did not even think of capturing. This is the picture, closed eyes and all, that is printed in the employee publication. (All the subjects requested extra copies of it.)

Spontaneity can make a group portrait become more than just a pleasing arrangement of bodies. It can turn a group of authority figures into people with feelings. But causing spontaneous responses sometimes takes courage. It was, after all, Brown's own performance that drew the laugh. "Never give a damn about looking like a fool when you're shooting," she says. Brown also suggests perseverance. "Hang in there to the last. The event was just about over. I was about to leave for dinner, but I decided to stay to watch the other photographer's techniques. I never did get to dinner, and I'm not sorry now."

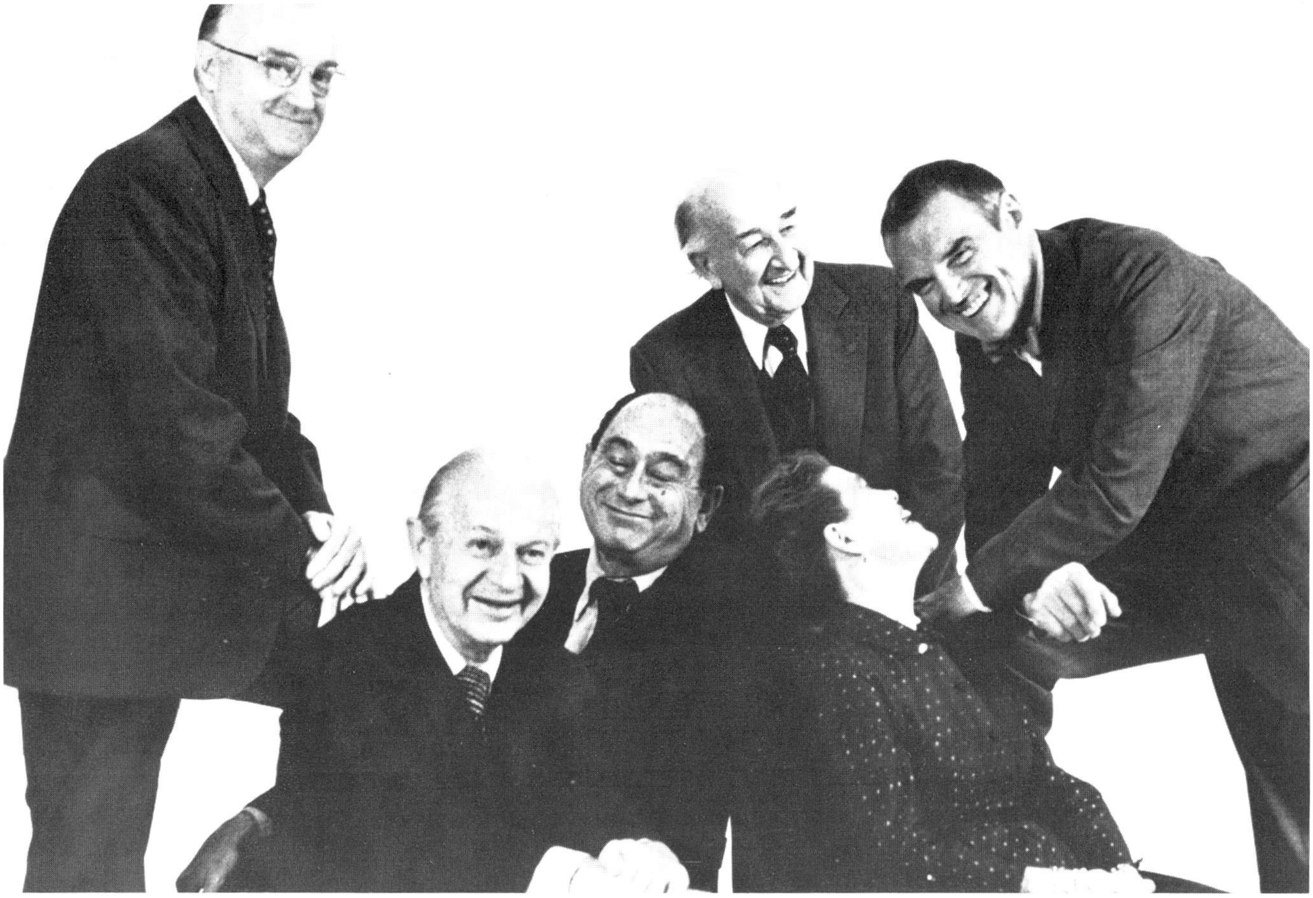

Citizens of Obidos, Portugal

Curt Kregness, editor
Conservative Baptist Foreign Mission Society
Wheaton, Illinois

It is possible to make a group portrait without the group even knowing the shot was taken. Curt Kregness shoots this photo of four men resting on a wall from the inside of a van parked across the street. He uses a telephoto lens, waiting for their postures to fall into a rhythmic progression before shooting.

None of the men even seems to know the others are there. Three are awake, one is not. But each seems to dream his own dreams. The very fact that these men sit together in the Portugese sun makes them a group. The bond that ties them together is the freedom to pass the time in this manner. And that is what Kregness may be trying to say to us with this picture.

There is a bittersweet quality to the image. While these men are free to do nothing but doze in the sun, their body language suggests that they may also be bored, perhaps leading lives without a sense of direction or purpose. I am not sure Kregness, or his organization, wants to say this to readers of his publication. But if he did, this photo hits the mark.

Photographic communication does not have to bring the same message to everyone at the same time. A picture such as this can represent just four fellows sitting on a wall to some. And it can be a statement on boredom to others. Who is right? We all are. For there are no universal answers in photography. Each viewer has the right, and indeed, the obligation, to come to his or her own conclusion. A message that causes various reactions is a strength in a photo, not a weakness. For it causes people to think, and thinking can lead to infinite benefits.

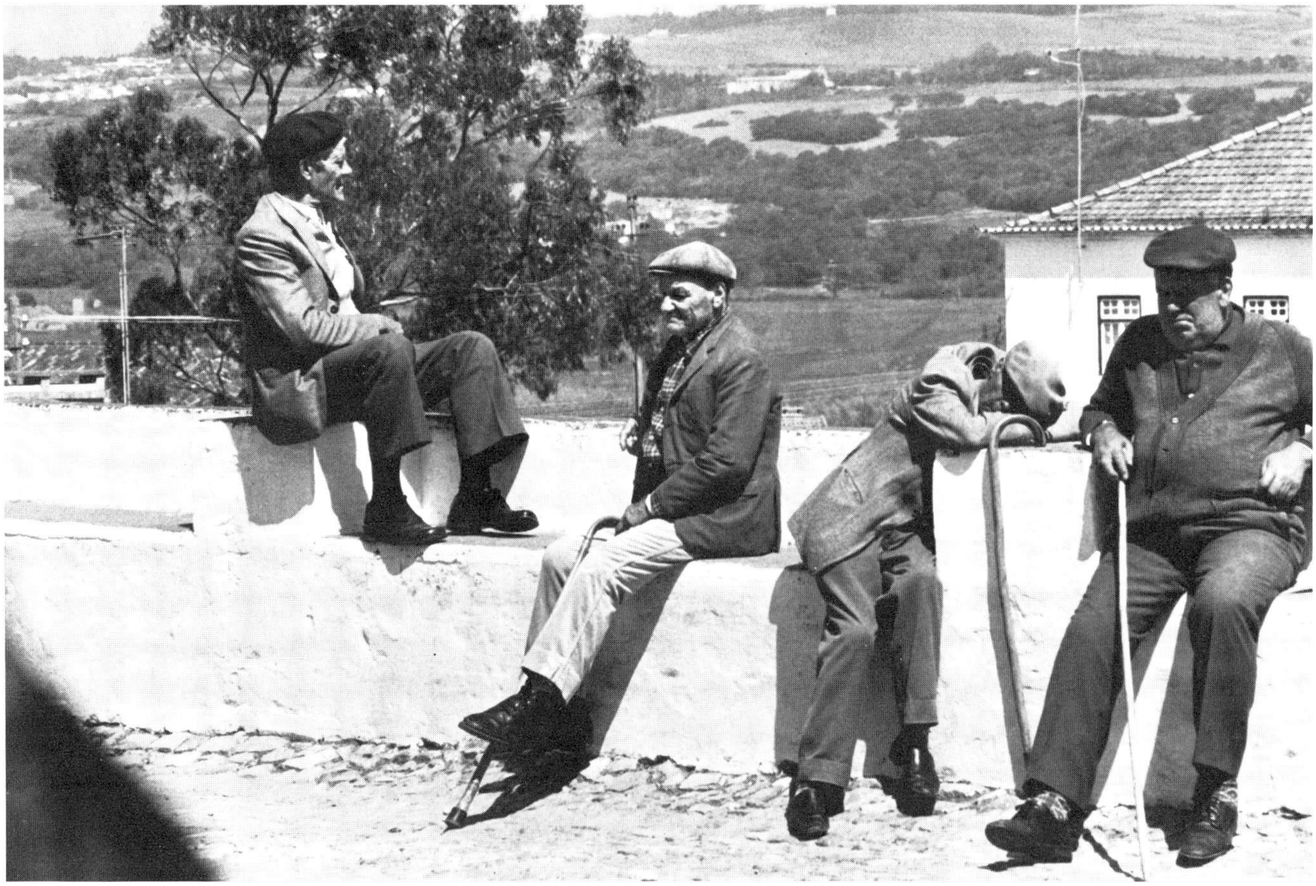

Members of Ile Ife Black Humanitarian Center, Philadelphia

Bruce Stromberg, freelance photojournalist
Client: Ile Ife Black Humanitarian Center
Philadelphia, Pennsylvania

It's fairly easy to make effective group shots of small numbers of people. But it's much more difficult to organize group shots when there are more than ten people in the group. The more people in a picture, the smaller the details in the faces become. The large group photo must depend more on postures and the overall design of the picture, rather than facial detail, to convey meaning.

Stromberg organizes 18 members of the Ile Ife Black Humanitarian Center into a pattern of horizontal rhythms. He chooses a location rich in rhythmic pattern: the balcony of the center's building, with its corrugated roof; the railing; and a backdrop of the center's brick wall. Now all he has to do is to fit the rhythms of body language into it.

He selects a low vantage point, shooting up at the people. He asks them to arrange themselves. Each person assumes the stance they feel most comfortable with. Some lean on the railing, others sit on it, still others stand away from it. Our eyes flow horizontally across the picture, moving upward slightly at far right when we reach the guitar player and the peak of the balcony roof.

Stromberg divides the photo into six horizontal bands. From bottom, we see a line of bricks, then shadow, the railing with people behind it, the shadow under the corrugated roof, then more bricks, and finally, in the shadows at the top of the picture, the dark struts of the building's overhanging roof. The entire photo is glued together by these horizontal panels, welding form and content into a coherent study of the group.

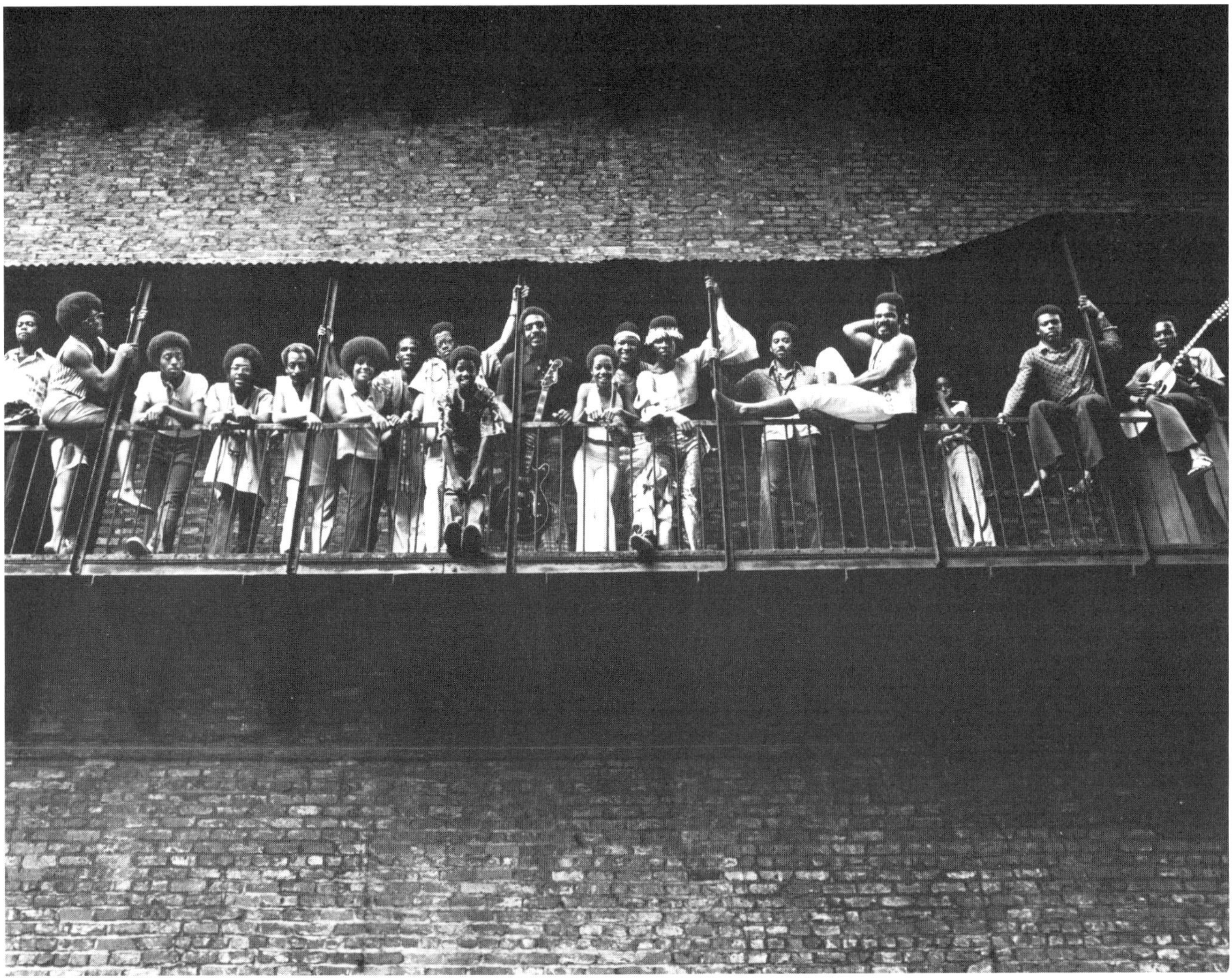

Farm children, Kenya

John Gerstner, editor, *JD Journal*
Deere & Co.
Moline, Illinois

Photographers can't just walk up to a group and make a picture of it. They must come to know the group, and let the group know them. That's how John Gerstner made this group study of the children of a Kenyan farmer, who had been saving for ten years to make a down payment on a John Deere tractor.

Gerstner wants to imply that their lives are primitive by our standards but also quite happy. He carries a Polaroid camera when he travels, and he begins by making pictures with it, giving them to the children as gifts. The children are thrilled by the Polaroids. Gerstner says he will never forget their astonished looks as they watched the pictures develop in their hands. From that moment, the group belongs to Gerstner.

The picture ran in color with a story on Africa's first farmers. Gerstner is able to obtain exquisite interaction among the children. The boys wear blue shirts; the girls, pink dresses. They stand before the crumbling, dun-colored entrance to their home. Each personality is unique, yet as a group they display a closeness that only a family can share. They are independent yet dependent at the same time.

The emotions coming at us are the result of something that happened *before* the picture was made. Any photographer can benefit from this lesson. By understanding our subject and by increasing our subject's understanding of us, we can build a human chemistry which results in effective photographs.

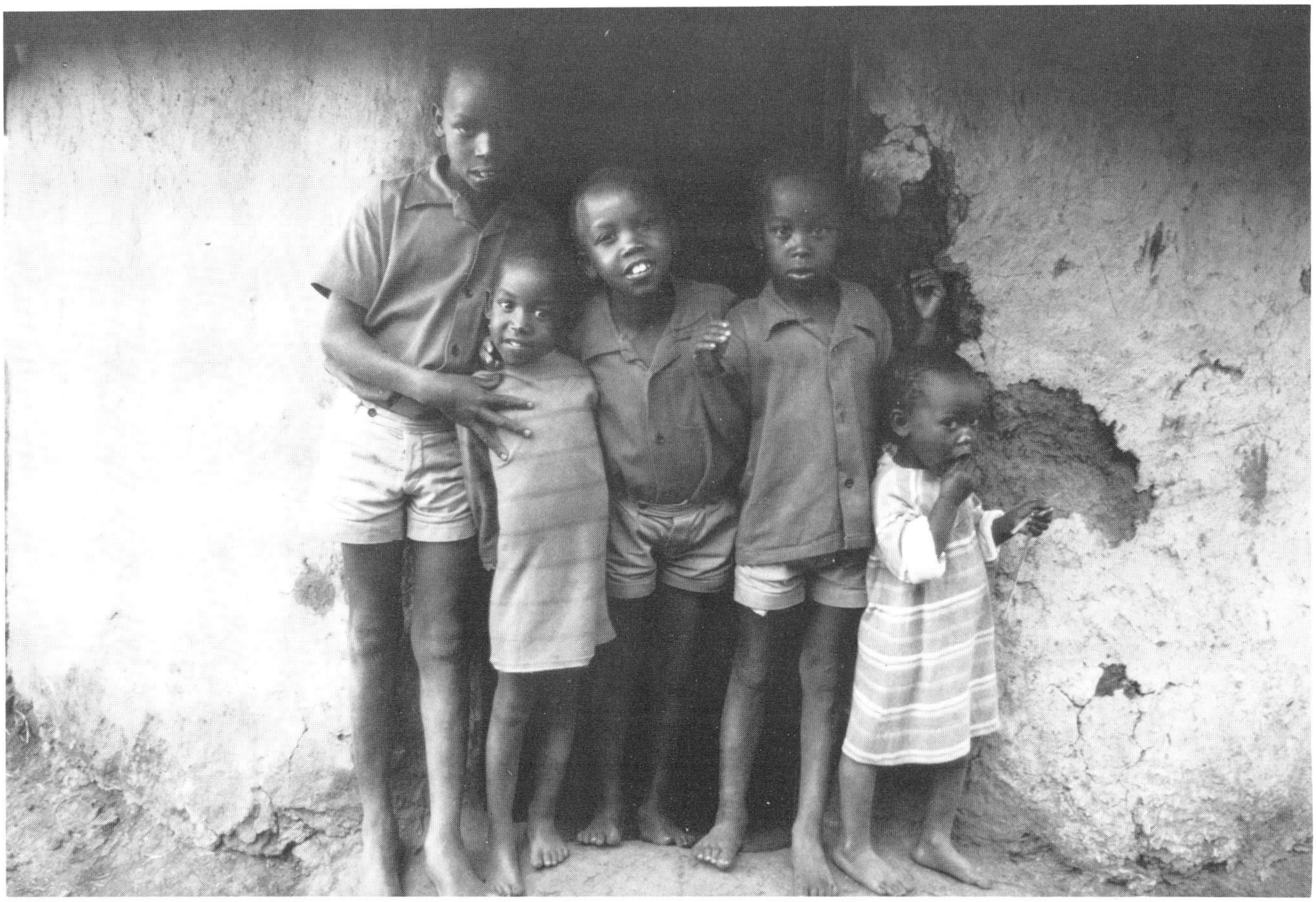

Acoustic technicians, York division of Borg-Warner

Michael Mauney, freelance photographer
Client: Borg-Warner Corporation Chicago, Illinois

The editors of *Perspective*, one of the most visually effective management publications in the country, draws heavily on environmental group portraits to relate employees to their jobs. In choosing Mike Mauney to create such portraits, Borg-Warner is going with consistency. For few professional photographers are as skilled as Mauney in structuring the staged portrait.

And staged is the word for it. Mauney uses a sense of theatre to weld people to the symbols of their work. Yet, the bond he creates between them is credible. Subject and environment seem to belong together. Nobody ever seems out of place in a Mauney portrait.

In this portrait of the engineers and technicians who check all of York's new products for sound ratings, Mauney gathers his cast around a new heat pump in the sound lab. They have been carefully placed; there is no spontaneous body language and little emotion. For these are precise, technical people; the formal arrangement underscores their expertise. The equipment they use flows around and among them. The carefully controlled lighting becomes part of the picture itself. The photograph—like the work of these men—is carefully engineered.

The equipment is complex, even bizarre. It takes technical skill to understand and use it. Mauney is able to mesh the formally relaxed postures into a display of self-confidence among all this complexity. The message comes home to us: These experts know what acoustics are all about. And that is why the picture is being used.

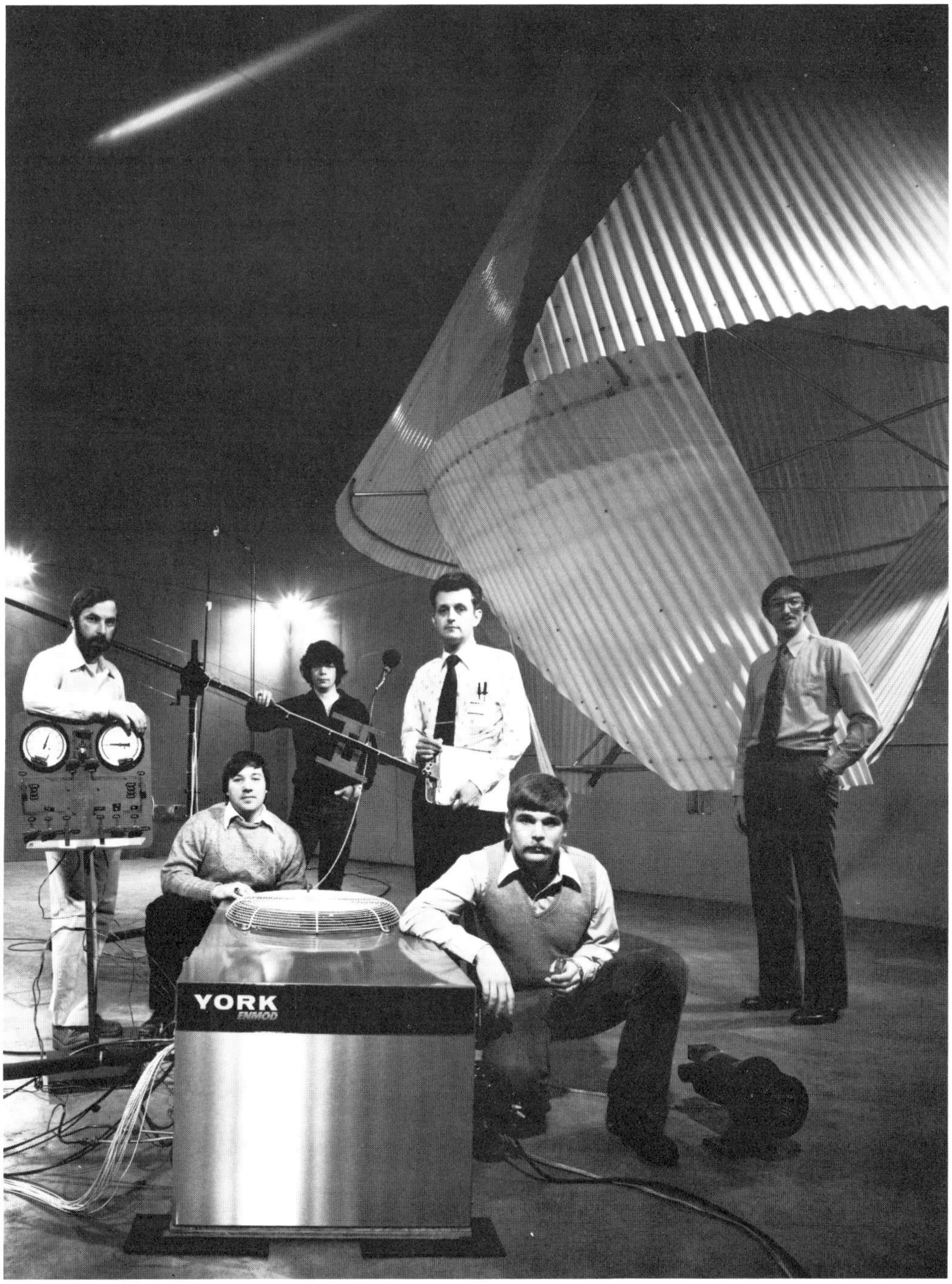
YORK
ENMOD

Wells-Fargo coin room employees

Michael Mauney, freelance photographer
Client: Borg-Warner Corporation
Chicago, Illinois

These men sort, roll, and bag coins for federal reserve and commercial banks. They work in the Miami, Florida, coin room of Wells-Fargo, part of Borg-Warner's Baker Industries protective services group. *Perspective* uses this environmental group portrait to symbolize, in human terms, the nature of such services. Mike Mauney resists the temptation to go with gimmicks here. He could have stressed guns and guards or used incongruity to emphasize the disparity between great wealth and ordinary working men.

But instead he plays it straight. For that is how these people play it. There is no joking, no grins, no stress on the money itself. Mauney draws on relaxed body language, the informality of the grouping. He infers, in spite of the awesome symbols of wealth, that protection and security remain an ongoing, everyday job.

It is a low-key portrait in a high-key situation. The caption tells us that "security minded employees aren't saying much about the coin room in Miami." But the picture, on the other hand, does a lot of talking. Mauney's portrait is able to tell us that these people have a respect for the obvious responsibility that comes with their jobs. While they may casually sit on bags containing thousands of dollars, they do not treat it lightly. All this money may not belong to them, yet their casual possessiveness tells us that, for the moment at least, it is their responsibility.

THE FIRST STATE BANK
OF MIAMI
Miami, Florida
FDIC
PHILA.
DIMES
$1.000
1977
DIMES

Corporate lawyers, Borg-Warner headquarters

Michael Mauney, freelance photographer
Client: Borg-Warner Corporation
Chicago, Illinois

The most typical of organizational group shots is the portrait of office workers gathered around a table. Most of them say little to us about the group as a group. They merely describe appearance and leave it at that. But Mauney goes far beyond that kind of photo with this group portrait of 30 Borg-Warner lawyers. He groups them around a huge, empty table; surrounds them with books; and lets the environment lend impact to the responsibility they carry as corporate decision-makers.

Mauney's subject matter is identical to the gather-round-the-table cliche that defaces many a corporate publication. But he is able to alter this subject matter effectively and thereby makes it work as communication. By choosing a wideangle lens, he creates distortion which emphasizes the symbolic thrust of the empty table, with its impressive texture and grain. The careful placement of the 30 executives rhythmically repeats the shape and thrust of the table. They represent corporate responsibility and the necessity of maintaining it.

Within the group, we see great diversity—in age, gender, appearance, body language. They are fascinating in their individual demeanors; and when they are viewed as a collective force, that fascination is intensified. The portrait is formally conceived and executed, but we are left with the feeling that these are not stuffed shirts. They are individuals, charged with a collective responsibility that gives the group its identity and purpose.

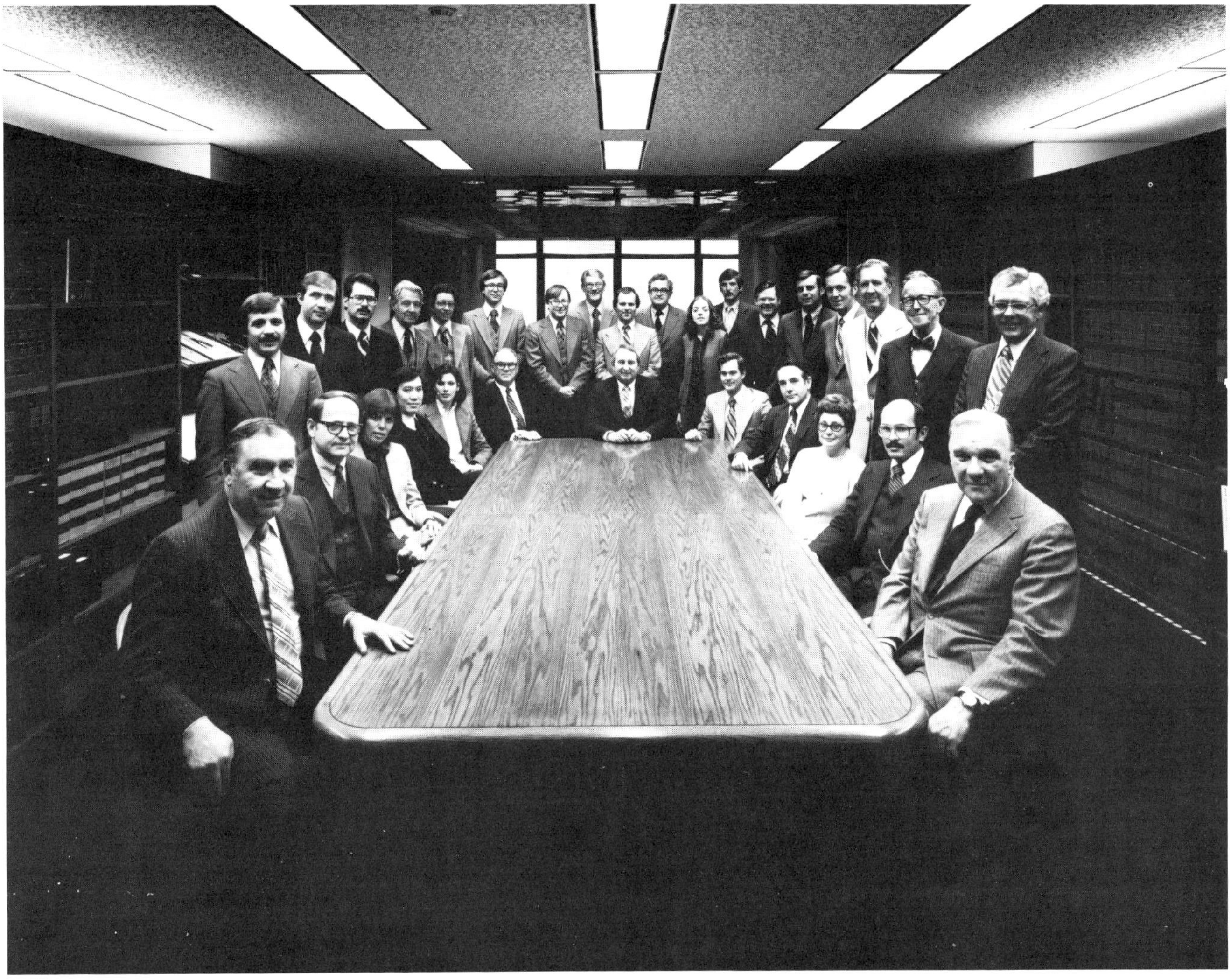

Chapter 15

The sequence: when the sum means more than any part

Photographs in sequence involve the editor, photo-editor, or designer as much as they involve the photographer. In order for sequences to work, great care must be taken in picture selection, relationship, and display.

One type of sequence involves a constant environment which offers striking changes as we proceed from photograph to photograph—from opener to transition to climax. The photographer must be thinking in terms of a sequence while shooting, keeping in mind that the stage remains constant as the players develop the story within.

Another form of sequence can be developed by the editor from a particular batch of photographs involving the same subject. The settings need not be constant (as long as consistency of setting is not important). We can develop the progression of an idea through the actions of people as they proceed through a situation, react to it, are changed by it.

The greatest pitfall in sequential photography is the failure to change the photographs enough from picture to picture. If, for example, we shoot a person talking and the only thing that changes in subsequent photos is the shape of his or her mouth, we have nothing but redundancy. Somehow, somewhere, a sequence must change the person or situation, cumulatively making a point. The whole must ultimately prove of more value than any of its parts.

Leukemia patient and mother, Memphis, Tennessee

**Mark Sandlin, manager, photographic services
Home Mission Board, Southern Baptist Convention
Atlanta, Georgia**

This four-picture sequence of leukemia patient Timmy Davis and his mother was shot as the boy awaited a painful spinal tap. He knew what was coming and is asking his mother if they can leave and not wait for the doctor to come in to do the tap. Timmy's quiet pleadings are met with understanding and compassion by his mother.

To appreciate this sequence, we must have this context. Otherwise it is simply another distraught child in a doctor's office. Mark Sandlin, shooting the story for *Missions USA*, tells us that the marks on Timmy's face are to help the radiologist at St. Jude's Children's Hospital align the machine for the cranial radiation the child is receiving. It is important that we know this, as well, or the marks become a bewildering distraction.

The first shot is the only photo clearly defining the appearance of four-year-old Timmy and his feelings. His mother is secondary. In the second picture, the emphasis is shifted to the mother and her gesture of understanding. The third image records an emotional crisis, and the final shot, the mother's response to that crisis. Each picture has a different job to do. While Sandlin remains in a fixed position, the scene before him changes enough to avoid redundancy, the greatest enemy of the picture sequence.

Sandlin came to know Timmy and his mother earlier that day. He establishes enough trust so that when he picks up his camera, he is ignored. That is the only way he could have come away with a sequence as memorable as this one.

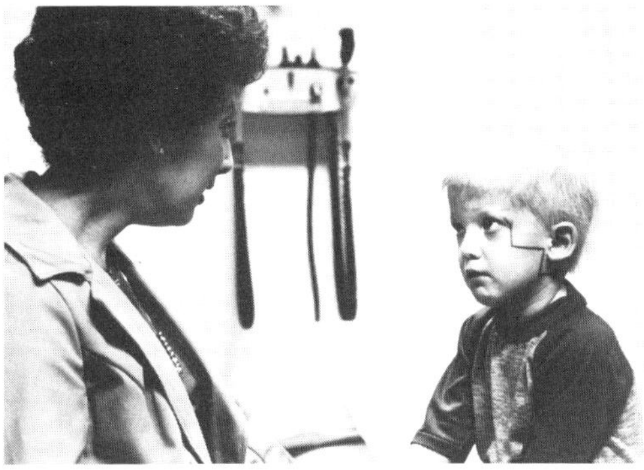

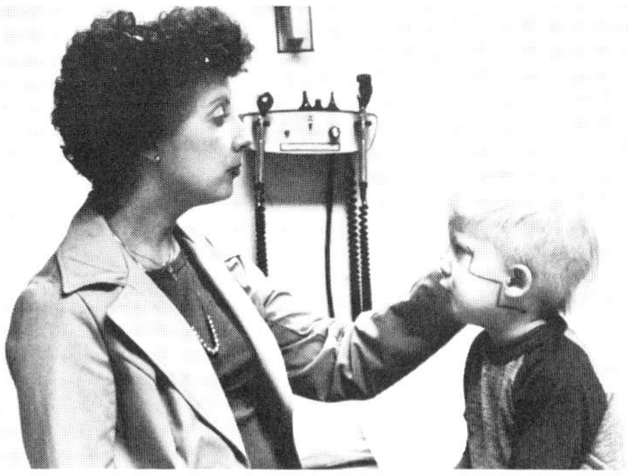

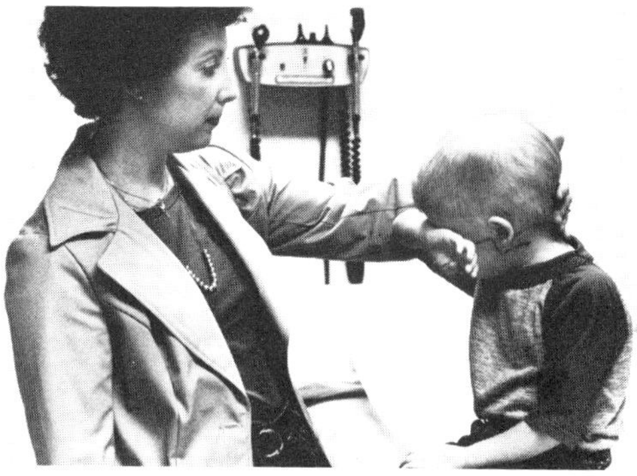

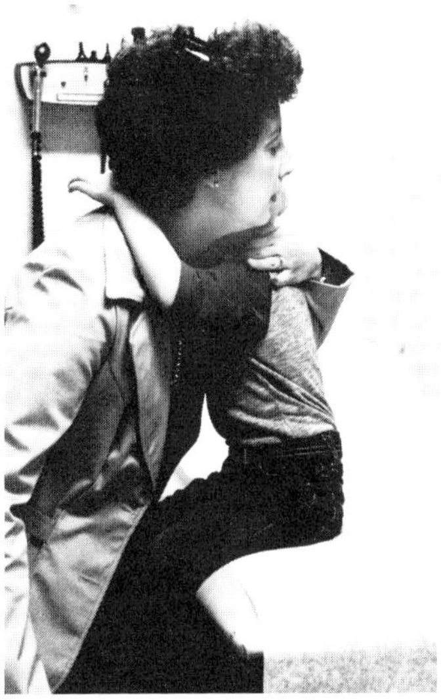

Wolf-man

Jim Visser, photographer
Six Flags over Mid-America
St. Louis, Missouri

Why is such an obviously contrived subject as this transformation of man into monster so fascinating? Because it is presented in sequence. Sequences allow us to see changes occur from picture to picture, to compare them, and finally to assess a result. They give us access to time as it unfolds before us.

Jim Visser made this sequence to promote the haunted house attraction at a Midwestern amusement center. The series was widely distributed by the UPI and later used in the employee newspaper. Visser uses a beginning, a middle, and an end—or what editors call an opener, a transition, and a closer—to create his sequence. It is a staged form of illustration. Yet it is chillingly effective because the contrasts from picture to picture are so great.

Seventeen-year-old Doug Kincaid is seen as himself, more or less, in the first frame. Yet the sinister sidelighting, emphasizing hair growing incongruously out of the shadows on his face, already heralds the hideous changes to come. The transition is horrifying. Kincaid is already a monster even though we can see it is actually a man wearing a mask. His hair remains normal, as does his shirt. The lighting is constant; the context is consistent; yet the subject changes within that context from frame to frame.

The final shot is a "grabber." The completed wolf-man, rising up at us from that familiar plaid shirt, stares us down. Although we know it is still Kincaid underneath, we allow our imaginations to accept the fact that he has changed into a monster before our eyes.

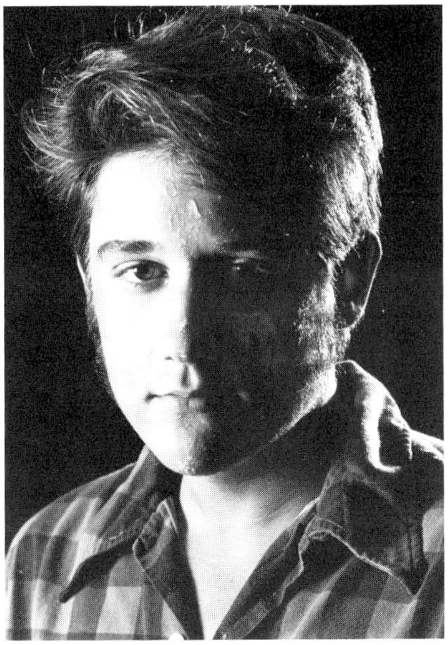

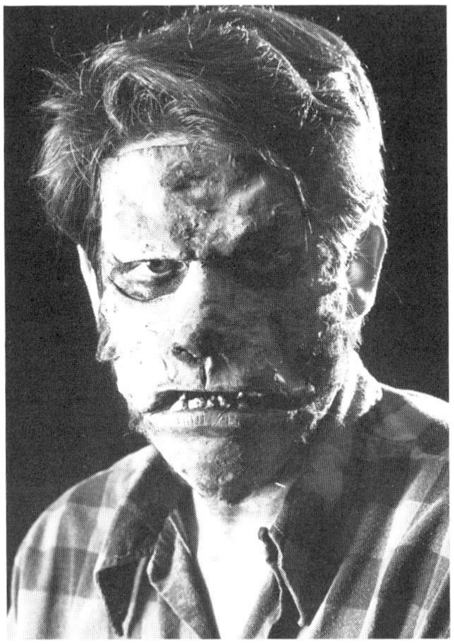

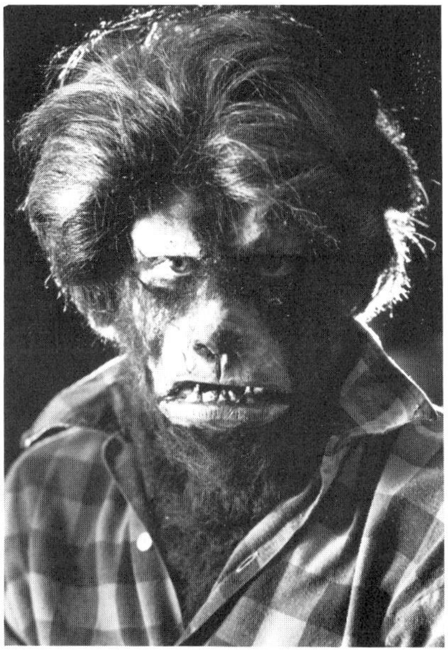

The little kid with the big heart

Paul Obregon, senior photographer
Home Mission Board, Southern Baptist Convention
Atlanta, Georgia

Unlike the other sequences in this chapter, this three-picture portrayal of Ricky Thatcher's open heart surgery does not use a constant setting for context. The scene shifts from pre-operative snuggling to intensive care anxiety to post-operative response. Yet Paul Obregon produces a strong sequence, originally used as part of a larger photo-essay in *Missions USA*.

While Mark Sandlin's sequence on leukemia patient Timmy Davis was shot within a few moments, Obregon must follow Ricky Thatcher's ordeal over many days. Sequences can be used to condense long time periods into the whisk of an eye scan. This ability to condense, extend, freeze, and contrast moments in order to develop our ideas, offers us a powerful visual communication tool.

In the first picture, Obregon uses a wideangle lens to stress the tiny slippers at the foot of the bed as a symbol of the child's vulnerability. He also portrays the relationship between the understanding mother and the sleeping child. The second shot still finds the child in bed. But now the surgery is over, and the bed is covered with a plastic tent. Ricky's face is deathly still. We sense softly focused anxiety of the parents through their body language. Obregon is permitted just this one shot in the intensive care unit. He makes it count.

The final picture is Ricky's response to Obregon and his camera, and thereby to us. We see past the context of the obvious stitching on his chest and into his expression. From his body language and its contrast to the pictures preceding it, we measure the distance Ricky Thatcher has had to travel.

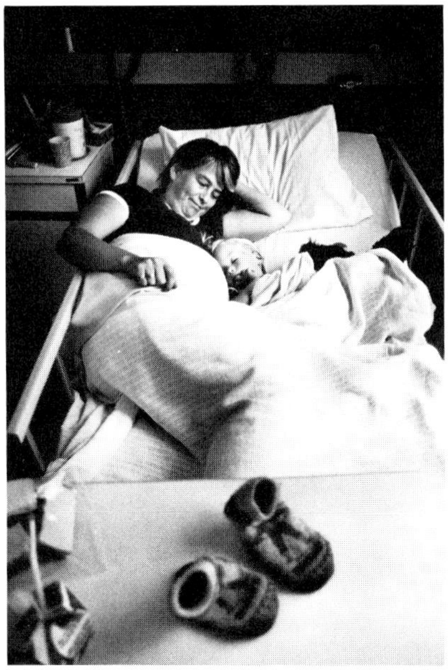

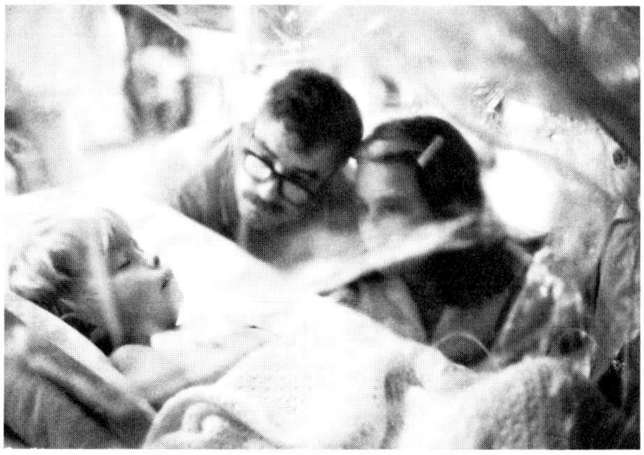

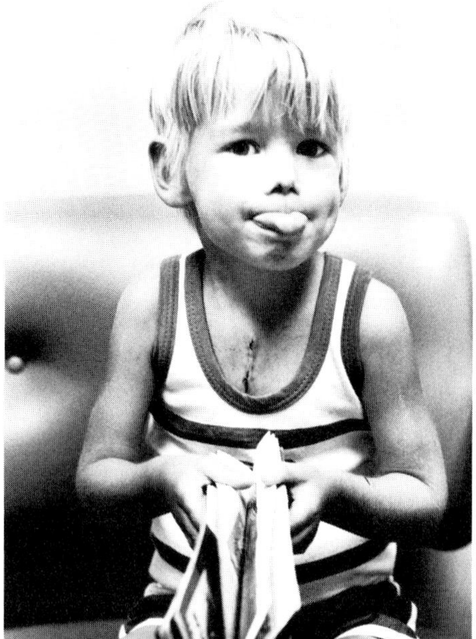

The photographers

Gordon Baer, freelance photographer
Box 2467
Cincinnati, OH 45201

Melissa Brown, internal communications manager
Herman Miller, Inc.
8500 Byron Road
Zeeland, MI 49464

Karen Copenhaver, editor
U.S. Bancorp
Box 8837
Portland, OR 97208

Chris Craft, freelance photographer
Box 1605
Albany, OR 97321

Dave Denemark, publications coordinator
Medical College of Wisconsin
8701 Watertown Plank Road
Milwaukee, WI 53226

Ed Eckstein, freelance photographer
200 E. 33rd St., 31E
New York, NY 10016

Kay Engelsen, public information officer
Tacoma Public Schools
Box 1357
Tacoma, WA 98401

Stormy Fitzgerald, chief photographer
Methodist Hospitals of Memphis
1265 Union Avenue
Memphis, TN 38104

Kurt Foss, photojournalist
Hennepin County Public Affairs
Northeast Street Level
Government Center
Minneapolis, MN 55487

Beverly Freeman, senior editor
Transco Companies, Inc.
Box 1396
Houston, TX 77001

Dale Geffs, staff photographer
Oilfield Products Group
Dresser Industries, Inc.
Box 6504
Houston, TX 77005

John Gerstner, editor, *JD Journal*
Deere & Company
John Deere Road
Moline, IL 61265

Mike Jenkins, communications manager
Burger Chefs Systems
College Park Pyramid
Box 927
Indianapolis, IN 46206

Curt Kregness, managing editor, *Impact*
Conservative Baptist Foreign Mission Society
Box 5
Wheaton, IL 60187

Michael Mauney, freelance photographer
1485 Judson
Evanston, IL 60201

Wm. Franklin McMahon, freelance photographer
1352 Elmwood Avenue
Wilmette, IL 60091

Robb Mitchell, editor, *Living*
Methodist Hospitals
  Foundation
1265 Union Avenue
Memphis, TN 38104

Paul Obregon, senior
  photographer
Home Mission Board,
  Southern Baptist Convention
1350 Spring Street NW
Atlanta, GA 30367

Mark Philbrick, university
  relations photographer
Public Communications
C-335 ASB
Brigham Young University
Provo, UT 84602

Bob Reznik, assistant director
Public Relations
Comshare, Incorporated
Box 1588
Ann Arbor, MI 48106

Don Rutledge, special
  assignment photographer
Foreign Mission Board,
  Southern Baptist Convention
Box 6597
Richmond, VA 23230

Mark Sandlin, manager,
  photographic services
Home Mission Board,
  Southern Baptist Convention
1350 Spring Street NW
Atlanta, GA 30367

Bruce Stromberg, freelance
  photographer
1818 Spruce Street
Philadelphia, PA 19103

Tom Treuter, supervisor,
  publication photography and
  design
William Beaumont Hospital
3601 West 13 Mile Road
Royal Oak, MI 48072

Jim Visser, freelance
  photographer
10812 Olive Street
Creve Coeur, MO 63141

Baron Wolman, freelance
  photographer
361 Magee Avenue
Mill Valley, CA 94941

The organizations

Albany General Hospital, Albany, Oregon
American Medical Affiliates, Valley Forge, Pennsylvania
Atlantic Richfield, Philadelphia, Pennsylvania
William Beaumont Hospital, Royal Oak, Michigan
Borg-Warner Corporation, Chicago, Illinois
Brigham Young University, Provo, Utah
Burger Chef Systems, Indianapolis, Indiana
Church Pension Fund, Philadelphia, Pennsylvania
Comshare, Incorporated, Ann Arbor, Michigan
Conservative Baptist Foreign Mission Society, Wheaton Illinois
Deere & Company, Moline, Illinois
Dresser Industries, Houston, Texas
Episcopal Community Services of Philadelphia, Philadelphia, Pennsylvania
Girard Bank, Philadelphia, Pennsylvania
Haverford College, Bryn Mawr, Pennsylvania
Hennepin County, Minneapolis, Minnesota
Herman Miller, Incorporated, Zeeland, Michigan
Home Mission Board, Southern Baptist Convention, Atlanta, Georgia
Ile Ife Black Humanitarian Center, Philadelphia, Pennsylvania

International Association of Business Communicators, San Francisco, California
Levi Strauss & Co., San Francisco, California
Medical College of Wisconsin, Milwaukee, Wisconsin
Methodist Hospitals of Memphis, Tennessee
Moore McCormack, New York City, New York
Philadelphia College of Optometry, Philadelphia, Pennsylvania
Philadelphia Corporation for the Aging, Philadelphia, Pennsylvania
Philadelphia National Bank, Philadelphia, Pennsylvania
Procter & Gamble, Cincinnati, Ohio
Otto Riechart Associates, Philadelphia, Pennsylvania
Saturday Review, New York City, New York
Six Flags over Mid-America, St. Louis, Missouri
Tacoma Public Schools, Tacoma, Washington
Transco Companies, Incorporated, Houston, Texas
U.S. Bancorp, Portland, Oregon
University of Pennsylvania, Philadelphia, Pennsylvania

Technical notes

The pictures in this book were made, in large part, with equipment now considered standard in the field of editorial photography. Here is a general summary of the cameras, lenses, films, and accessories used to shoot subject matter we usually encounter in organizational photojournalism.

Cameras: All the photographers featured in this book use 35mm systems (a body and at least two lenses). Photojournalists no longer use large format cameras for editorial assignments. Most choose *manually* controlled Nikon or Olympus single lens reflex systems. A few prefer Leica systems. None use cameras designed for the amateur market, which usually feature battery-powered shutters. Such automatic cameras are more likely to encounter battery failure, rendering them as useless as paperweights. Some automatic cameras also deny photographers the right to choose both lens opening and shutter speed.

These photographers choose such systems as Nikon FM, Nikon F-2, Nikkormat, and Olympus OM-1. (The F-2 and Nikkormat are no longer manufactured, but many professionals claim they are more durable than later models.) Some carry an extra body, allowing them to shift back and forth between wideangle and telephoto lenses without having to change lenses.

Lenses: None of these photographers regularly use the standard 50mm lens that "comes with the camera." All rely on wideangle lenses, generally 24mm and 28mm, with f/2 and f/2.8 maximum apertures. And all use medium telephotos for portraits and similar subjects, generally f/2.5 or f/2.8 lenses of 85mm, 90mm, 100mm, and 105mm focal lengths. Only a few use 135mm lenses or longer for indoor work. Outdoors, some employ 70-205mm zoom lenses. For sports, 300mm lenses are usually essential.

Film: Most use Kodak Tri-X ASA 400, 36-exposure, black-and-white film as a standard indoor and outdoor film. Many "push-process" this film with virtually no loss of quality, using ASA 800 and ASA 1600 ratings to gain flexibility in low-light situations and allowing greater control of depth of field outdoors. For color work, the majority use Kodachrome 64 for maximum color saturation, and rely on Ektachrome 400, often pushed to ASA 800, for indoor color work.

Lighting: All of these photographers work with available light to obtain the most natural results, allowing the light within a scene to become part of the message of the picture. Available-light shooting is also less obtrusive, allowing photographers to work without calling attention to the picture-making process. Fast lenses, fast film, and push-processing helps them make pictures in locations as dark as a coal-mine or a hotel ballroom. Available-light techniques require steady camera-holding and movement-free shutter release. This group of photographers, rarely, if ever, uses flash.

Accessories: Very few of these photographers use tripods, filters, or other trademarks of studio and commercial photographers. They must work quickly and flexibly, unobtrusively, and naturally. They shun artifice, concentrating on becoming invisible, in order to make the kind of pictures we see in this book. Many, however, will protect their lenses with a skylight filter. Some may use a polarizing filter now and then to reduce reflections. Most use lens shades to avoid flare. A few require motor drives for sports or other subjects where speed is essential. But all of them are aware that motor drives make noise, and noisy photographers do not get pictures such as these.

Selected resources

Books on photography:

Life Library of Photography: Time-Life Books, Chicago, IL

Visual Impact in Print, Gerry Hurley and Angus McDougall. Visual Impact, Inc., 161 W. Harrison, Chicago, IL 60605

Photographer's Handbook, John Hegecoe. Alfred A. Knopf, Inc., New York, NY

Beginner's Guide to the Single Lens Reflex. Nikon Educational Services, 623 Stewart Avenue, Garden City, NY 11530

Photojournalism, The Professional's Approach, Kenneth Kobre. Curtin & London, Inc.

The Photographer's Eye, John Szarkowski. The Museum of Modern Art, New York, NY

Looking at Photographs, John Szarkowski. The Museum of Modern Art, New York, NY

Magazines on photography:

American Photographer, 1255 Portland Place, Box 2833, Boulder, CO 80302

News Photographer, National Press Photographers Association, Box 1146, Durham, NC 27702

Columns on editorial photography in organizational publications:

Douglis on Visuals, Philip N. Douglis. *The Ragan Report,* 407 S. Dearborn St., Chicago, IL 60605.

Photo-Critique, Philip N. Douglis, ABC. *IABC News,* International Association of Business Communicators, Suite 940, 870 Market St., San Francisco, CA 94102

Workshops on editorial photography for organizational communicators:

The Douglis Visual Workshops, 212 S. Chester Road, Swarthmore, PA 19081. Presented in 20 cities nationwide.

Ragan Report Workshops, 407 S. Dearborn St., Chicago, IL 60605. Presented in various cities nationwide.

IABC communicators seminars, Suite 940, 870 Market St., San Francisco, CA 94102. Presented in various cities nationwide.

About the author

Philip N. Douglis is the country's most widely known photographic consultant and workshop leader in organizational communication. As director of The Douglis Visual Workshops, headquartered in Swarthmore, Pennsylvania, he has offered since 1970 more than 500 workshops in photography, visual creativity, and photo-editing, including sponsored presentations to more than 200 in-house groups and editorial associations.

This is his second book. His first, *Communicating with Pictures*, was published by Ragan Communications in 1976 and is now out of print. This basic guide to editorial photography was written specifically for editor/photographers working for organizations.

Douglis has been a regular columnist on editorial photography for *The Ragan Report* since its inception in 1971. He also writes the monthly photo-critique column for *IABC News*, publication of the International Association of Business Communicators. His articles on photojournalism have also appeared in *The National Press Photographer*, *Technical Photography*, *The Professional Photographer*, and *Writer's Digest*.

He brings to his books, columns, and workshops a comprehensive viewpoint. A journalism graduate of the University of Michigan, he has directed internal and external communications programs for The Franklin Mint; managed award-winning publications for Smith Kline & French Laboratories; and was among the first in the nation to be accredited by the International Association of Business Communicators. In 1981, Douglis was elected an IABC Fellow, the association's highest honor.

He offers his introductory workshops in approximately 20 cities across the country each year. All participants in these workshops acquire eligibility to participate in his special continuing three-day workshops in visual creativity, photo-editing, layout, and design, offered several times a year in various sections of the country. The Douglis Visual Workshops also provides its past participants with an ongoing publication critique service and a monthly newsletter—*The Douglis Letter*—covering developments and trends in visual communications within organizations.

Philip N. Douglis
Director, The Douglis Visual Workshops,
Swarthmore, Pennsylvania
Photo by Chris Craft, Albany, Oregon

TR 820 .D68 1982

DATE DUE		
JAN 1 1 1993		